A SMALL CORNER OF HELL

A SMALL CORNER OF HELL
DISPATCHES FROM CHECHNYA

ANNA POLITKOVSKAYA

TRANSLATED BY
Alexander Burry and Tatiana Tulchinsky

WITH AN INTRODUCTION BY
Georgi Derluguian

THE UNIVERSITY OF CHICAGO PRESS
CHICAGO AND LONDON

The University of Chicago Press, Chicago 60637

The University of Chicago Press, Ltd., London

© 2003 by The University of Chicago

All rights reserved. Published 2003

Paperback edition 2007

Printed in the United States of America

19 18 17 16 15 14 13 12 11   5 6 7 8 9

ISBN-13: 978-0-226-67432-2 (cloth)
ISBN-10: 0-226-67432-0 (cloth)
ISBN-13: 978-0-226-67433-9 (paperback)
ISBN-10: 0-226-67433-9 (paperback)

Politkovskaia, Anna
    A small corner of hell: dispatches from Chechyna / Anna Politkovskaya; translated by
Alexander Burry and Tatiana Tulchinsky; with an introduction by Georgi Derluguian.
        p. cm.
    ISBN 0-226-67432-0 (cloth : alk. paper)
        1. Chechnia (Russia)—History—Civil War, 1994–. 2. Chechnia (Russia)—History—
Civil War, 1994– —Personal narratives, Russian. I. Title.

DK511.C37P654   2003
947′.52—dc21   2003010001

Originally published as *Vtoraya chechenskaya,* © 2002 by Zakharov Publishers

♾ The paper used in this publication meets the minimum requirements of the American
National Standard for Information Sciences—Permanence of Paper for Printed Library
Materials, ANSI Z39.48-1992.

CONTENTS

All Nature seemed filled with peace-giving power and beauty.

Is there not room enough for men to live in peace in this magnificent world, under this infinite starry sky? How is it that wrath, vengeance, or the lust to kill their fellow men can persist in the soul of man in the midst of this entrancing Nature? Everything evil in the heart of man ought, one would think, to vanish in contact with Nature, in which beauty and goodness find their most direct expression.

War? What an incomprehensible phenomenon! When reason asks itself, is it just? is it necessary?, an internal voice always answers no. Only the permanence of this unnatural phenomenon makes it natural, and only the instinct for self-preservation makes it just.

Who would doubt that, in the war between the Russians and the mountain people, justice, stemming from the instinct for self-preservation, is on our side? If not for this war, what would protect all our neighboring rich and enlightened Russian territories from robbery, murder, and raids by savage and warlike peoples? But let us consider two particular people.

Who has the instinct for self-preservation and, consequently, justice on his side? Is it on the side of some pauper named Jemi who, hearing of the approach of the Russians, swears, takes his old rifle from the wall, and, with three or four rounds that he doesn't intend to waste, runs to meet the giaours? Of Jemi, who has seen how the Russians keep advancing toward his planted field, which they will trample, toward his hut, which they will burn down, and toward the ravine where his mother, wife, and family, trembling with fear, are hiding? Who thinks that they will take everything from him—everything that gives him happiness? Who, full of impotent rage, utters a cry of despair, tears off his tattered homespun coat, flings his rifle to the ground, pulls his cap down over his brows and, singing his death song, hurls himself headlong against the bayonets of the Russians with only his dagger in his hand?

Is justice on his side, or on the side of the officer from the general's staff who sings French songs so well just as he passes us? Back in Russia he has a family, relatives, friends, serfs, and responsibilities to them, he has no cause or desire to fight with the mountain people, but he has come to the Caucasus . . . to show how brave he is! Or is it on the side of an aide-de-camp I know, who wants only to attain the rank of captain and a cushy job, and has therefore become an enemy of the mountain people?

—From an early draft of "The Raid: A Volunteer's Story," written 150 years ago, in 1852, by the twenty-four-year-old army officer Count Lev Nikolayevich Tolstoy

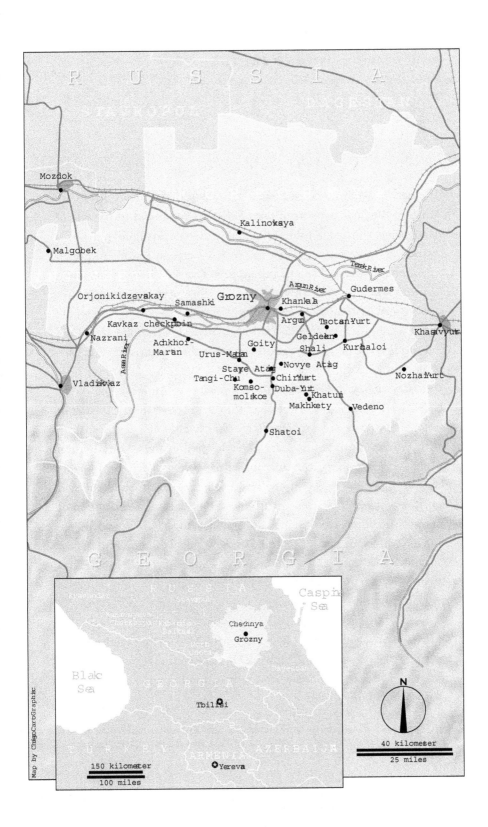

The first question to be addressed inevitably is, why read this book? Much of the book consists of personal stories; many of the people of whom those stories are told are no longer alive. Anna Politkovskaya is unsparing in presenting the brutal realities of war, and reading such a book requires moral labor. Perhaps this is because by learning about Chechnya we learn not only about a wretched corner of postcommunist eastern Europe, but something important regarding the whole world where we all live. It is a substantially more complex and often more tragic world than suggested by the upbeat futuristic portrayals of globalization during the market boom of the 1990s. Acts of terrorist violence, such as the attacks of September 11 in America, the recurring suicide bombings in Israel, and the seizure of a Moscow theater in October 2002, present a spectacularly ghastly facet of a new global reality. Whatever might be the fashionable opinion, the world situation is not reducible to a clear-cut conflict of backward fanatical terrorists assaulting the realm of civilized urbanity.* Fortunately, the real world is more complex; fortunate indeed, because the realization of the world's complexity and interdependency might allow us to discuss and seek different ways of coping with new global dilemmas than propagandistic calls for all-out war on terror would suggest. Politkovskaya accomplishes her task by showing the contradictory complexity of the human condition in an otherwise absolutely inhuman situation.

Is this account of the war in Chechnya to be trusted? Or, in the language of social science, how valid are the data and analysis that organize the presentation? This is a very contentious question. Many important people in Moscow routinely call Politkovskaya's reporting

---

*For one of the most authoritative and sophisticated expressions of this view, see Ian Buruma and Avishai Margalit, "Occidentalism," *New York Review of Books*, January 17, 2002, 4–7.

too sensationalist and lacking in patriotism, especially as Russia fights what they describe as the threat of Islamic terrorism. And indeed, the radical wing of Chechen insurgency under the command of Shamil Basayev uses Islamic rhetoric to justify acts that many would call terrorist: hijackings, taking hostages, car bombings.

As in all violent conflicts, the belligerents present diametrically opposed versions of events in support of their political claims and tactics. It would be naïve to seek the truth somewhere in between these mirror-image extremes. It is equally futile to assume that outside observers—third-party diplomats, aid providers, scholarly experts, or investigative journalists—could be totally unbiased in their presentations. Then how can we decide which truth about the war in Chechnya is better?

The French sociologist Pierre Bourdieu suggested a promising way out of this conundrum. To decide consciously, we must make an effort to know what kind of people or organizations produced the accounts of events and what might be their agendas, and then we should ask ourselves how it relates to the kind of person we think we are and what shapes our own attitudes. Instead of striving for abstract objectivity (which usually ends in pretentious hypocrisy and sermonizing), Bourdieu advised us to *grasp the whole field* of social relations, for example the intersecting field of politics or journalistic production.

Furthermore, the stakes proper to each field must be clarified. For instance, the stakes in capitalist markets clearly are monetary profits; in science it might be the thrilling sensation of making a discovery and recognition of one's intellectual stature by colleagues; in the arts it is the acclaim of fellow artists, critics, and spectators. Public acclaim and professional recognition surely matter in political journalism too. But in this field the importance of such considerations might fade away during periods of acute political struggle, when people come to consider the stakes much more important than their personal interest or even life itself. For the sake of professional success Politkovskaya could have chosen a less grievous and dangerous topic to write about. More than two dozen journalists have been killed in Chechnya since the beginning of the first round of war in 1994. Many more have been abducted, harassed, imprisoned, and severely beaten— which Politkovskaya herself knows from personal experience (briefly described in the book). She also has been the target of death threats that have caused her to flee Russia for a time. Nonetheless, she continues to travel to Chechnya and bring back accounts of a horrific war—accounts that we would otherwise not have.

Therefore, I propose the following hypothesis. This book represents a political position in a struggle where the stakes are exceedingly high. The author wants us to appreciate this because she hopes to enlist our support in her cause. Her cause is stopping a small but very cruel war and perhaps saving Russia's nascent democracy.

My hypothesis is consistent with what is publicly known about Anna Politkovskaya, a leading investigative journalist from Russia. She belongs squarely in the generation of the democratic intelligentsia who in 1989 led the popular surge of questioning the communist bureaucratic authority. Anna Politkovskaya writes for Moscow's *Novaya gazeta*, one of the last major newspapers in Russia that sticks to the agenda of the democratic intelligentsia. This weekly (and now, in hard times, biweekly) specializes in exposing political and financial machinations, discussing social problems, and helping all sorts of honest mavericks who stand against the tide of postcommunist corruption. *Novaya gazeta* has been reporting on the dirty side of the war in Chechnya from the outset. Almost every issue provokes a public uproar, so it is little wonder that the newspaper is constantly being sued for libel and subject to threats of a hostile takeover (the new weapon of choice in controlling the Russian press). This is key to characterizing Politkovskaya's kind of journalism and identifying her proper place in the big picture of postcommunist Russia.

Let me first clarify this picture by cutting through the tenacious underbrush of popular clichés regarding "failed democratic transitions" and "demons of ethnonationalism." Second, I am going to briefly outline what on earth Chechnya is—and here the clichés get even denser, as is always the case when we discuss Islamic militancy these days.

The current political scene in Russia and the conflict in Chechnya date back to the events of 1989–1991, that is, to the ways in which communist rule ended throughout the Soviet bloc. In some former socialist countries, like Hungary and Poland, the questioning of authority by dissident intelligentsia brought the collapse of communist party dictatorships followed by a robust democratization.* This achievement became possible for three intertwined reasons that explain why things turned out differently in Russia and, for that matter, in Chechnya. We must not forget that during 1989–1991, Russia experienced a widespread revolutionary situation; nor must we forget that Chechnya experienced a classical revolution in August–October 1991, with jubilant crowds storming palaces, opening prisons, and throwing the most hated officials of the old regime out of windows. How could the postcommunist transitions turn out so different in the end?[†]

First, in the socialist states of Central Europe there were formidable intelligentsias that could rely on national cultures to mobilize the civil societies against the communist apparatchiks who were viewed as Soviet-imposed stooges. In these countries the vector of national pride coincided with democratization. This juxtaposition sustained the popular revolutionary challenges that had been rehearsed in previous rebellions like the Hungarian uprising of 1956, Prague Spring of 1968, and the powerful Solidarność movement in Poland during the early 1980s. Second, by 1989 the communist rulers in these countries were feeling very insecure because their economies had been stagnating since the 1970s, and because their patrons in Moscow had grown increasingly reluctant to subsidize the comfortable levels of consumption among the Poles or Hungarians with the proceeds from Soviet oil exports (which Moscow now needed to use at home). This shift removed the economic and political props. Third, all sides felt a strongly restraining sense of common European identity and the obligation to behave in a "civilized" manner. After all, the main attraction of leaving the Soviet bloc was to join a prosperous and peaceful Europe.

---

*A deep and fairly readable analysis of Central European democratic transformation, including its many paradoxes and ironies, is provided by Gil Eyal, Ivan Szelényi, and Eleanor Townsley, *Making Capitalism without Capitalists: The New Ruling Elites of Eastern Europe* (London: Verso, 1998). To get a better and more sobering sense of what was actually achieved even by the most successful countries of the former Soviet bloc, add to your reading list the excellent article by Lawrence King, "Making Markets: A Comparative Study of Postcommunist Managerial Strategies in Central Europe," *Theory and Society* 30 (2001): 493–538.

[†] Here my discussion of how similar revolutionary processes led to divergent outcomes follows the theorizing of Doug McAdam, Sidney Tarrow, and Charles Tilly, *Dynamics of Contention* (New York: Cambridge University Press, 2001).

By contrast, in the critical moments leading to war, both Bosnia and Chechnya felt abandoned in a desperate situation.

Rabid nationalists surely can be found in Hungary and Poland, as in any country. But the utterly simplistic and violent solutions typical of a fundamentalist mentality do not hold a wide appeal in a society that remains fairly secure in its normal way of life and expects life to get better soon. Why would, say, Hungarians wish to fight for a chunk of Romania (even though many ethnic Hungarians might live there) when it is clear that such pursuit of national aggrandizement would destroy the prospects of joining the prosperous European Union— which, luckily for the Hungarians, is virtually next door?

In fact, the same "pro-European" realization was the key factor in Gorbachev's restraining the Soviet generals and the party hardliners during the revolutions of 1989. The last Soviet president sought to reduce the military and political tensions of Cold War, restructure a Soviet economy that was burdened by the gigantic military-industrial complex, and foster in its place a more dynamic and consumer-oriented economy based on some combination of market and state planning mechanisms. In this way, he thought, the citizens would regain their faith in the political leadership and the Soviet system, and the country would become more "normal": that is, like France after decolonization, postwar Germany, or Spain after the death of Franco.

Of course, no one at the time thought that instead of honorably joining Europe, within the next decade Russia would plummet to nearly Third World levels of poverty and state corruption. And almost nobody could have imagined the firepower of the former Soviet army unleashed on Grozny, a quaint provincial capital in the south of Russia, and people disappearing into secret graves like in the times of the gulag. How did Russia get there?

The first goal of Gorbachev's perestroika reforms after 1985 was to shake up the stolidly bureaucratic apparatus of the Soviet Union by subjecting it both to public criticism in the newly liberated press and to the pressures of competitive elections. This is how the civic-minded journalists of Politkovskaya's generation got the opportunity to pursue the story of lifetime. Perestroika-era journalism was mostly of the kind that Americans call muckraking; plenty of ugliness accumulated around the Soviet system over the decades, first from the Stalinist terror and then from the long comfortable reign of Brezhnev, with its bureaucratic incompetence, vested interests, cynicism, and corruption.* After the loosening of press controls in 1986, the circulation of the most daring publications soared to stratospheric heights and their journalists became public heroes.

At first, the communist bureaucratic elite was frightened and disoriented. With Gorbachev going increasingly liberal and pro-Western, the old elite was left with neither leaders nor a political program; who would trust them after all that the journalists had dug up? The popular antibureaucratic agitation reached its peak in 1989, when the first competitive elections to the Soviet parliament clearly demonstrated that the best winning strategy was to claim that the candidate was never a member of ruling elite.

But the Soviet dissident intellectuals had time neither to politically organize to take power nor to figure out how they would use state power. No less important, the Soviet economy consisted of mostly big and very big industrial enterprises. Running them required considerable insider knowledge and interpersonal bureaucratic connections— something that the big Soviet bosses had but were not prepared to share with the intelligentsia upstarts. In the critical moment of 1989 the Soviet intelligentsia showed sufficient capacity to push the reforms close to the breaking point of revolution, but it had not yet acquired the capacity to govern a large state with an extensive state-organized economy. In Russia, the revolutionary situation of 1989–1991 ended in a stalemate, opening a prolonged period of destructive chaos.

In a bitter irony, the salvation of communist bureaucracy came unexpectedly in the rapid disintegration of Soviet economy. Once Moscow ceased being the command center, the planned economy lost its bearings and began to fall apart. Shortages of all kinds reached proportions unheard of since the war, while speculative black markets sprang up all over the place. A majority of Soviet citizens now had to concentrate on solving such daily problems as getting milk for

---

*See Michael Urban with Vyacheslav Igrunov and Sergei Mitrokhin, *The Rebirth of Politics in Russia* (New York: Cambridge University Press, 1997).

their children. The intellectuals who continued speaking about human rights and democratic procedures seemed to many ordinary people to be far removed from their daily plight.

In the last months of 1991 a daring group of young oppositional economists led by Yegor Gaidar convinced the new Russian president, Boris Yeltsin, to start a market transition through the overnight "shock therapy." They also insisted on dissolving the Soviet Union mainly for pragmatic reasons: the profitable republics were leaving it anyway, so why stay in the union with unprofitable ones? Instead the neoliberal economists proposed to shake up the whole economy, see the old industrial bosses perish in bankruptcies, and hope for self-regulating market forces to jump-start economic growth on a trajectory that would soon bring Russia up to Western standards in everything, from the quality of consumer goods to the mechanisms of liberal democracy.

Specialists are still arguing about whether the market shock therapy was at all a viable strategy of transformation. We need rather to look at what the actual results were because, indirectly, the war in Chechnya was one of them. In mitigation, it should be recognized that as long as Gaidar enjoyed any clout in Yeltsin's administration, there was no war in Chechnya. But by the end of 1993 Gaidar had perished in the backlash that his policies had provoked.

Politically, what neoliberal market economists presented as their major virtue proved to be their biggest fault: the hard-nosed insistence that the economy must be left to the globally connected technical experts like themselves and certainly not to the soft-hearted humanistic intellectuals and common populace, whose demands of stable jobs and living wages endangered monetary stability. This neoliberal elitism coupled with economic depression deeply alienated the Russian citizenry. The neoliberals believed that once the rich emerged from the creative destruction of the postcommunist transition, they would use their money to start new businesses and lift the country out of depression. Rich Russians did appear, but of a quite different kind.

The powerful and ostentatiously rich persons who began emerging from the shade in the mid-1990s invariably preferred to obfuscate their origins for one big reason: the mechanisms of their ascent were thoroughly dishonest, if not downright criminal. Investigative reporters

and scholars have compiled much evidence about such mechanisms.[*]
No, there was no secret conspiracy. Simply, it was a "bank run" situation in which the officials who were once highly positioned in the
collapsing Soviet structure simultaneously rushed out in panic; quite
a few took whatever lay close at hand. Ironically, those best served by
the neoliberal ideology of privatization proved to be the former communist bosses. Those who used to run the state banks and factories
were in the best position to arrange the insider buyouts. The economic
depression, however, rendered most enterprises unprofitable. In this
situation it made rational sense to strip the assets and transfer the
money to a tax haven abroad. Such machinations invariably required
the connivance of police and local politicians, especially the governors
of provinces. The latter went corrupt on a massive scale because their
own ability to stay in power now hinged on political machines of the
kind that Chicago's mayors of yesteryear would have immediately
recognized.[†]

Faced with this reality, President Yeltsin chose to turn his administration into the supreme machine of political machines. He also felt
that this transparently cynical move warranted a veneer of imperial
splendor and patriotism. In this, a small victorious war could help.
What he did not realize is how deeply his army was affected by the
pervasive disorganization and moral rot.

In the language of social science, the war in Chechnya appears terribly overdetermined. That is, there are too many factors, each of
which should suffice to cause the war: historical legacies, imperial
geopolitics, political instability, oil, Islam, organized crime, and now,
atop of all, al Qaeda. Different scholars have proposed sophisticated
explanations based on any combination of these factors. And then
there is the informed opinion of General Alexander Korzhakov, the

---

[*] See Chrystia Freeland, *Sale of the Century* (New York: Crown Business, 2000); David
Hoffman, *The Oligarchs* (New York: Public Affairs, 2002); and Vadim Volkov, *Violent
Entrepreneurs: The Use of Force in the Making of Russian Capitalism* (Ithaca: Cornell
University Press, 2002).

[†] Two books are particularly useful to understand the character of Russia's privatization: Steven Solnick, *Stealing the State: Control and Collapse in Soviet Institutions*
(Cambridge: Harvard University Press, 1998); and David Woodruff, *Money Unmade:
Barter and the Fate of Russian Capitalism* (Ithaca: Cornell University Press, 1999).

vile former chief of Yeltsin's bodyguards and the president's reputed drinking buddy, who confided shortly after his ouster that decisions that continue to puzzle political analysts were, in fact, influenced by hangover or indigestion.* Which type of explanation is more valid? All of them and none of them, I believe. Surely there are structural factors that make Chechnya so contentious. Yet, in the profound words of French historian Fernand Braudel, history and geography propose, but people dispose.

The first stage of the war in Chechnya started at the end of 1994 after a series of bewildering and mostly contingent events. A year earlier, in October 1993, the confrontation between President Yeltsin and the Russian parliament resulted in fierce rioting in downtown Moscow that was put down by tank fire.† Boris Yeltsin, an ambitious and inordinately lucky adventurist politician of humble provincial origins, drew his own lesson from this close encounter with civil war. He sacked his highbrow, neoliberal advisers, surrounding himself instead with "simple tough guys" like General Korzhakov who were ready to split a bottle with the boss, laugh at his jokes, and quickly send in tanks to protect him if necessary.

Thus in 1994 the postcommunist regime acquired the quasi-monarchical traits of Bonapartism. Yeltsin's men flattered the new emperor by openly calling him "tsar." The Kremlin's chief of supplies, Pavel Borodin, in the face of the economic hardship plaguing the country, spent several billion dollars to restore the former imperial palaces, including the thrones, to their original splendor—actually to more than their original splendor; he plated the interiors with more gold than was used in the time of the tsars.

Admittedly, social science is ill equipped to deal with the human aspects of Yeltsin's self-transformation from the populist politician assaulting the privileges of the communist establishment into the potentate who evidently believed, at least for a moment, that his destiny was to become a tsar. Such a task probably calls for a Balzac or a Dostoevsky. Nonetheless, I must note that Bourdieu's sociology takes

---

*Interview with Alexander Korzhakov, *Argumenty i fakty*, no. 34, August 1996.
† See Lilia F. Shevtsova, *Yeltsin's Russia* (Washington: Carnegie Endowment for International Peace, 1999).

us further than other theories in relating Yeltsin's decision to invade Chechnya to the contemporary atmosphere of imperial restoration in the Kremlin. Yeltsin's decision, which many judged irrational, was consistent with his atmosphere of imperial restoration. Should the tsar negotiate with rebellious "mountain shepherds," or should he wage a "small victorious war"? These exact expressions were proffered at the fateful session of Russia's national security council in December 1994.[*] Therefore, we should reformulate our question. Instead of asking why Yeltsin used force against the Chechen separatists, we should ask why it had to be Chechnya when it came to the show of force.

Let me now provide a brief overview of Chechnya's geography and history. The place is tiny, especially when compared to the immensity of Russia. Most of the fighting today is taking place in an area of forty by seventy miles. But this area contains a very varied landscape, from the snow-capped mountain peaks of the Caucasus ridge, across the numerous densely populated valleys in the foothills, to the fertile steppe plains that eventually turn into arid semidesert. Mountains offer nooks and crannies where many different communities can co-exist without mixing and preserve their own identities and traditions. Chechen and many other languages of the Caucasus, like the Basque language in Spain, have no surviving relatives in the modern world. The likely explanation is that in the past the Caucasus provided refuge for small peoples that otherwise would have been conquered and ab-sorbed either by the ancient civilizations of the Middle East just to the south of the Caucasus or by the nomadic invaders from Inner Asia who dominated the open steppe lying to the north. Squeezed between these two grinding wheels of world history, the peoples of the Cauca-sus could survive because they successfully adapted to its difficult but protective environment.

Their social and economic adaptations were akin to what we com-monly observe among such mountain peoples as the old-time Swiss, the Basques, the Albanians, and the Scots of Europe and the Kurds and

---

[*] The best-researched journalistic account of the origins and the course of the first Chechen war is Carlotta Gall and Thomas de Waal, *Chechnya: Calamity in the Caucasus* (New York: New York University Press, 1998).

the Pashtuns of Asia.* The highlanders must be resourceful, tough, and economical because their environments are poor. The men are usually good fighters and their most prized possession would be a weapon: a dagger, a sword, and later in history a gun. Hospitality, friendship, loyalty, and family honor are as sacred to the highlander as is blood revenge. In the mountains a reputation as a valued friend, a generous host, and a fearsome foe is the precarious guarantee of one's life. After the first war, Chechen propaganda featured a leaflet with the photograph of a wolf (Chechens' favorite self-representation to their enemies) and the caption "Think twice before messing with me!" This bravado, no doubt supported by many genuine examples of ferocious valor, nonetheless betrays profound insecurity. Mountain peoples tend to be small because mountainous terrain cannot support large populations. Similarly, they have no states of their own because state organization cannot take root in such terrain, among pervasively armed populations, and with such small economic surpluses to appropriate through taxes. The typical social organization of highlanders is stateless clan society. Clans serve as the collective repository of reputation that plays a key role in structuring the social interactions and creating trust among the people. Clan reputations are assiduously cultivated and transmitted in legends from generation to generation. And these legends motivate people to perform great deeds, above all deeds of courage and honor.

A warning: all this pertains to what sociologists call the ideal type. The highlanders are complex and contradictory human beings like the rest of human race. I am only suggesting here some elements toward a rational explanation of the ethnic and cultural traits that invariably captivate the imagination of outsiders: the highlanders' sense of pride, independence, toughness, and violence.

Now, imagine what happens when in the early 1800s the Russian Empire descends on the clan societies of the North Caucasus region. From imperial Saint Petersburg, Chechnya looked like a small rock on the road to the riches of Persia and India that all European conquerors so coveted at the time. From its standpoint the demands placed on the

---

*See Allen W. Johnson and Timothy Earle, *The Evolution of Human Societies: From Foraging Group to Agrarian State*, 2d ed. (Stanford: Stanford University Press, 1998).

natives of the Caucasus seemed natural. The natives were expected to provide the manpower to build the imperial outposts, roads, and bridges to make their lands accessible, pay taxes, supply auxiliary troops, and generally to display subservience to the European masters. In case the natives thought of some "treachery," hostages were taken from locally prominent families.* These were typical colonial practices of the epoch: the British in India and the French in Algeria did much the same. And as in so many other territories subjected to European imperial domination, the native peoples revolted.

In 1818 the Russian general Aleksei Yermolov built a fortress in the foothills of Chechnya and called it Grozny, literally Fort Terrifying. By preventing the natives from taking their herds to the winter pasturage, the new fortress threatened the highlanders with starvation—just as General Yermolov expected. When the Chechens tried to burn the hated fortress, they were met with artillery fire, and in the common practice of the time the rebellion was followed by a punitive expedition against a nearby village. To the astonishment of Russian troops, the villagers, even the women and children, preferred to die fighting. The fate of that village endures in Chechen folk ballads. Insisting that the "Asiatic savages" respected only the arguments of superior violence, General Yermolov proceeded to methodically burn the Chechen villages (reportedly while reading Julius Caesar's *Gallic Wars* for inspiration).

Yermolov's toughness achieved the opposite: instead of submission, the numerous small peoples of the North Caucasus began to unite against the common enemy. Since the Russian Empire espoused the official Orthodox Christianity, the resistance found inspiration in the Islamic teaching of holy war against infidels, or jihad. It was a simple yet vigorous faith of independent peasants who rose in a tremendous movement of resistance to empire. Islam provided two crucial mechanisms required by a rebellion: first, a powerfully unifying ideology for the disparate and often feuding mountain clans and, second, the

---

*See the detailed and penetrating study of Michael Khodarkovsky, *Russia's Steppe Frontier: The Making of a Colonial Empire, 1500–1800* (Bloomington: Indiana University Press, 2002).

flexible but robust network of Sufi preachers who inspired and coordinated the struggle.

In the 1830s an energetic and capable preacher called Shamil started building a centralized state in the neighboring Dagestan and proclaimed himself its leader, or imam. Shamil's imamate lasted twenty-five years, during which it acquired its own government, built strategic roads, and even developed its own armaments industry. Chechnya provided perhaps the majority of fighters for Shamil's rebellious state.

What started for the Russian Empire as a minor frontier operation unexpectedly grew into its longest and costliest war up to that time.* The Caucasus war left an indelible imprint on Russian classical literature, from Alexander Pushkin and Mikhail Lermontov to Leo Tolstoy, who wrote such moving stories as "Prisoner of the Caucasus" and "Haji Murat." Among the peoples of the Caucasus the cultural imprint of that war, of course, is even stronger.

Having said that, I hasten to warn against the extremely common pitfall of viewing the Caucasus war of yesteryear through the prism of romantic literature. To a considerable extent, today's war in Chechnya seems a replay of Imam Shamil's jihad of 150 years ago only because both sides read Tolstoy at school and built their expectations on imagery from the past. Yeltsin and Putin, along with their generals, consider Yermolov a wise and tough patriot of great power (as I tried to show, calling Yermolov tough is an understatement, and wise is sheer nonsense). Today's Chechen fighters, a majority of whom would otherwise be unemployed and without a purpose in life, launched themselves from obscurity to military glory by the conscious emulation of the legendary warriors of Imam Shamil. Since I resolutely protest against this sort of historical memory propagated by the belligerents, I am going to focus on the less heroic side of history that is not preserved in legends but still can be excavated by historical sociology.

---

* The best account of this war in English remains John Baddeley, *The Russian Conquest of the Caucasus* (London, 1908). Also see Moshe Gammer, *Muslim Resistance to the Tsar* (London: F. Cass, 1994).

The truth regarding Imam Shamil is that he surrendered in 1859 because the Russian side finally realized the futility of Yermolov's terroristic strategy and offered very comfortable terms to Shamil and his circle to end the hostilities. Shamil was taken to Saint Petersburg and introduced to the tsar, who magnanimously gave him a generous pension. Many of Shamil's local officials received equivalent ranks in the Russian colonial administration. By this time the common people were worn out by the decades-long destructive fighting. In Chechnya, Dagestan, and Circassia the war produced bands of professional warriors who fought mostly for personal glory and gain: raiding for booty and trading hostages for ransom eventually became more important than protecting their villages. In this sense the destructive dynamic of the war today is indeed comparable to that of the past.

The Bolshevik revolution of 1917 gave the peoples of the Caucasus another opportunity to rise against imperial domination. Many Chechens joined the Reds, who promised to restore land to the peasants and liberate the oppressed colonial peoples. Quite possibly, the Chechen partisans saved the Reds when in 1919 they dealt a strong blow to the rear of General Denikin's White army, stopping his advance on Bolshevik-held Moscow. After victory in the civil war, the Bolsheviks created for the Chechens an autonomous republic within the framework of the Union of Soviet Socialist Republics.* A few dozen such republics were created in the former colonial peripheries of the Russian Empire. Each one was endowed with its ethnic schools, theaters, publishing houses, and eventually universities, and official policy gave preference in admissions and hiring to the native nationalities. The early Bolshevik transformation produced the new group of modern-educated native specialists and brought considerable improvements to the quality of life through public works, free health care and education, and modern cultural amenities.

Here we encounter a major contradiction of Soviet history. On the one hand, the Soviet state promoted urbanization, education, industrialization, equality between the sexes and ethnic groups, and generally

---

*For the ultimate analysis of the Soviet nationality policies, see Terry Martin, *The Affirmative Action Empire: Nations and Nationalism in the Soviet Union* (Ithaca: Cornell University Press, 2001).

all that was regarded as progressive. On the other hand, it was a harshly dictatorial state, born in a brutal civil war and committed to survival through militarization: beginning with Lenin, the Soviet leaders deeply envied the effectiveness of German bureaucracy, and thus their inspiration was Bismarck perhaps even more than Karl Marx.

The Chechen peasants resisted the state expropriation of their livelihood during the collectivization of 1929–1932 just like the Russian and Ukrainian peasants. But the Chechen peasants, being highlanders, traditionally possessed weapons, which resulted in a bloody cycle of rebellion and state repression. This is a grim and obscure period of modern history. Evidently many Chechens still believed in the promise of the modern socialist project and felt tragically at a loss trying to reconcile the progressive and the brutal dictatorial sides of Stalinist regime.* As happened elsewhere in the Soviet bloc during the Stalinist purges of the 1930s–1940s, most victims either were taken at random or else were true believers who considered Stalin's policies a deviation from the original idea. This may help to explain the tragically contradictory reaction of the Chechens to World War II.

In 1942, when the German armies surprised the Soviet command by forcefully advancing simultaneously on the Caucasus and on Stalingrad, tens of thousands of Chechens and other North Caucasians enlisted in the Red army and fought bravely. But we also know that during spring and summer of 1942, the Soviet command was in disarray, and many units at the battlefront were sacrificed senselessly. Only later in the midst of the battle of Stalingrad did Stalin realize that instead of issuing draconian orders he should let the soldiers do their job of defending the country. For the Russian soldiers the survival of their country was clearly at stake.

Many North Caucasians, however, could not feel as patriotic, especially the peasants from small mountain villages, many of whom barely spoke any Russian and regarded the Germans as just another European invader. Some escaped back into their villages with stories of mayhem reigning near the battlefront, which the Soviet authorities

---

*See Valeri Tishkov, *Ethnicity, Nationalism, and Conflict in and after the Soviet Union* (Thousand Oaks, Calif.: Sage, 1997).

considered desertion and spreading panic. On the German side, a few senior officers who had served in the African colonies used the familiar strategy of fomenting "tribal sentiments" to recruit native scouts and police for the Nazi-occupied territories. Their efforts were successful to some extent before the German advance was rolled back a few months later. On balance, a majority of Chechen soldiers fought in the Soviet army, a minority probably evaded the draft or deserted, and a few joined the Germans either for opportunistic reasons or to take revenge on the Soviets.

The events of this dark period come to us distorted by old rumors and wild accusations. In February 1944, an entire year after the Germans retreated from the North Caucasus, Stalin ordered the wholesale deportation of the Chechens and several neighboring peoples from their homelands. Close to half a million people were crammed into freight trains and, in brutal cold, sent on a long journey to Central Asia. Between a quarter and a third of them did not survive the trip. Stalin's motives remain as murky as ever. After all, many times more Ukrainians and Russians also had joined the enemy during the early disastrous period of Nazi invasion. Likely, the typically small size of the Caucasus peoples made feasible their wholesale forced relocation. It's possible too that Stalin and his chief of secret police Lavrenty Beria, who were both ethnic Georgians from the other side of the Caucasus, shared the stereotype portraying the Chechens as dangerous bandits from the highlands. Stalin, who came to believe that historical accomplishments required a ruthlessness of equally gigantic proportions, seemed little troubled that there were many more women, children, engineers, teachers, and decorated veterans of the Soviet army than traitors and bandits among the deportees.

Importantly, almost every Chechen family has a story of how during the deportation some Soviet soldier or railwayman shared a piece of bread with them. Minutka Square in Grozny, the site of fierce fighting during recent wars, officially bears the name of Khrushchev—a token of Chechen gratitude to the Soviet leader who in 1957 allowed them to return from exile. This kind of popular memory served to reconcile the Chechens to the acute contradiction of their situation under Soviet rule. On the one hand, they suffered from Stalinist terror as immensely as any group in the USSR. But on the other hand, they joined the modern world through the Soviet institutions of education and industrialization in which a great many Chechens achieved considerable success. Key figures of the Chechen revolution in 1991 were a military pilot, a writer, a journalist, industrial managers, engineers, professors, policemen, a few inevitably shady businessmen—but there was not a single traditional peasant, clan elder, or Islamic preacher among them.

The Chechen revolution of 1991 above all sought to eradicate the humiliations and injustices of Soviet period. Its original promise was a secular and democratic national state that, in a typical hope of the times, would develop a modern market economy and, in a particular Chechen apprehension borne by their history, would secure the survival of the nation. The Chechen revolution was directly inspired by the analogous pro-independence movements in the Baltic republics. General Dzhokhar Dudayev, who until March 1991 served as the commander of a Soviet Strategic Air Force wing of nuclear bombers near Tartu, Estonia, left his military career and became the revolutionary leader and soon the Chechen president by popular acclamation. At innumerable revolutionary rallies and political meetings he impressed his countrymen by arguing that Estonia and Chechnya were roughly the same size, had distinct ethnic characters, and suffered terribly from the Stalinist outrages. What then prevented Chechnya from becoming an internationally recognized democratic state like Estonia? Similarly, just as Estonia could benefit from her location on the Baltic Sea close to Scandinavia, so could Chechnya benefit from its oil reserves and proximity to the Caspian Sea.

Like all politicians carried away by their populist rhetoric, Dudayev wildly exaggerated Chechnya's potential wealth and geopolitical importance. But the sudden collapse of communist rule bred similarly high hopes across the entire Soviet bloc, including within Russia itself. Moreover, in the weeks after the defeat of the reactionary coup attempt of August 1991, Moscow was embroiled in its own revolution. At the time, Yeltsin was busy consolidating his presidency and preparing the dissolution of the Soviet Union. Only when Dudayev declared Chechnya's independence from Russia did Yeltsin realize that this could start the chain reaction of further declarations of independence.

The old Soviet Union was structured like matryoshka doll. It contained the fifteen republics, like Estonia, Ukraine, and Russia, which theoretically enjoyed the constitutional right to leave the union—which they all took advantage of by the end of 1991. But Russia itself contained a number of lesser-status ethnic autonomous republics and provinces like Chechnya that had been created by the Bolshevik founders back in the early 1920s. In Moscow they now feared that the example of Chechnya would be followed by the more important provinces like Tatarstan or Yakutia. Considering that more than half of Russia's trucks were made in Tatarstan and virtually all diamonds were mined in Yakutia, their independence could spell an end to both the Russian state and the economy.

The nightmare of the domino effect rarely materializes in real life, but it is always a potent argument for military hawks and political hardliners. Moscow rushed to proclaim the independence of Chechnya unconstitutional, imposed a blockade on the separatist province, and called on the international community not to recognize it. However, Russia was not in a position to dislodge Dudayev from his self-declared presidential palace in Grozny (formerly the communist party headquarters). In 1992–1993 Russia's main preoccupation was the economic shock therapy conducted by Gaidar's neoliberal government, which for two years left Dudayev's regime in a limbo: neither truly independent nor subordinate to Moscow's policies.

In Chechnya the revolution went sour even faster than in Russia and for largely the same reasons. The economy and public order fell apart, forcing many educated Chechens and Russians who had lived in Chechnya before 1991 to seek a safer and better place to live elsewhere. Just like Yeltsin, Dudayev quarreled with his parliament, elected in the wake of Chechen revolution. A few months earlier than Yeltsin, Dudayev disbanded the parliament, also with tank fire and bloodshed. Afterward, Dudayev surrounded himself with a coterie of personal loyalists, many of whom proceeded to loot the state coffers even more brazenly than did Yeltsin's cronies. Just as Yeltsin did, Dudayev grew tougher in his pronouncements, blaming all the problems of Chechnya on enemy forces and calling his nation to prepare for war. Dudayev, always a general, relished military parades.

Many political analysts believed, with good reason, that Dudayev was on his last legs and would sacrifice the unrecognized independence of Chechnya in exchange for a legal and economic deal of the kind that Moscow offered to many other ethnic republics within Russia, such as Tatarstan. But Yeltsin, after all his failures and humiliations in the previous two years, desired a decisive victory. His minister of defense, General Pavel Grachev, was delighted to be useful and famously promised to win with "one paratroop regiment in two hours," while Yeltsin's legal and diplomatic advisers predicted that a small war would not cause objections from Western governments because Chechnya was a Russian internal matter. Unfortunately, Yeltsin's diplomats were and still remain correct in their assessment of the official Western reaction, but the eager General Grachev went badly wrong and started the cycle of warfare that seems to have no end.[*]

Shamil Basayev, the most daring and uncannily lucky among the Chechen rebel commanders, admitted to a Russian journalist that to him the most difficult moment of the war was the first three days, when nobody knew whether the Chechens would be able to resist the invading regular army.[†] Then volunteers began pouring into Grozny, many of them with their own weapons bought at the town market. (In Dudayev's Chechnya, the weapons looted from the former Soviet arsenals were bought and sold as easily as used cars.) The volunteers were organized into small mobile units and assigned defense positions all around the town according to the brilliantly simple plan devised by Aslan Maskhadov, who until 1992 was an artillery colonel in the same Russian army that he was now set to defeat in the streets of Grozny. This spectacular slaughter of the Russian forces has been described by many journalists and military analysts.[‡] Let me concentrate on the sociological side of this war and especially on why the Chechen fighters didn't stop fighting even after their incredible victory.

---

[*] The most updated, sober, and thorough analysis of the two Chechen wars from the perspectives of politics, law, and international ethics is Matthew Evangelista, *The Chechen Wars* (Washington: Brookings Institution Press, 2002).

[†] *Komsomolskaia pravda*, January 24, 1997.

[‡] See Gall and de Waal, *Chechnya*, or Anatol Lieven, *Chechnya: The Tombstone of Russian Power* (New Haven: Yale University Press, 1998).

The first generation of Chechen fighters consisted of volunteers who rose in the patriotic defense of their homeland. They fought not only for themselves and their families but also for the ancestors who perished in the deportation of 1944 and in the Caucasus war of the nineteenth century. There is perhaps a special emotional state known only to the peoples that have been subjected to genocide in the past—the "never again!" sentiment that reduces the whole world to the dilemma of survival. It provided the extraordinary determination and moral edge to the Chechen fighters in the first war. In August 1996 they recaptured their ruined capital of Grozny from the badly disorganized and demoralized Russian troops.

It is necessary to mention that Russian society was overwhelmingly opposed to the first war, not to a small degree because Russian journalists in their last moment of professional glory exposed, with great passion, the war's senselessness and ghastly reality. The resulting popular indignation nearly cost Yeltsin his presidency. He proved his inordinate survival skills by firing his hawkish advisers and "buddies" like General Korzhakov and suing for peace.

With the withdrawal of Russian troops in the fall of 1996, the first round of war came to an end, and a durable peace looked possible. Chechnya in effect became an independent state though its formal status vis-à-vis Russia was to be decided in 2001 after a five-year cooling-off period. The chief guerrilla commander, Aslan Maskhadov, whose judiciousness and discipline earned him wide respect, was elected Chechnya's second president (the flamboyant General Dudayev was killed by a Russian rocket during the war).

As the new Chechen leader, Maskhadov faced two problems. First, he had to reestablish decent relations with Yeltsin's Russia, which remained the primary provider of goods and money to the devastated Chechnya. Maskhadov tried earnestly but failed, apparently because many officials in Moscow could not forgive him the humiliation of the lost war. But perhaps there was a dirtier reason: maybe many more Russian officials expected kickbacks that Maskhadov would not provide. The guerrilla hero turned president proved insufficiently pliable.

His second task was to demobilize the Chechen fighters who, after two years of war ending in an astonishing victory over Russia, remained euphoric with little thought to what they were going to do in the future. As part of his demobilization policy, Maskhadov asked the National University of Chechnya (which was in fact a group of surviving professors and students meeting in the gutted wreck of a building) to admit the former fighters without exams and retrain them for civilian professions.*

As part of this same effort, President Maskhadov offered the portfolio of prime minister to his younger competitor in the presidential race, Shamil Basayev, whose wartime exploits had become legendary. To the Russians, Basayev was the arch-terrorist who in 1995 seized over a thousand hostages, mostly the patients, nurses, and doctors, in a town hospital in Budennovsk, in southern Russia. It was his way of demanding immediate peace talks. (The same Basayev took responsibility for planning the seizure of a Moscow theater in October 2002.) But in 1997 even in Moscow they grudgingly agreed that by promoting the former terrorist to lead the government, President Maskhadov was neutralizing a serious internal opponent. For a while Basayev earnestly tried to act like a statesman. He even donned a business suit and mused about Internet ventures. However, Basayev's incompetence in the civilian job soon became embarrassingly obvious.

Basayev quit the Chechen government in utter frustration and reverted to his warrior image and lifestyle. Basayev's move into the self-proclaimed opposition attracted many former fighters to him, especially the young men who during the war had become, in effect, professional warriors. They insisted that the struggle with Russia was not yet over and refused to demobilize. Seeking an ideological banner, Basayev and his band of unemployed veterans turned to religion and began propagating the world Islamic revolution as the only true way of overcoming foreign domination and establishing moral order. Russian officials and some journalists citing CIA sources suggest that Osama bin Laden provided inspiration and funding for these activities. As the above should make clear, however, the situation in Chechnya cannot

---

* The dean told me that when he asked Maskhadov to provide a budget to support the students with some sort of stipends, Maskhadov sadly joked that he could rather make him a brigadier general so that he would get some respect from the veteran-students.

be ascribed so much to Islamic traditions as to Islam becoming the last resort of desperate politicians and society when the promises of the 1991 revolution were replaced by grim reality.

Instead of enjoying peace, by the end of 1997 Chechnya was plunged into violent chaos as various private armies sought the sources of income in a totally ruined small country. The few remaining rackets included oil refineries, gun running, and increasingly the abduction of hostages for ransom. Maskhadov desperately sought to counter Basayev's accusations of betraying the national character of Chechnya by invoking Islamic sharia law and instilling order by dispatching his own small army against the unruly warlords. Failure to restore peace and order weighed heavily on Maskhadov, whose public pronouncements grew sullen and strangely incoherent.

By spring 1999 Chechnya was effectively in a state of internecine war. In August Basayev, operating from his native stronghold in the mountains, invaded neighboring Dagestan, ostensibly to spread his Islamic revolution to this republic that had remained part of Russia. But Shamil Basayev, who was emulating the legendary imam Shamil of the nineteenth century, failed to unite Chechnya and Dagestan by force—the local Dagestani militias resisted the unwelcome Islamic liberators with unexpected determination and, with the help of Russia's regular army, soon forced Basayev to retreat.* The Dagestanis clearly wanted to avoid what they saw happening across the border in Chechnya.

The campaign seemed to be over in a matter of days. But in September a series of apartment block bombings in Dagestan and Moscow and other Russian towns brought Russian society to a state of shock and indignation akin to what Americans experienced on September 11, 2001. Shortly before the bombings, President Yeltsin, to everyone's surprise, anointed as his successor the little-known former KGB officer Vladimir Putin. The new leader unleashed a ferocious war on the purported Chechen terrorists (although the Moscow bombings remain unsolved to this day) and promised to return Russia back to normalcy.

---

*This episode is analyzed in detail in Georgi Derluguian, "Che Guevaras in Turbans," *New Left Review*, I/237, September–October 1999, 3–27.

Putin's tough, sober, and businesslike image appealed to a great many Russians. The paradox is that now, three years later, Putin has achieved remarkably little, yet his popularity remains very high. Apparently part of the explanation is the much tighter control exercised by the Putin regime over the Russian mass media. The fortunes of Putin and his associates seem secure as long as the Russian economy is not collapsing into another crisis and the war in Chechnya is kept at low profile. Yet both pillars of Putin's stability seem shaky: the high energy prices that benefited Russia cannot last forever, and the "antiterrorist campaign" in Chechnya is still far from over after three years. If anything, the war in Chechnya has degenerated into a quagmire.

Nobody knows for sure what the actual situation in Chechnya is because today it is probably the single most dangerous place on earth to do research. Here lies part of the value of this book by Anna Politkovskaya. She shows in graphic detail the conditions of civilians caught in the vicious fighting; what motivates the brutality of the Russian troops; the role of pervasive venality in this horrible tragedy; and why the higher echelons prefer to cover up the war crimes committed by their subordinates. Politkovskaya documents two interrelated processes: first, the weakness of Russia's central government, which must (or thinks it must) tolerate war atrocities in order to attain minimal compliance from its junior ranks, and, second, the entrepreneurial strategies of various military and state officials who form an extensive, inchoate, and perennially feuding informal network that is making a profit on this war. This seems to me sound sociology no less than a damning indictment.

Let me get back to Bourdieu's method, with which I started this exposition. Politkovskaya certainly writes from a partisan position—as passionately partisan as the Russian democratic intelligentsia has always been. A century earlier Chekhov traveled to the far-off island of Sakhalin to expose the prison hell there; Korolenko stood up to reactionary opinion to expose the falsity of anti-Semitic accusations in the Beilis affair; and later in the 1960s Solzhenitsyn fought to bring out the truth about the gulag. I am not comparing public stature or literary talent here. It is the enduring motivation of the Russian intelligentsia that leads them to fight against what they consider the horror and the shame of their own country. In this respect, Politkovskaya's revelations about the war in Chechnya follow a long and dignified tradition.

It also takes a woman to get at this kind of truth. In collecting information, Politkovskaya benefits from her gender: she can gain access to the inner spaces of Chechen women, which remain off limits to a male sociologist like myself. Thus, Politkovskaya could document the massive and possibly routine incidence of rape committed against both Chechen women and Chechen male prisoners by Russian security personnel.

Politkovskaya's narrative moves from basic empirical observations to broader generalizations. The first part recounts the structures of everyday life in the midst of the war. The second part offers an insider's view of how the war has affected Russian society and its army and the impact it has had on neighboring states. The book's final part analyzes the markets generated by war: who gets what from the warfare, how some (mostly those armed) people on both sides are profiting from the war, and the incentives they have for it to continue.

The reader will notice that Politkovskaya avoids the two-sided bias that characterizes a great many Western accounts of this war. She does not romanticize the Chechen guerrillas and barely refers to their purported struggle for national independence. Her sympathy is with the civilians, the medical personnel and especially the women, both the ethnic Chechens and Russians who had lived in Chechnya since Soviet times and now find themselves trapped in this war. This remarkable woman finds the moral strength to pity the brutalized Russian soldiers and police, many of whom indeed suffer from severe psychological disorders, alcoholism, and drug abuse. It could be regarded as encouraging that Politkovskaya could still find in this war the decent or just sufficiently professional Russian officers and military attorneys who make courageous efforts to stop the atrocities or at least to report them to their superiors. But many of these officers end up being killed, usually under suspicious circumstances.

Politkovskaya spends little time discussing what is going on in Chechen politics and among the armed factions. Such information might be important if there were a peace process. But at the moment (spring 2003) such prospects seem improbable as both sides are seeking to escalate the violence, apparently in the hope that they might yet win the war. Politkovskaya chooses to describe what this escalation does to the people on the ground. In doing so, she gives us good reason to see why and how international solidarity, or at the very least international outcry, could make a difference in this forgotten war. If we live, as many of us believe, in the new global world, then we shall and we should be building transnational solidarity with fellow humans regardless of their race, faith, or location. This book does just that. Through inhumane empirical detail she shows us the crooked aspects of humanity expressed in the brutal and generalizable character of Russia's declared "antiterrorist campaign" in Chechnya; at the same time, she shows us how complex and contradictory the war is—exceedingly cruel and violent, yet there are sublime moments of human effort to just stay humane.

Now it is up to us to take our position in the global field.

Georgi M. Derluguian
Department of Sociology
Northwestern University

PROLOGUE

Who am I? And why am I writing about the second Chechen war?

I am a journalist—a special correspondent for the Moscow newspaper Novaya gazeta—and this is the only reason I've seen the war; I was sent there to cover it. Not, however, because I am a war correspondent and know this subject well. On the contrary, because I am just a civilian. The editor in chief's idea was simple: the very fact that I'm just a civilian gives me that much deeper an understanding of the experiences of other such civilians, living in Chechen towns and villages, who are caught in the war.

That's it.

For that reason, I've been going to Chechnya every month since July 1999, when the so-called Basayev* raid on Dagestan took place, which resulted in torrents of refugees from mountain villages and the whole second Chechen war. Naturally, I have traveled far and wide through all of Chechnya. I've seen a lot of suffering. The worst of it is that many of the people I've been writing about for the past two and a half years are now dead. It has been such a terrible war. Simply medieval, even though it's taking place as the twentieth century passes into the twenty-first, and in Europe too.

People call the newspaper and send letters with one and the same question: "Why are you writing about this? Why are you scaring us? Why do we need to know this?"

---

* Shamil Basayev (1965–): A former unskilled worker who became famous in 1991 with the hijacking of a Russian plane in Turkey. A comrade in arms of President Dzhokhar Dudayev. A field commander of the resistance army of the Chechen Republic of Ichkeria, a brigadier general, a terrorist, an organizer of kidnappings. Trained in the special camps of the Main Intelligence Department of the Russian Federation General Staff. Participated in the Georgian-Abkhazian War (1992–1993) as a mercenary for the Abkhazians, who were helped by the Kremlin. In 1995, he and his militants organized a bloody raid on Budennovsk (in the Stavropol district), with the seizure of personnel and patients from the district hospital and maternity hospital as hostages.

I'm sure this has to be done, for one simple reason: as contemporaries of this war, we will be held responsible for it. The classic Soviet excuse of not being there and not taking part in anything personally won't work.

So I want you to know the truth. Then you'll be free of cynicism.

And of the sticky swamp of racism that our society has been sliding into.

And of having to make difficult decisions about who's right and who's wrong in the Caucasus, and if there are any real heroes there now.

London, May 2002: The Beginning

It is the eve of the summer of 2002. We are in the thirty-third month of the second Chechen war. The end of this hopeless war is nowhere to be seen. The "purges"* never stop; they resemble mass autos-da-fé. Torture is the norm. Executions without a trial are routine. Marauding is commonplace. The kidnapping of people by Federal soldiers in order to conduct slave trading (with the living) or corpse trading (with the dead) is the stuff of everyday Chechen life.

"Human substance" disappears overnight, without a trace, à la 1937.

And in the mornings, on the outskirts of town, there are cut-up, disfigured bodies that have been thrown out after curfew.

And for the hundredth or thousandth cursed time, I hear children in the village streets routinely discussing which fellow villager was found, and in what condition.... Today ... yesterday ... scalped, with sliced-off ears or chopped-off digits....

"So he had no fingers?" one adolescent asks, matter-of-factly.

"No, Alaudin had no toes," the other answers apathetically.

This is state versus group terrorism. Wahhabi† bands attack villages,

---

*Special operations conducted by Russian subdivisions in Chechen territory to check passports and hunt bandits. However, the Russian forces have departed considerably from the initial goals and tasks of the purge, and the term has become a symbol for murder, kidnapping, and marauding.

† A Muslim religious sect that has existed in what is now Saudi Arabia since the eighteenth century. Wahhabi emissaries appeared in the Russian North Caucasus in the period between the first and second Chechen wars. They promised the people that the Islam they were preaching was the pure one, unlike the traditional local Islam. The Wahhabis were especially active in Dagestan, Ingushetia, Kabardino-Balkaria, and Chechnya. The term "Wahhabis" means something a little different in Russia today: terrorists. Most

demanding money for a jihad.* The army and police, nearly one hundred thousand strong, wander around Chechnya in a state of complete moral decay. And what other response could one expect but more terrorism, and the recruitment of new resistance fighters?

Who is to blame? President Maskhadov,[†] who was chosen by the people and is therefore responsible for their fate? Maskhadov is in the mountains. To his people, he's a leader in name only, and as a rule, he keeps his silence on every issue.

Maskhadov's comrades in arms? They're scattered all over the world. Basayev? Gelayev?[‡] Khattab?[§]

What about Putin? He's in the Kremlin, enjoying the respect of the world community as an active member of the international "antiterrorism" VIP club, the so-called coalition against terror. It's May 2002, and Bush is in Moscow . . . fraternization . . . a "historic visit" . . . but barely a word about Chechnya, as if the war didn't exist.

The world capitals flash before my eyes as I campaign for support. This spring I've been in Amsterdam, Paris, Geneva, Manila, Bonn, Hamburg . . . Everywhere they invite me to make a speech about "the situation in Chechnya," but there are zero results. Only polite Western

---

of the Chechen population thinks very badly of the "Wahhabis" or "bearded ones," as they're called here. They blame these newcomers for drawing Chechnya into the second, bloody war.

*An Islamic war against infidels. Originally, the term meant "struggle with unbelief within one's own soul." But in Chechnya it is used to mean war to the death against Russia.

[†] Aslan Maskhadov: The second president of the Chechen Republic of Ichkeria (elected in 1997). Commander of the resistance forces in the first Chechen war; continues to lead the resistance forces. A brigadier general and a former colonel of the Soviet army (an artilleryman).

[‡] Ruslan Gelayev: A former tractor driver. A field commander of the resistance army of the Chechen Republic of Ichkeria. A brigadier general, and later commander of the Chechen Special Task Detachment. He is famous for entering his native village of Komsomolskoe of the Urus-Martan district, which fated it to destruction, while retreating from Grozny with his units in winter 2000 on his way to the mountains. The storming of Komsomolskoe was the second most brutal operation of the second Chechen war, after the attack on Grozny of winter 1999–2000. More than a thousand Chechens were killed. Gelayev himself left the village secretly, and now lives in Georgia.

[§] Omar ibn al-Khattab: Field Commander of the Chechen resistance forces. A mercenary, born in Saudi Arabia, who fought in Afghanistan. One of the bloodiest figures of the second Chechen war. In March 2002, his comrades reported his death in the Chechen mountains. He was buried there.

applause in response to the words: "Remember, people are continuing to die in Chechnya *every day*. Including today."

It's a clear, obvious, unbelievable worldwide betrayal of human-itarian values. The Universal Declaration of Human Rights, a lit-tle more than half a century old, has fallen in the second Chechen war.

From Geneva, after some sluggish sessions of "official human rights advocates" (the UN Commission on Human Rights), I go on a trip to Urus-Martan, a district center in Chechnya. The situation there is bloody and stagnant, the same as a year ago. "Death squads"—Federal units belonging to an unknown department—are rushing all over the district destroying the "enemies of Russia." These enemies consist of anybody who fought for or sympathized with Dudayev* and Maskhadov, or anyone who happens to be on hand.

May 2002 reeks of despair.

... Finally, England. A decent hotel on a nice street. There is a magnificent, elderly aristocratic-looking doorman in a dignified ma-roon uniform. A gray-haired man with a fixed expression slowly gets up to meet me. He's wearing a baggy, light gray suit that only under-scores his tragic weariness. His weak shoulders are slumped.

This man is a Chechen, a native of Urus-Martan, who hasn't been there for two years. He can't be there—that's the kind of war this is. He glances around too much, as if he were homeless. His life is not comfortable, despite the doorman, the fancy hotel, and the cosmopoli-tan English surroundings. I search his face for the man I remember. The world knows this gray-haired man completely differently from the way he appears now. They know him from photographs in the newspapers, in news agency reports, and on TV: a dashing, zealous, alert man with a khaki bandanna tied in back of his head, always next to Maskhadov.

---

*Dzhokhar Dudayev (1944–1996): The first president of the Chechen Republic of Ichkeria (1992–1996), killed by a self-guiding missile in April 1996, during a phone conversation using a satellite communication system. An officer of the Soviet army, a pilot who took part in the Soviet invasion of Afghanistan. A major-general (his last rank), and a commander of the Division of Strategic Bombers of the USSR air force. He ended his military career in March 1991 in order to head the Chechen national liberation movement.

This legendary figure is Akhmed Zakayev. He is a brigadier general of the Chechen resistance forces, a comrade in arms of Dudayev (under whom he served as minister of culture) and Maskhadov, an active participant in the Khasavyurt agreements* at the end of the first Chechen war, and the commander of a special force brigade in the second Chechen war. He was wounded in March 2000, carried off the battlefield through the mountains across the border, and has not returned to Chechnya since. Today, Zakayev is Aslan Maskhadov's special representative to Europe.

Our meeting has been rescheduled several times, from country to country. Zakayev's name was handed over to the Interpol by Russia and uses an assumed name.

"I brought you some presents," he says after we greet each other, and shows me a book and a videotape.

"Thank you."

But Zakayev doesn't put them into my extended hand. He slowly turns the book with its pages down and deliberately shakes it.

"See, there's nothing else here," he says, in a completely normal tone of voice. "No white powder. Don't be afraid."

I'm not afraid, but I realize that I'm watching his hands carefully anyway. The recent war has damaged both of us. Although we're in England, we behave as if we were in Russia, where Chechen terrorism is strongly feared, and Chechens try to dot their "i"s right away, before they're asked to. That's why Zakayev shakes the book. But this doesn't satisfy him. He takes a key chain from his pants pocket and unseals the videotape.

"Nothing here either."

"Akhmed, is all this really necessary?"

"Yes, it is."

He says this without a smile and without malice.

There is an uncomfortable silence.

"When were you in Urus-Martan?" Zakayev asks. Moisture glimmers inside the half-closed eyelids of this man who's been driven into a

---

*The Khasavyurt peace treaty (1996) between Russia and Chechnya is considered the endpoint of the first Chechen war. Khasavyurt is the little village in Dagestan where the treaty was signed.

corner and is used to constantly checking to see if someone is following him. This isn't the interview yet—we're just chatting. Urus-Martan is Zakayev's native village, so it is especially important for him; it's the Chechen tradition.

"About ten days ago, at the end of April."

Zakayev's eyes are expressionless, as before, but a tear flows from one of them.

I have to say something . . .

"They showed me the street where your house was."

"Yes?"

"It's been destroyed, you know . . . "

"Not completely?" Zakayev allows himself hope.

But we both know that it's been razed to the ground.

"Of course not," I say. "Not completely."

It's time to start the interview. About the war we've left behind. An interview as long as the war. Or perhaps, as long as life itself. Definitely as long as our lives.

It will be hard to understand what we talked about, considering the massive prowar and anti-Chechen brainwashing on the part of our government. You'll be able to understand only if you know what happened during the war.

It's Nice to Be Deaf

The war began the way wars usually do, with the bombing of villages and cities, which led to torrents of refugees. Thousands of people, grabbing their children and elderly, fled wherever their feet would carry them. They were coming and going every which way, a trail of people many miles long following the main highway of Chechnya, the Rostov-Baku Federal Route. But this trail got bombed too.

September 1999. We are lying on withered autumn grass. To be more precise, we want to lie on it, but for most of us all that's left is the dusty Chechen ground. There are too many of us—hundreds, and there are not enough amenities for everyone.

We are the people caught in the bombing. We didn't do anything wrong; we were just walking toward Ingushetia along the former highway, which is now all torn up by armored vehicles.

Grozny is behind us. We run as a herd from the war and its battles. When the time comes, and you have hit the ground face down, assuming a fetal position, trying to hide your head, knees, and even elbows under your body—then a kind of false, sticky loneliness sneaks up on you, and you start to think: "Why are you crouching? What are you trying to save? This life of yours that no one but you cares about?"

Why is it false? Because you know perfectly well that this isn't really true: you have a family, and they are waiting and praying for you. And it's sticky because of the sweat. When you're clinging to life, you sweat a lot. Some people are lucky, though. When they feel that death is near, all that happens is that the hair rises on their heads.

Still, there is loneliness. Death is the one situation where you can never find companionship. When the diving helicopters hover over your bent back, the ground starts to resemble a death bed.

Here are the helicopters, going for another round. They fly so low that you can see the gunners' hands and faces. Some say that they can even see their eyes. But this is fear talking. The main thing is their legs, dangling carelessly in the open hatches. As if they didn't come to kill, but to let their tired feet get some fresh air. Their feet are big and scary, and the soles almost seem to touch our faces. The barrels of their guns are squeezed between their thighs. We're frightened, but we all want to see our killers. They seem to be laughing at us crawling comically down below—heavy old women, young girls, and children. We can even hear their laughter. But no, this is just another illusion; it's too noisy to hear that. Automatic weapon fire whistles in the air around us, and someone always starts to wail along. Has anyone been killed? Wounded?

"Don't move. Don't raise your head. That's my advice," a man next to me says. He dropped to the ground right where he was, in his black suit with a white shirt and black tie.

My neighbor Vakha starts talking nonstop. This is a good thing; it's better to talk now than to be silent.

Vakha is a land surveyor from Achkhoi-Martan, a big village not far from Ingushetia. In wartime Chechnya, everyone is afraid of everything. This morning, Vakha left his house wearing his suit and carrying his folder as usual, so as not to attract attention, as if he were going to work. In fact, he had decided to flee.

"Every time," Vakha mumbles, because you can't help mumbling with your mouth pressed to the ground, "every time the helicopters come, I take my folder, get out some paper, and pretend to write. I think it helps."

People nearby start to laugh quietly.

"How can paper help? What are you talking about?" a tiny, skinny man to his left mutters in a loud whisper, spitting out dirt.

"The pilots see that I'm working, that I'm not a terrorist," the land surveyor retorts.

"And what if they think just the opposite? That you're taking down their license plate numbers?" a female body in front pipes up, gingerly shifting a bit. "I'm all numb. When will this all end?"

"If they think that, then you're done for." We can't see who says this. He is behind us. And it's a good thing: his words are tough, sharp, and pitiless, like an ax.

"There you go again. Enough of that." An old man's voice cuts the tough guy short. Then he asks Vakha, "Show me your folder, please. I'll tell the others."

The bodies, who have been silenced by the tough guy, are eager to clutch at straws again, to enjoy an unexpected gift of momentary happiness, the last for some.

"Go ahead, show us . . . "

"We'll all get these folders . . . "

"The Russians will run out of them . . ."

"Putin will wonder, why are all the Chechens running around with folders during the war? They should be carrying automatic weapons . . ."

"And he'll give out folders to the Feds* too. All of Chechnya will be carrying folders . . ."

"Vakha, what color should the folders be?"

The helicopters don't stop circling around. The children's crying shakes the ground that is studded with people, machine guns are shooting—why don't they shut up for just a moment?—and the explosions of falling mines croak the whole time, introducing a banal note into our stay on the death bed. That's all we need!

Still, people joke around. Vakha defends himself meekly.

"It's all in Allah's hands," he says. "But say what you want, I've never been wounded with this folder. Not in the first war, and not in this one. It's always helped me."

"So you had the folder in the first war too?" someone bursts out laughing, in a kind of nervous spasm, "Then why are you lying on the ground, man? Why don't you get up?"

Vakha is tired of that.

"Everyone's lying on the ground. Why should I be the one to get up? Why should I make myself into a target?"

---

*Representatives of Federal troop units and military departments. The term is used both by them and by civilians. In Chechnya, the term is synonymous with "Russians."

"But you have your folder." It's the old man who cut off the tough guy, who, by the way, has been silent ever since. The old man laughs somewhere behind us, if you can call body movements and raspy sighs against the ground laughter. "You don't know how lucky you are, man; they might think you're counting us. And that means you're on their side."

Vakha is silent now; it's no time for jokes. Everything in its place. He starts blowing dust from his dirty black sleeves, breathing from somewhere under his body. After all, this is the only thing he can do in the fetal position we've been forced to assume.

In twenty-four hours, Vakha and his magic folder will be destroyed, blown up by a mine about a mile from where we are now lying. He'll take just a few steps away from the road, into an untidy, un-harvested field from that first wartime autumn. There were already too many mines to count, and everyone to a man, including soldiers and militants, was wandering around Chechnya without a map of the minefields. It's like playing Russian roulette.

Vakha walks to that side not because he has to, but simply be-cause he's exhausted from waiting. The line to the passport check-point was too long. It consisted mostly of us jokers, the new family he'd been prepared to die with the day before, lying on a different field.

Now dead, Vakha lies on a field again, but this time fearlessly, with his wounded face looking up and his hands spread wider than they've ever been in his life. The left hand is about ten yards from his black jacket, which has been torn to pieces. The right hand is a bit closer, about five steps away. And Vakha's legs are quite a problem: they disappear, most likely turning into dust at the time of the explosion and flying away with the wind. His folder with its blank sheets of paper meets the same fate. It saved him from the helicopters, but it can't save him from the mines.

Then two soldiers carefully approach Vakha from the checkpoint with the long line. One of them is young and scrawny; he looks like he's fifteen years old, and his helmet and boots are too big. The second is a bit older and bigger, well-built, with his hands in the pockets of his camouflage pants. The first starts crying softly, dirtying his face as he wipes his tears, and turns around, not having the heart to look. The second smacks him on the back of the head, and the first soldier shuts up immediately, like an alarm clock that's been turned off with a slap of the hand so that a person can continue sleeping in the morning. The Chechens in line buy an "emergency reserve" big black plastic sack for "Cargo 200"* from these soldiers' lieutenant. Then they gather Vakha's remains and spend quite a while discussing where to bring them. To his mother, wife, and children in the camp at Ingushetia? Or to his empty house in Achkhoi-Martan? Reason prevails—the body should be brought to Achkhoi, of course. It will be buried there anyway, in the family cemetery. So why waste money lugging it to Ingushetia? You need to bribe a lot of people to get there. At the Kavkaz checkpoint, the border between this war and the rest of the world, you need to pay twice, once each way. And you'd have to pay two or three times as much for a corpse, depending on the commander's mood that day.

. . . But for now, Vakha will be alive and well for twenty-four hours. And we continue to lie on the field on the outskirts of Gekhi, hoping to get away from the helicopters, and almost believing in a happy future. After all, it's only the beginning of the war, the first days of October 1999. It seems to us that the fighting won't last too long, and that the refugees will soon be able to return to their homes. All we have to do is survive this day, and things will straighten themselves out.

At one point, Vakha becomes bolder—after all, when there is danger for too long, everything gets to be dull and boring. Ignoring the helicopters, he suddenly turns over onto his side. And in a normal, human way, without earth in his mouth, he begins to talk about his family—his six children, who had left Achkhoi a week ago for Ingushetia along with his mother, wife, and two unmarried sisters. They're the ones he's trying to make his way to.

Off to the side, Gekhi is being bombed. Probably as fiercely and continuously as Königsberg was in World War II. Vakha turns face down again.

---

*Army jargon for a corpse. "We have a Cargo 200" means that there are dead people.

"There were so many refugees from Grozny gathered there—a real nightmare," he says, distracted from the topic of his family and engrossed in the rhythm of the attackers' mounting, irrational bombing of their own people. "Thousands, probably. In the last bombing, a week ago, a hospital was destroyed, and the sick and wounded were taken away. Where will they take the wounded now?"

The women are quietly wailing, and shushing the children so they don't wail, as if the children weren't people too. The splashing sounds emitted by the weapons swarm around us from all sides, not letting our minds rest. Although it's been only about half an hour since the beginning of the helicopter attack, it seems like half a day, enough time to recall most of your life. People gradually start to lose their self-control. Cries of desperation can be heard; men are sobbing. But not all of them. Among us are some thirteen- or fourteen-year-olds. They are excitedly and joyfully discussing which weapon is being used at a given moment. And what else can they do besides demonstrate their thorough knowledge? They've been learning modern weapon terminology their whole conscious lives, since the Chechen war began, for nearly ten years.

Between the teenagers and us, a little boy is quietly crawling around. He is probably six years old, thin and sad-looking. He isn't screaming, crying, or grabbing his mother, but looking around thoughtfully and saying "It's nice to be deaf" in a simple, calm, even everyday voice. As if he were saying "It's nice to play ball."

Right then the "hail" overtakes us. There is no greater torture for a person's hearing, not to mention life, in war. The hail comes from the late twentieth-century version of the Katyusha* rocket launcher. It whistles and hisses for a long time. But if you can already hear it, that means it's past you, and death, though it was nearby, has chosen someone else for the time being. And you laugh about this. The hail turns you into an inhuman beast that has learned to rejoice in someone else's misfortune.

The boy, who is lying comfortably on a grass bush pillow despite the circumstances, sums it up this way:

---

*An artillery rocket launcher with high striking capacity. It was actively used during the second Chechen war. Its fire was commonly called "hail."

"The deaf can't hear any of this. And so they're not afraid."

Vakha quietly pulls the boy closer, hugs him, and gives him some candy from the pocket of his black jacket.

"What's your name?" Vakha asks, crying softly.

"Sharpuddin," the boy answers, surprised to see a grown man crying.

"It would be even better, Sharpuddin, if we could become blind, mute, and stupid." Vakha's eyes dry up under the boy's gaze. "But we're not. And yet we have to survive anyway."

The helicopters fly away after about five minutes, and the hail falls silent. The raid is over. People begin to pick themselves up at once and shake themselves off. Someone praises Allah. The field becomes lively. The women run to look for trucks for the wounded, and the men carry the dead to one place.

A day and night pass. The boy, Sharpuddin, goes up to the men who are collecting Vakha's remains in a black bag, and silently begins to help them. They sternly shoo him away like a dog, for his own good, but his mother objects. She says that her son was the last child that Vakha caressed in his life. And then Sharpuddin is allowed to help.

The Chiri-Yurt Settlement

Chiri-Yurt is a big Chechen village. It was industrial in Soviet times. It had a large cement factory with many thousands of workers, cultural centers, hospitals, schools, libraries, a developed infrastructure, and a high percentage of educated people. Chiri-Yurt's geographical position, which was so advantageous for industrial development during the epoch of "strategic heights" and "command points," doomed it in the second Chechen war. The factory is now completely destroyed, the people have no work, the infrastructure is in total decay, and all the educated inhabitants have fled wherever they could. However, the population of Chiri-Yurt has gotten several times bigger. That's because it is located at the edge of the Argun valley, or the "Wolf Gates," as the Feds call it. If you're coming up to the Argun valley and Chiri-Yurt from Grozny, about fifteen miles away, you pass a plain with oil rigs and a refinery, which both the Feds and the militants want to control. Beyond Chiri-Yurt and the Argun valley are the mountains of the Nozhai-Yurt, Vedeno, and Shatoi districts, the headquarters of Basayev and Khattab's forces. These are precisely the places that their detachments went through in the summer of 1999 to get to Dagestan; this is in essence what started the second Chechen war. They came back here too, and as a result the people living here learned about modern politics not from television, but directly, firsthand. Back then, in 1999, people could watch the monstrous provocation and betrayal, with all its consequences. Basayev and Khattab's troops returned from Dagestan to Chechnya accompanied by Federal aircraft, and nobody touched the troops. However, as soon as they disappeared into the mountain forests, intensive bombing of the villages they passed through to get to their bases began. As a result, 98 percent of Duba-Yurt (another village with a population of many thousands, not far from Chiri-Yurt, but deeper in the foothills) was destroyed, and the majority of its inhabitants, deprived of the roof over their heads, went to Chiri-Yurt. It is no accident that in this area between Chiri-Yurt and Duba-Yurt, the events that became the primary cause of many future tragedies occurred. The fierce battles for the Wolf Gates took place right here in February 2000. On the Feds' side, these battles were conducted by (among other units) the tank regiment under the command of Yury Budanov, which was considered one of the best units of the Russian armed forces. This was the same Budanov, a colonel with two Orders of Bravery on his chest, whose experience has clearly shaped the new face of Putin's promilitary and neo-Soviet Russia, where the ends once again justify the means. Right here, in the field between Chiri-Yurt and Duba-Yurt, in February 2000, several of Budanov's officers were killed, among them his best friend Major Razmakhnin. It was here that Budanov swore to avenge himself against those snipers who killed his comrades in arms. After the battles there, at the end of February, his regiment was transferred about fifty miles deeper into Chechnya, at the edge of the village of Tangi-Chu, which the whole world now knows in connection with the "problem of war crimes by Federal servicemen in Chechnya." Here, on March 26, 2000, the night after Putin won the presidential election, the colonel got drunk and decided that the time had come for payback for the battles at the Wolf Gates. He kidnapped, raped, and strangled an eighteen-year-old Chechen girl named Elsa Kungayeva, who he thought was the sniper responsible for everything. On this basis, he was "acquitted," both in the eyes of Russian public opinion and by the Russian system of justice, which ruled that if the colonel was socially motivated, then it was a justifiable murder.

However, this was a later chapter of a war that completely tore up our lives. Now, let's return to Chiri-Yurt. To the burning, torturous, nearly 120-degree summer at the end of the first year of the second Chechen war. To the crowd of people who were driven away by Budanov's troops from their homes and turned into outcasts. Hungry, dirty, humiliated people deprived of their rights.

Khazimat

For the first time (except in the movies), I saw an old woman who was swollen from hunger, and nothing will ever wipe this image from my memory. It happened nearly a year after the beginning of the war, in the very center of Chiri-Yurt, amid an overcrowded mass of people. We were in High School No. 3, which hurriedly stopped classes eight months ago, as the bombing got closer, and was transformed into one of five refugee camps.

Woodcuts, as everyone knows, are drawn in one color. Khazimat Gambieva, a withered old refugee with swollen joints and an inflated stomach, looks exactly that way—as if she had been drawn in black and white, with her black wrinkles standing out on her parchmentlike skin. Her tightly drawn nose is just another line of blackness; so are the dark circles around her angular cheekbones. She looks like a victim of the siege of Leningrad, only this is taking place at the turn of the millennium, in a Europe that is more concerned with luxurious centennial celebrations than with Chechnya, one of its territories.

Khazimat is very sick. And she's actually not even an old woman; she is fifty-one, and her youngest daughter is only thirteen. The disease that has turned her into a living woodcut is called dystrophy, or chronic hunger.

The self-sacrificing Khazimat, who has worked as a nurse at a children's hospital for twenty years, gives everything that comes the way of her family of eleven to her children and grandchildren. Apples go to her four little grandchildren, since they have caught tuberculosis from hunger and cold. Flour for bread goes to her unmarried teenage daughters.

When they first came to Chiri-Yurt, the Gambievs had money. One by one, the girls brought their earrings to the market. For some time the family was also able to support itself from her oldest son selling their little television set, the only thing the Gambievs were able to save from their burning house. But that was the last money they saw.

"What are your hopes for the future?" I ask.

"I don't have any. We survived another day, Allah be praised," Khazimat answers, holding her neck with her right hand, as if to help herself breathe. "There's no help from anywhere. We're dying little by little. My oldest son can barely move—there's nothing to eat. And my youngest girl fainted from hunger yesterday. Our camp neighbors acted like they didn't understand why she fainted. But they had bread and tea that day—I could smell it. People have turned into beasts."

As we approach the end of the first year of the war, it is no longer possible to hide one of its major effects. Because of the havoc wreaked by desperate hunger and unrelieved tuberculosis, the likes of which were unheard of last winter at the huge refugee camps of Ingushetia, the Chechens are rapidly losing their soul as a people. Back in the winter, most of the refugees would firmly, defiantly snap: "We'll survive *this* from you too, no matter how much you abuse us! We're united, and we're strong." But now, they're liable to grab your hand in some nook of a camp, and say in a quiet, despondent voice: "We can't survive *this*. We're beasts, even to each other."

The G-4 Syndrome

In the backyard of the former food factory in Shali (a district center about twenty miles from Chiri-Yurt), hundreds of people are cursing and fighting with each other in a frenzy. They came here at the crack of dawn with a "G-4" stamp in their documents testifying that they are homeless refugees within their own country and are entitled to three cans of evaporated milk and a can of processed meat for each person still alive.

"G-4" is humanitarian aid from the Russian government for those who have suffered from antiterrorist operations.

Right now they are giving out G-4, the fourth such crummy handout during this year's war. Each handout contains a "three-day ration," a supply of food worth fifteen rubles a day. The third, G-3, took place a couple of months ago. These are the rations that the Chiri-Yurt refugees, including Khazimat Gambieva's family, will get in the coming days.

I stand in the backyard of the Shali food factory among the starving crowd of people who are struggling for the cherished containers, and recall Putin's well-groomed assistant Sergei Yastrzhembsky announcing that a humanitarian disaster does not exist.

Aishat Junaidova, the head of the Shali regional migration services (there are almost sixty thousand refugees registered here) says:

"Call Moscow's attention to the fact that this government handout is not enough to live on. Many of our refugees are for all intents and purposes condemned to starvation."

Of course, I promise to tell them this. But I promise very quietly. I don't even actually promise, but just nod and whisper something. And I don't explain anything either. It's hard to tell the condemned that, first, the Kremlin doesn't give a damn about my report and, second, the situation in Moscow regarding the war in the Caucasus is very complicated, and no one knows anything about it, because they don't want to. Third, even close friends don't believe my stories after my trips to Chechnya, and I have stopped explaining anything, and just sit silently when I'm invited anywhere. And finally, not even my newspaper, which opposes the current party line, is eager to print my reports from Chechnya. And if they do, they sometimes cut out the toughest parts, not wanting to shock the public. There are fierce arguments within the editorial staff over this issue, and it is more difficult than ever for me to publish the whole truth.

But I am silent about this, simply because for the people around me, who have suffered so much, I am the first civilian from *there*, from the other, nonwar world. No journalists come here. There's no one else they can tell what's going on.

To tell me about the starvation, Aishat has to shout over the howls of some women who are out of their minds with hunger and are cursing and ripping a three-day ration out of each other's hands. I also see some people in the crowd spitting at others. They are tubercular. Out of eternal bitterness toward the world, they're trying to infect those who are not yet coughing up blood. Or perhaps they're hoping that the healthy ones will jump aside out of fear and let them through to the boxes of canned goods.

A cordon of soldiers surrounds the trucks with G-4. With their automatic weapons tilted forward, they try to establish some kind of order among the exhausted people. But they have a strange expression on their faces too. Not of sympathy, but not of dumb cruelty either. It's more like a stupor from the kind of war they have to fight, against a crowd of hungry people. Later, month after month, I would see this many more times; most of the soldiers' faces in the second Chechen war would be just like these.

Another hungry crowd is storming the locked iron gates of the factory. The gates won't yield, and then the crowd's pent-up anger boils over. People start to yell unearthly things—how they'll stab and hang each other, what body parts they'll cut off, and to whom they'd hurl them to be eaten.

But why should they want to hang someone or cut off body parts? Only because whoever has ended up slightly ahead will get to eat his or her canned meat half an hour sooner. This is an utter loss of human feeling, total alienation. It's impossible not to notice the extent to which the traditional Chechen mentality has been destroyed here, with the people crushed and depraved by war and hunger. Seeing them and mingling with them, you don't find one bit of their legendary fortitude, their guarantee of survival on the winding historical crossroads of the past. No Chechen businessmen (far from the poorest people on earth) are willing to give up a tenth of their wealth to their tribesmen. The poor Chechens—and everyone in the settlements is poor—are alone with their poverty, hopelessness, and G-1, G-2, G-3, G-4 . . .

Has this close-knit nation, which would stick up for a man simply because he is "one of their own," become a myth?

How could this have happened, in front of the whole world? Under the "supervision" of international observers, the Red Cross, Doctors without Borders, Doctors of the World, the Salvation Army, human rights advocates—our own and foreign? Even in the presence of Putin's presidential special ambassador for the observance of human rights in the zone of antiterrorist operations?

As soon as you enter the former dormitory of the old cement factory in Chiri-Yurt, which has been turned into a refugee settlement, you hear wailing. A protracted half-animal monotone evoking the farthest reaches of despair. When these people find out that you're a journalist, they cling to your clothing, your hands and feet, as if you were a magician, as if something essential depended on you, such as a gigantic truck with more than enough flour for everyone who is trying to survive.

Who is to blame for this national disgrace? You can't help thinking about this, because you are a human being too, and you need to find a guilty party.

Of course, the greatest blame falls on Putin, and the government that is carrying on this war, ignoring the fact that its inevitable result is these crowds of hungry, sick, homeless people.

But what about the rest of the blame? Here, the unbelievable becomes real. In the fall of 1999 and the winter of 2000, despite the heavy battles, there was always a kind neighbor to be found near the poor and downtrodden. Sometime around the summer, all this changed. The people who at the beginning of the war had been courageously helping each other stay alive have abandoned their principles. Khazimat tells of the hypodermic needles that crunch underfoot in the evenings, of the tremendous amount of marauding and stealing—of kitchen utensils, for example, even though most people had found them in the garbage—of the growing number of Chechen prostitutes serving the troops, of refugee families selling their teenagers into slavery to survive. Chiri-Yurtans who earlier had taken children from the settlement into their homes to feed in the winter now turn away even infants and pregnant and nursing mothers.

In this way, Chiri-Yurt, a beautiful, cozy little village in the foothills of the Caucasus, has turned into a cold, unpleasant settlement point, where bullets fly around like the wind. The key word is "point." A point for thousands of refugees to eat and sleep. A point of round-the-clock pain. Anything you like, except a place to live.

"We can't take everyone who comes to us, the way the law says to—we're in no position to do so," says Adam Shakhgiriev, the head of migration services in Chiri-Yurt. "We can't handle them. It's a disaster for the village when eleven thousand displaced people are forced on our five thousand inhabitants. All of Duba-Yurt has descended upon us, all six thousand! And everyone is utterly demoralized. It's hard to put up with these people. They're all in terrible shape."

Observing Death

The villages of Chiri-Yurt and Duba-Yurt are a couple of miles apart. From the outskirts of Chiri-Yurt you can easily see the other village. That's exactly what happens at night: the women stand by the farthest houses of Chiri-Yurt as though waiting for their men to come back from a long, distant war. They look over there, at the remains of their homes. Most of them wail as they would at a funeral. When Khazimat feels stronger than usual, she is among them.

Duba-Yurt resembles a huge scarecrow: dead, ragged, riddled with holes from "hail" and artillery shots. Even the mountains above it look unkempt and shabby, like street dogs. Bald patches reaching deep into their mountain bones, right down to their chalky Mesozoic skeletons, are scattered all over like shingles, marking the spots of fierce bombing.

The same can be said about the Duba-Yurtans. They are a lost tribe, unclear as to how to restore their lives, 98 percent of which has been bombed and burnt. They recall again and again how painfully their village was dying. The Feds have been attacking the Argun valley for several months. Both they and the militants have passed through it in turn, leaving the plains and coming back like the Whites and the Reds. And a nightmarish, all-consuming artillery shelling on December 31, 1999, the very night when the whole world was joyfully ringing in the millennium. And continuous artillery bombardments for the next two months.

People ran from Duba-Yurt to Chiri-Yurt for shelter in small groups. But when the militants took position and started to dig in on the southern edge of Duba-Yurt, and the senseless, haphazard aerial bombardment of their position became routine, the whole community fled for their lives: the first group on January 27, 2000, and the second, the most stubborn, on February 5–6. Under bombs and hail, without any safe passage, they filed toward Chiri-Yurt. Some fell down, killed; others picked them up and carried them to give them a burial in Chiri-Yurt, but they just kept on walking.

The Duba-Yurtans planned to wait nearby until the battles were over and come back right away. But the refugees were forced to experience the cruelest of all tortures: being faced with their own graves. On February 6, when not a single person was left in Duba-Yurt, the

Feds started to burn down the houses that had survived the bombing. Why? Out of revenge and bitter sorrow for their perished comrades. From the outskirts of Chiri-Yurt, the Duba-Yurtans watched it happen.

"I was one of them," says Raisa Amtayeva, the mother of two teenagers, son Islam and daughter Larisa, who had both become mute during their February flight from the bombardments. "That was the end of everything. I don't have a single photo left of our past."

The destruction of Duba-Yurt was shocking even for the soldiers of the military unit that was stationed there after that fiery pogrom. After the deputy commander of military unit 69771, Lieutenant Colonel S. Larichev, had seen the place of his new deployment and realized that he would now have to be face to face with the village residents, who were crazed with grief, he did something unusual for the Feds. Together with the V. Yakhyayev, head of the village administration, and Colonel Y. Voichenko, the representative of the Russian Ministry for Emergency Situations, Lieutenant Colonel Larichev issued a report on "an examination of the village of Duba-Yurt." It stated that "the military convoys that pass through the village systematically rob and burn the houses of civilians." This document, unprecedented during this war, is verified by the stamp of military unit 69771.

But it did not help. None of the military prosecutors who visited Duba-Yurt to "verify the facts" spoke of the main thing: compensation to the villagers for the army's marauding. And no one demanded a trial for the marauders either. Because the Russian heroes in Chechnya are above suspicion.

It's difficult to remain human when everything has been burnt to ashes, your whole life lies in ruins, and the bandits who were the reason for all this have gone into the mountains again anyway. And when the soldier who, out of anger at the Chechen people, poured oil over Khazimat's house, has let those militants go.

Afterword: Two Years Later

Today Duba-Yurt still lies in ruins, now covered with hothouse plastic. Under the plastic, some people who returned from Chiri-Yurt have made their homes. Most residents remained up there, in the village that once was home to a cement factory.

The story of Chiri-Yurt, forced to shelter the Duba-Yurtans, is typical for a Chechen village. With time, its consequences grow still more severe. Wandering around the war-stricken Chechen villages and towns for months, I met more and more people who, like the refugees from Duba-Yurt, obey only one law, the biological law of survival. The war hasn't just damaged the Chechen land—it has also scarred the people's souls. Hundreds of thousands were driven out of their homes, into the camps, into the fields, or just to the middle of nowhere, and forced to adopt new laws of life, the camp laws. Seemingly united, they are in fact horribly split. Informers are everywhere, and their sole aim is to survive, even at the price of others' lives. When this becomes blatant, a nation is as good as dead.

Makhkety: A Concentration Camp with a Commercial Streak

I received a petition from ninety families living in several villages in the Vedeno district—Makhkety, Tovzeni, Selmentausen, and Khatuni. In it, several hundred people pleaded with me to assist them by arranging speedy transport out of Chechnya. The reasons were constant hunger, unbearable cold, a lack of doctors or any ties to the outside world, and the cruel punitive actions of the soldiers stationed near Khatuni. The facts seemed unbelievable. My trip there began on February 18, 2001.

I've heard dozens of horrible stories and seen the exhausted faces of people who have experienced torture from soldiers accomplished in the fine art of harassment. My pen simply refuses to move from all the horrible things that I have to record. And suddenly, the same thing happens to you. Now they're yelling at you: "Stop! Forward!" And a Federal Security Serviceman, a wet-behind-the-ears senior lieutenant, with the nasty smile of his professional predecessors of 1937, whispers— to you, not to your recent interviewee—"Basayev sent you, you're a militant . . . Shooting is too good for you . . . You blink too much, that means you're lying."*

---

*The Federal Security Service (FSS): a new name for the KGB in democratic times; a symbol of the repressiveness of the Soviet regime. Putin was the head of the FSS in the period between the first and second Chechen wars, when banditry and kidnapping were most frequent in Chechnya, and when camps for terrorist training were functioning in its territory.

Scene One: Torture by Electric Shock

Rosita, from the village of Tovzeni, is barely moving her lips. Her eyes, as if reversing their natural function, are motionless and turned inward. It's still hard for Rosita to walk—her legs and kidneys are aching. A month ago, she had to pass through a filtration point* (that's what they're called) because she "sheltered militants in her home." That's exactly what the soldiers screamed at her.

Rosita is no longer young. She has many children and some grand-children. The youngest, a three-year-old, couldn't speak Russian earlier, but seeing how her grandmother was dragged on the ground, now constantly yells, in Russian, "Down! On the floor!" Rosita was taken from her home at dawn, while everyone was sleeping. Her home was surrounded and she wasn't given time to get dressed properly. They threw her into a pit on the military base.

"They shoved and kicked you?"

"Yes, just as they always do."

Her legs drawn up under herself, Rosita sat on the earthen floor of the pit for twelve days. The soldier guarding the pit took pity on her one night and threw her a piece of carpet.

"I put it under myself. That soldier is a human being too." Rosita's lips barely move.

Her pit was no more than four feet deep. It had no roof, but it was impossible to stand straight up, since logs were placed over it. So for twelve days she crouched or sat on the carpet. And all this in the winter, too! The whole time, Rosita was not charged with anything, although she was taken out for questioning three times. The officers, who were young enough to be her sons, told her they were Federal Security Servicemen. They connected bare wires to the fingers of both her hands and threw the wires across her neck, from behind.

"I really screamed when they switched on the current. But I took all the rest silently. I was afraid to anger them any further."

---

* Part of the purge operation, a place for illegal detainment of people. The detained are brought to a "filtration point" (the Feds usually organize them around half-destroyed, abandoned buildings at the outskirts of the purged villages). A filtration takes place there ("passing through a filter," in military terms), in which people who have been detained are subjected to interrogation, torture, and humiliation with the aim of getting information about the whereabouts of militants. Filtration points are essentially mobile concentration camps during the second Chechen war.

The FSS men kept saying, "You're dancing badly. We need to add a little more," referring to Rosita's convulsions. And they added some more.

"What did they want?"

"They didn't ask me anything."

During this time, Rosita's relatives were given a task by these very officers through go-betweens: to come up with ransom money. The officers explained that they needed to hurry. Rosita was doing badly in the pit; she might not survive it. At first they asked for a ransom that was so high that the villagers (here it has become traditional to collect ransom money from the whole community) responded that they wouldn't be able to pay it even if they sold the entire village. The officers, surprisingly, turned out to be amenable, and set the sum at one tenth the original amount. The money was brought to them, and Rosita, dirty and unwashed, barely able to walk, came up to the base command checkpoint. She fell into the arms of her children.

On the territory of the military base, laid out at the edge of Khatuni in the Vedeno district, where the 45th airborne and the 119th paratroop regiments of the Ministry of Defense are being deployed, as well as Ministry of the Interior, Ministry of Justice, and FSS units, there is a concentration camp. With a commercial streak.

Scene Two: A Leader of Pigs

Colonel Aleksei Romanov, the commander of the 45th regiment, is a very charismatic, strong-willed person. He has been through the Afghanistan war and the first Chechen war. Like most officers fighting in the second war, he curses it, thinking out loud about his children, who continue to grow up without their father, and is ready for it to end as soon as possible. He is really sick of it. But right now, at the end of February 2001, on the eve of Defenders of the Fatherland Day, we are strolling through the regiment base. The commander takes me to a mess hall that is nicer than you expect, given the field conditions. He leads me to a warehouse, fully stocked with canned meat and all kinds of food that he thinks fully prevent the men entrusted to him from stealing the local residents' cattle.

We make our way to the main part of the tour. The commander shows me the pits Chechens are thrown into after purges. He is solicitous with me, holding me by the arm so I don't fall into the twenty-foot depths. The pit looks just the way the numerous people who sat in it have described it. It's about ten by ten, and a rope hangs down into the indiscernible netherworld, so people can climb up for interrogation. Despite the frost, there is a distinct odor. That's how they do things here—the Chechens have to go to the bathroom right in the pit.

The colonel tells me some amazing things. Once the division commander, General Baranov himself, arrived by plane to inspect the regiment. He saw some arrested Chechens standing in the fields and ordered them to be thrown into the pits, which had originally been dug for garbage. And they've been used for human beings ever since. Romanov is very uncomfortable about everything that's happened.

"We only put militants in there," he says.

"Then why do you let them out later, if they're militants?"

"You know very well," he forces out.

No, I don't know personally.

Scene Three: Waiting to Be Arrested

A fit fifty-year-old Chechen mountaineer named Vakha from the village of Tovzeni used to work for the KGB, and also as a teacher in the local high school. Now he works as a volunteer, collecting information on the atrocities committed by the Russian army. For that reason, he expects to be arrested and thrown into a pit every night.

Vakha knows how to answer the question dodged by the colonel. He tells me the most unbelievable stories about a short stay of Basayev's brigade in his village. The village residents had really hoped then that Basayev would finally be arrested. He and his men were exhausted; it could not have been easier. But the army, which had been positioned in a tight circle around the village, suddenly moved away, exactly for the time when Basayev stayed there.

And believe it or not, he left. But as soon as the bandits had gone to the mountains, the soldiers started to arrest and torture the village residents, who had had nothing to do with the militants, while leaving those who had actually taken part in the bloodshed alone. After all, the villagers know everything about everyone.

Scene Four: Nice Asses

Isa lives in Selmentausen. At the beginning of February he too was taken to the concentration camp on the outskirts of Khatuni. They put cigarettes out against his body, pulled out his nails, and beat him on the kidneys with Pepsi bottles filled with water. Then they threw him into a pit that they called a "bath." It was filled with water (in the winter, too). After throwing the Chechens there, they tossed in some smoke bombs.

There were six people in that pit. Not everyone managed to survive.

The lower-ranking officers who conducted joint interrogations told them they had nice asses and raped them. They explained that the reason was that "your bitches don't want to do it with us." The surviving Chechens now say that avenging themselves for the "nice asses" incident is the only purpose of the rest of their lives.

It's obvious that Isa hasn't quite recovered from the shock either. Like Rosita, he was let go for a ransom collected by all of Selmentausen. But first, the soldiers also had a good time taunting the relatives, who had gathered by the detachment command checkpoint hoping to find out something about their dear ones who had been taken to the pit.

In Chechnya, the marauding and racketeering routine masked as searching for bandits works nonstop. All that has changed in the second war are those who commit the crimes. The activities that the antiterrorist operation has sought to eradicate—violent hostage taking, slavery, ransoms for "live" goods—are now being performed by the new masters, the soldiers.

We are sitting in Isa's single tiny room. It has nothing but a plank bed and a stove. The family is terribly poor. Isa's four-year-old daughter stares at me with horror. His wife explains:

"She can tell you're not one of us. You look like the ones who beat her father right in front of her, and then took him away."

Scene Five: Firsthand Experience

Just two minutes after parting with the commander of the 45th airborne regiment, I was detained.

First they ordered me to stand right in the middle of a torn-up field for more than an hour. Then an armored vehicle arrived, carrying armed personnel and a first lieutenant of unknown military origin.

Pushing me with rifle butts, they put me in a vehicle and drove off. "You have false papers, that Yastrzhembsky of yours is Basayev's toady, and you are a militant," they announced.

Hour after hour of interrogation followed. A succession of young officers, reminding me insinuatingly, by way of introduction, that they work for the FSS and answer only to Putin, completely took away my freedom. I was not allowed to make a phone call or walk around, and I was forced to put all my personal belongings on the desk. I choose to omit the nastiest details, since they are completely indecent. However, these details are the main proof for me personally that all the reports of harassment and torture in the 45th regiment are true.

From time to time, the zealous young officers were joined by their senior officer, a lieutenant colonel with a swarthy face and dull dark bulging eyes. He would send the youngsters out of the tent, turn on music that he considered romantic and hint at a "favorable outcome" of the affair if I were to comply in certain ways.

Between the lieutenant colonel's visits, the young officers tortured me, skillfully hitting my sore spots. They looked through my children's pictures, making a point of saying what they would like to do to the kids. This went on for about three hours.

Finally, the worldly-wise lieutenant colonel, who would boast now and then that he was giving his life here for the Motherland, glanced at his watch and said in a businesslike tone, "Let's go. I'm going to shoot you."

He led me out of the tent into complete darkness. The nights here are impenetrable. After we walked for a while, he said, "Ready or not, here I come." Something burst with pulsating fire all around me, screeching, roaring, and growling. The lieutenant colonel was very happy when I crouched in fright. It turned out that he had led me right under the hail rocket launcher at the moment it was fired. "Well, let's go."

Soon I saw steps going down in the dark. "Here's the banya. Take off your clothes." Seeing that his words had no effect, he got very angry: "A real lieutenant colonel is courting you, and you say no, you militant bitch."

Another FSS officer—as he introduced himself—entered the banya. "She doesn't want to bathe," the lieutenant colonel summed up. The FSS man put the bottles that he had brought on the table and said, "I'll take her then." Again, I was led for a long time around the dark base. Finally, he told me to go downstairs into a bunker, where I stayed until February 22, when I was freed. There was a flyer on the bunker's wall that read "119th Airborne Parachute Regiment." The flyer also said that eighteen of the regiment's men were honored with the title of Hero of Russia.

They brought me some tea. I took a sip, and my head immediately started to swim, my legs grew weak, and I had to beg to go out, as I was vomiting violently. To the bathroom? All right, but with an escort. "We have to make sure you don't get rid of your bugging devices there," they explained.

I demanded that they tell me my charges, write their report, and send me to prison so that my family could at least bring me a tooth-brush. "No!" they said. "You're a militant! You came here to look at the pits! Slut! Bitch! Basayev paid Yastrzhembsky for you, Yastrzhembsky paid your editor, and your editor sent you here."

On the morning of February 22, an officer entered the bunker and announced that he would accompany me to Khankala, and that he had all my papers and belongings, which he would "submit to the FSS." The same lieutenant colonel was standing by the helicopter. "If it were up to me, I'd shoot you," he said as a good-bye.

When we landed in Khankala, some soldiers jumped out at us right by the hatch, taking me away from my escort. They turned out to be officers of Grozny's Military Prosecutor's Office, for which I am very thankful. If not for them, I'd have had to spend more time under the charge of yet another FSS man who had gone a little nuts from the antiterrorist operation. In the prosecutor's office, I explained everything. They also interrogated the officer who brought me, and it turned out that the regiment men had stolen everything except for my journalist ID 1258. My escort did not bring anything—no personal belongings, no cassettes, no rolls of film.

Dzhokhar

A tiny baby, wrapped in dirty rags, calms down only after poking around and finding its mother's breast. The rest of the time, the thin lit-tle body squirms and twitches spasmodically. Is it crying? Trembling?

"What is—uh—its name?" It's hard to ask if it's a boy or a girl without sounding insulting.

Toita, the mother whose breast the baby demands every ten or fifteen minutes, is silent, as if it were an interrogation.

"Doesn't she understand Russian?"

"Sure, she does," the women say, hiding their eyes. There is a long pause. Why wouldn't you want to say what a tiny, sick infant's name is?

"His name is Dzhokhar," Toita finally forces out, harshly and decisively. "It's just that I've gotten out of the habit of saying his name out loud. What if the soldiers hear? They'll kill either him, because his name is Dzhokhar, or me for naming him that. He'll be two years old soon."

"But why is he . . . like this? . . ."

"He isn't growing at all. He was born right when the war started."

Toita and Dzhokhar's home has a hole facing the sky. A year ago, in February 2000, a shell pierced their roof. No one was there to repair it and little white snowdrifts piled up. Toita is a widow. Her husband was lost in action when she was still pregnant. Now the mother and her son live in a terrible place, where hardly anyone would move voluntarily. It is a Vedeno mountain village forgotten by the world, with a "pro-German" name that is very unusual for these parts: Selmentausen. There is no water, light, gas, or heat here, and there are no telephone lines or doctors either. All that's here is the war, which has already been going on for eighteen months. Toita is one of the people who couldn't stand it and signed the petition from dozens of Vedeno families asking to be moved anywhere at all outside of Chechnya. Nothing like this has ever happened in the history of the present war. Chechens are too tied to their land to ask for deportation.

A Zone within a Zone

Even within the special zone called Chechnya, the Vedeno district stands out. It increasingly resembles the U.S. Indian reservations at the beginning of the twentieth century, which became more and more isolated from the outer world. Inspectors don't come here from the government or the head of administration in Grozny. The big shots from Moscow also don't show up here—they're afraid to. Vladimir Kalamanov, Putin's special representative for the observance of human rights in Chechnya, doesn't drop by either. Nor do humanitarian aid convoys. For the residents of Vedeno, the whole outside world boils down to automatons in masks and white overcoats (because of the mountains, winter, and snow) with no epaulettes, carrying automatic weapons, hungry, mean, and cruel.

The soldiers hate Vedeno with a passion, because they think that its mountains are full of militants. Therefore, they have to fight and incur losses on a daily basis. They hate it ten times more since it is the birthplace of Basayev, who they're unable to catch no matter how hard they try. They imagine that at any moment he could stop by a neighboring village to warm up by the stove, but he never appears, and this is very frustrating. Akhmad-Khaji Kadyrov,* the head of the republic, can't stand the region either, since it is the birthplace of his personal enemy, the very same Basayev.

However, Vedeno is a heterogeneous reservation. Some people and villages are worse off than others. Within the region there is another zone. The villages of Makhkety, Tovzeni, Selmentausen, and Khatuni are in this zone. They are laid out very near each other in a ring surrounding the largest, Makhkety, where about seven thousand people live.

The Makhketians are outcasts even in the outcast region of Vedeno. The other Vedeno residents dislike them for their opposition to the town of Vedeno, the district center, opposition that also stems from the war. The Makhketians did not support Basayev and, even worse, organized a militia against him. As a result, even the limited humanitarian aid that does get to Vedeno doesn't make it to this village. Only once in the eighteen months of the war has the public organization Echo of War, based in Nazrani (in Ingushetia) brought rice, sugar, and oil here, and then only for orphaned children.

Run away! Leave! It's the only way out.

However, it's not so easy to leave the Makhkety reservation. According to the village passport officer, Aina Makayeva, the issuance of IDs

---

*Appointed under military pressure by Putin in July 2000. One of the bloodiest figures of modern Chechnya. A former mufti (elected religious leader) of Chechnya and one of the organizers and inspirations of the gazavat (religious war with the infidels) against Russia during the first Chechen war. Was Dudayev and Maskhadov's closest comrade in arms; he later betrayed them.

has been suspended pending some kind of special orders. That's what they told her in Vedeno. They didn't go into details as to the reason. The village passport officer's duties are to gather and prepare papers so passports can be issued, and then to bring them to the district center and pick up the passports from there. Several months ago, Aina ran into an obstacle when the head of the Vedeno district passport and visa service refused to accept documents from her, especially if they were for teenagers. And at this moment, Aina has 250 sets of documents in her hands, mostly for youths from fourteen to eighteen years old. Outraged, Aina tells about her fruitless conversations with that boss, a Ministry of Internal Affairs officer:

"I tell him, our teenagers have been tortured by the purges. They've been grabbed and put in pits at the edge of Khatuni, and their relatives have to buy them out of there! Some of them have already been tortured to death! Under these circumstances, a passport is life itself, and not to have one means death. But the boss answers: 'That's not my problem. I don't have time for that—I'm going to the banya.' And the same thing happens every Friday. Because they accept documents only on Fridays."

Nobody has any doubts anymore that artificial conditions are being created in their villages, a special system to hold all the inhabitants here and gradually destroy them.

Woodcutting

When you don't have anything, you become capable of irrational behavior. Everyone here knows that you can't go to the forest, the lifesaver for the villagers. You can't cut wood or gather wild garlic, the local source of vitamins.

But people go there anyway, even though they know that many of those who decided to cut some wood were shot dead and are now buried at the village cemetery.

Here's what Vakha, a Selmentausen resident, says:

"There was intense shooting for two days. Then it stopped. I got up very early in the morning, listened carefully, thought it over and decided to go to the edge of the forest. My wife was crying for me not to, but we had run out of wood a few days before, and I just had to go. You die either way. You can freeze to death with your kids and not be a man, or get shot by a bullet. I prayed and set off. Everything ended well that time. I brought enough wood for three days—it took five trips. Feel how warm it is here?"

"But in just a couple of days you'll have to tempt fate again?"

"I'm ready." Vakha answers shortly and sternly like an officer standing in line. Readiness to die is the main requirement of their existence, which flits between life and death every minute. Rumors about which neighbor died how, under what circumstance and from what number of shell fragments serve as a lullaby before the kids go to sleep.

"Remember how on January 5, 2001, they dropped a bomb from a plane?" Makka Jabrailova from Makhkety asks her companions. On that day, her father and brother Gasikhaji and Gasali Akhmadov, her only means of support, were killed. Before that, on December 12, 2000, Makka's home was completely destroyed by five shells. On that day her neighbors were killed too, the whole Tagirov family of eleven. There was nothing left to bury—just some earth from the place where the man-made meteorites fell; that's what they put into the grave. Makka is crying, but the women continue:

"On February 16 they shot at the school, right around 2 P.M., and that wasn't the first time, either."

The Makhkety village high school has the misfortune of being located close to the military base, right across the field. When the parents ran to the base, the soldiers told them they didn't know who had been shooting; it was not their shells.

The head of the Makhkety administration, Abdullah Elbuzdukayev, has the look of a man who has been frightened and crushed forever. He used to be the Vedeno district judge, but now he admits he can't do anything at all for the village residents. Absolutely nothing. He's scared to death of the soldiers, who think he is an accomplice to the militants and could shoot him at any time. As a result, the parents decided to keep their kids out of school. It's not a real school anyway; there are no classes, and the kids just go there to socialize.

"Call Putin"

Malika Yunusova is a young woman, but her hair is all gray. Her recent story has shocked even the Makhketians, who have been through so much already.

Malika is a village nurse. She's always ready to help the wounded and sick, even though they haven't paid her at the hospital for years.

On the night of February 10–11, 2000, a bomb hit her house. It was totally destroyed. All the cattle were killed, and cows are your whole livelihood here. All the sheds were burnt down. The only things the family had left were their rubber boots and the clothes they had on.

Last summer, the Yunusovs built a new shed, and their neighbors gave them a cow. But on December 15, around eight in the evening, there was another shelling. The Yunusovs hid in their neighbors' basement. After a shell hit their new shed and started a fire, Malika's husband Said-Ali ran to put it out and save the cow. He was showered with shell fragments.

He spent the whole night lying unconscious on the neighbors' floor while the shelling went on. Early the next morning, Malika ran to the military base to ask for a helicopter to take her husband to the hospital. After all, it was their fault! They dawdled for a long time and refused in the end, saying she had to take him on her own. They did promise to call the Khankala hospital. The neighbors found a car and drove him there. But the Khankala doctor said they had to take him to the Mozdok hospital since the wound was very serious. They went there. The neurosurgeon told Malika that if her husband had been a militant or a soldier, he would have treated him as a participant in a military conflict. But since he was a civilian, he couldn't treat him for free. He wanted forty thousand rubles in cash right away—then he'd perform the surgery.

Malika didn't have any money. She saw them taking the wounded Said-Ali from the operating room out into the hall. They let her use the phone to call anyone who could bring the money.

"I have no one to call." Malika burst out crying.

And the neurosurgeon said:

"Call Putin."

Malika asked:

"What if I weren't here now—who would you ask to give you the money?"

"No one. I'd just send him over to the morgue," the doctor answered.

Malika went to look for a car. Luckily, she found a driver who agreed to take her and Said-Ali to Argun for free. There, he introduced her to people who took them to Grozny, to the Ninth Municipal Hospital. All this involved going through checkpoints and stopping for the night.

At the Ninth Hospital they finally operated on Said-Ali, three days after the deep skull and brain wound. Malika's husband lived for another month, but they couldn't control his sepsis. As the doctors explained, the surgery was too late.

After the funeral, Malika went to the Vedeno military prosecutor, but he refused to accept her claim. Soon after her trip to Vedeno, Malika was visited by the soldiers at her village—the prosecutor must have informed them of her complaint. They explained that the first few shells that hit the shed had not been fired by them, and they did not know who did it. They started shelling only after they saw a big fire at night and a man running around it.

Malika could only throw up her hands: of course there was a fire, and her husband was running around trying to save the burning cow. After the soldiers left, Malika realized she was lucky they hadn't shot her too.

The men in epaulettes have nothing to be afraid of and no one to have scruples about. There are still no trials or prosecutions in Vedeno—they are not needed in the zone—only irrational lawlessness, and whoever turns up in the wrong place at the wrong time is the one at fault. Like Malika's husband saving his cow.

Now Malika has no husband and no home. She lives with her three kids wherever she can find shelter. They have no food or clothes. Malika begs me to help her move, no matter where.

"People say they built a new refugee camp in Ingushetia. Please send me there. It can't be worse than here. I don't care which law I live under—Chechen, Russian, Korean, or Japanese—as long as there is some kind of law. And some food, too."

"I can't stay here any longer," Toita wails softly. She has to conceal the name of her own child, and is already sorry she has given him this name. She puts her withered nipple into Dzhokhar's mouth to keep him from crying. Other widows and wives from Selmentausen, Makhkety, Tovzeni, and Khatuni echo her sentiments:

"We haven't seen a doctor for years. We have nothing to eat or light the stove with. We're tired of being bombed. The soldiers take everything from us. We're exhausted."

Genocide

July 2001. I'm meeting with Aina as if she were an undercover agent and I were a liaison from the center. We take precautions worthy of a spy thriller. Aina made her way to our meeting place via secret paths, using a different route than usual and not telling even her neighbors where and why she was setting off. But the whole problem is that Aina and I don't have an underground mentality, and the position that the authorities have forced us into is downright revolting to us. Aina is a widow from Makhkety, and I am a journalist who wants to know why Makhkety has been cordoned off and isolated from the rest of the world for several months now.

"Did you know that the driver who ventured to go to Shali in February to tell the world outside of Chechnya about your arrest was just killed? They tried to talk him out of it, but he said, 'Someone must save her.'"

"What?! He was killed?"

"Soldiers drove up, asked him his name, and then shot him point-blank. It happened on June 30. His name was Imran."

So this means I am living at the cost of Imran's life.

"But didn't only people in the village know that Imran went to Shali? Your people? Doesn't that mean someone denounced him to the soldiers?"

"Of course. We have so many informers now that we don't know what to do. The Feds corrupt our people; they pay them for the deaths of their neighbors. I myself, coming to this meeting, feared the informers most of all, not the Feds. The soldiers come to the villages to follow up on tips. Eventually, the informers get killed too. Do you remember the old house in Selmentausen where we met four men who had just been bought out of the pits on the 45th regiment base?"

I remember it well. The house was very poor. The family was crammed into a narrow little room with a primitive stove fueled by brushwood gathered near the forest. The little children huddled up close to their mother and stared with fright at the guest. After all, I looked like the people who had once taken away their father; he had later returned home sick and beaten up.

The host himself had turned out to be a cheerful, witty man who was born the same year as me. He hadn't complained at all about the Feds torturing him, which surprised me. He'd merely laughed at them. Rubbing his fingers, which had been crushed by pliers, he had said, "Those poor bastards. They'll have to answer to God for everything they've done. What's the difference if we call him Allah?"

"He was killed too," Aina said quietly. "They came, took him, shot him somewhere, and threw the body onto the road. No one in the village has any doubt why it happened. It's because he told you about the torture. We decided to ask you not to reveal his name anywhere, so his family can survive. And do you remember that black-haired fellow who was sitting in the homemade trestle bed next to the host then?"

"Of course I do. He was also very cheerful. He tried to calm me . . ."

"Oh, yes, he kept telling you, 'Don't get so upset! We Chechens are tough. I can survive anything.'"

"That's how he answered the question whether he ever dreamed of the tortures he'd been through."

"He's dead too. They killed him the same way: they came in, asked his name, and took him away. Only instead of throwing away the corpse, they forced the relatives to pay ransom for it. Of the five men we talked to in Selmentausen then, three are gone. And do you remember that tractor driver? He was fixing a tractor by the farthest house in Selmentausen, and you talked with him for fifteen minutes. He told you about the Feds' raids, and you asked him, 'Did you see the militants a long time ago? When did they come here?'"

"Yes, and he answered, 'A long time ago, maybe a year. They stayed in the village for a day. This day, the Feds stopped their shooting, and the militants warmed up, washed, and left. And that's when the raids started here . . .' That was his story. I copied it down on my notepad."

"That tractor driver has also been shot . . . And how about the people you stayed and talked with at night in Makhkety? Twenty or twenty-five people were crammed into that room. And half of them are also no longer here. Remember Taus Tagirova? She was telling you so much, and crying. Two of her sons were taken right from their home into the 45th regiment, and it's been two months since they've been heard from. And how about the Mohammedkhajievs? Kharon and his wife? They took Kharon, beat him up right in front of his six children, dragged him away, and he hasn't been heard from for two months either . . . Nobody knows what to do. There are funerals every day," says Aina, and her eyes are dry.

I look at Aina, who has been driven into a corner, recalling her own children whom she's left behind in Makhkety every five minutes of the conversation. She shudders at the thought that while she's not there, anything could happen to them. What if someone turned her in?

The Hundredth Grozny Blockade
Run for Your Life!

Life in Grozny falls into two categories: "free" and "blockaded." The first category means the city is open for entrance and exit. Only relatively open, of course, because you still have to move through the interior network of dozens of predatory checkpoints that rob everyone walking, and especially driving, of ten or twenty rubles. Nevertheless, it is possible to visit your relatives in the village a little more than a mile from Grozny (impossible under the second category), or go to the Gudermes market. If you are lucky enough to pass through all the checkpoints on all the roads, you can even make it to Ingushetia on one side and Dagestan on the other. Then you are free! Within the limits of the war, of course. Students come from the villages to study at Grozny's partially open colleges and university. There are people in the streets. The ruins are seething with life.

The second category means the blockade, the "full stop" conditions. That's how the soldiers refer to the time when they close the city and start "special measures" in it—inspections and round-ups—whose aim is often difficult or even impossible to grasp. At that point, Grozny freezes, the markets empty out, the stores close, and armored vehicles rush through the streets at lightning speed, sweeping aside everything in their path, including chance passersby. Single shots and submachine gun rounds are heard. Parents take their sick children home right from the operating tables.

The city ruins can look happy too, when the sun suddenly shines brightly in the morning, after the night winds have scattered the ashes from the fires.

That's how September 17, 2001, begins in Grozny. People smile as they maneuver between the ruins—at the sun, at each other, at the fleeting, joyful sense of things being like "before." No one hopes for any other kind of joy here.

But by nine, the ruins grow somber. The sun seems to disappear. Pressing their chins against their chests, people try to sneak past checkpoints while the soldiers are setting up "biting snakes." These are special barrage devices, flexible metal bands with big thorns sticking out. Everyone knows that once you come across these snakes, you'd better run for your life, and look for shelter as fast as you can. They mean that the city is being closed to traffic, and this is the surest sign of a coming purge. Very soon Grozny becomes deserted, its residents driven to their homes, if they still have any.

By eleven, there is a deadly pause in the city's life. You can't move, even between the checkpoints. After rushing from one closed street to another, even those brave souls who winked joyfully an hour ago, saying that they could weasel their way through since they knew secret routes in the mined ruins and were not afraid of any checkpoints, acknowledge defeat.

The soldiers who guard the checkpoints are as bewildered as we who are stuck there are. They have received a strange order not to let through even the military and the police. Officers from some other department, not the one that initiated the blockade, stand nearby. Servicemen from the so-called Chechen police, units newly formed from local residents, are also among us, in a blockade. Schoolgirls, nine or ten years old, have also lost their right to walk the short distance to their destroyed School No. 41, which, despite everything, is open for classes.

Shooting at the Generals

At the same time, Prime Minister Stanislav Valentinovich Ilyasov* is frantically pacing his office in the Chechen Government Complex, a group of remodeled buildings behind a high, ugly fence the color of yellowish dirt, in downtown Grozny.

Other offices around him are empty: 80 percent of the officials didn't show up for work since they couldn't pass through the checkpoints.

---

*Chairman of the government of the Chechen Republic, appointed by Putin in 2001. Has a reputation as a tough manager and leader. His personal achievement is the basic normalization of the lives of people living in Chechnya under conditions of war and economic ruin.

Ilyasov grabs his many telephones, argues heatedly with some high-ranking military figures. A young lieutenant general stands next to him. This looks very strange: the general and the prime minister, important people here, are unable to cope with the army anarchy. The armored vehicles, the real rulers of Grozny, are still charging through the deserted streets. No one in the world cares one bit about Ilyasov. He himself doesn't yet know that he will be trapped in his office like this, almost alone, for a few more days. This will be a long blockade.

Around noon, the city turns into a fortress getting ready for an extensive special operation. Women whisper to each other: "Have the militants launched an attack somewhere?" All life stops, everyone tries to disappear. You can hear only the roar of armored vehicles, nearby or far away, and an occasional woman's shriek turning into crying: "Let me through, my child's there . . ."

The young lieutenant general starts to say good-bye to the prime minister. Ilyasov asks him to stay. But the general says that he has to be in Moscow by tomorrow morning to submit his report to Putin.

Everyone there looks at the general with respect, even admiration. A narrow circle of those in the know are aware of the special assignment, unprecedented in today's Chechnya, that the president has given him: to gather information about military crimes, draw conclusions, and submit a report.

The helipad is located right here in the government complex area, by the prime minister's office windows. Ilyasov walks the general and his people to the ladder. The helicopter immediately takes off; we can see it flying away for some time. Everyone stuck at checkpoints, especially in downtown Grozny, can see it as well. But the spectacle lasts for just a few minutes—the helicopter crashes in the city center.

Young Lieutenant General Anatoly Pozdnyakov, who was hurrying to make his report to the president, along with his assistants, another general and six colonels from the general staff, perish in the crash. And the pilots too, of course. All the material gathered by the presidential commission on the military crimes in the antiterrorist operation zone is lost.

That evening, all the TV channels and news agencies are screaming about a "tragic loss for the armed forces" and "another militant attack." They claim that the helicopter was shot down by a single bandit armed with a "ground-to-air missile launcher" of Western make, wearing "white pants," and unshaven for many days. He jumped out of the ruins and ran into the area adjacent to Minutka Square.

But I myself was standing right there. There were more checkpoints in that area than anywhere in Grozny. Anyone who "jumped out" of the ruins, especially carrying a Stinger, would be spotted right away at the heavily armed checkpoints. You can't even call it a square anymore; it's just a spot of land raked by shells and bombs. Just ruins and checkpoints and then more ruins. The soldiers can see each other and all the surroundings without binoculars. No one standing on Minutka would even think of making the smallest move—everything is completely under control. Even taking out your camera without the Feds' permission is a major violation that could end in submachine gun shooting without warning. You can't even imagine a "militant in white pants armed with a ground-to-air missile launcher."

It also turned out that the helicopter, "for some reason," did not have any military cover that time, despite the fact that there were high-ranking officers on board. The very officer who was striving for peace happened to die on Minutka. Too many suspicious details.

This is one of Chechnya's main problems. It's not the militants' craftiness or armaments or the foreign origin of their weapons, but the betrayal by its own "defenders." Those who want the war to go on are capable of anything. For example, the total blockade of Grozny that on September 17, 2001, created all the necessary conditions for antiaircraft rocket shooting at certain generals. Shooting without witnesses.

"Shut Up, Bitch!"

The downed helicopter served both as the reason to start a blockade and the pretext to continue it indefinitely. And it's not important who organized it, only who's going to have to pay for it.

On the night of September 17, Grozny was rocked by terrible purges. Men were grabbed from their homes, and the howls of women for their abducted sons, husbands, brothers, and neighbors rang out over the whole city, mixed with rounds from automatic weapons and the thunder of mortars.

Around 6 A.M. on the eighteenth, the blockade dawn displaced the night, saturated with firing. Armored vehicles covered with chilled, mean, sleep-deprived people in black masks awaited the Grozny residents as they crawled out onto the streets out of sheer necessity.

And there was only one necessity: some people absolutely had to go to work—doctors and nurses, for example. The sick were waiting.

I make a tiny peephole in the curtains. My hostess pleads with me in a whisper not to reveal myself. If the masks see us, they'll shoot.

I see an empty street past the window through the peephole. It is Staropromyslovsky Road. About fifteen feet from my peephole is an armored vehicle. And another one thirty feet away. They're everywhere you look. Soldiers sitting in the armored vehicle curse nastily and pointlessly. Some of them are obviously not sober. Others gulp water from plastic bottles, a sign of a hangover. A young nurse cautiously moves along the road with short steps, looking back and stopping often. She's wearing a white coat, which of course she put on so the soldiers can see that she's a medical worker and let her go. She's going to work; the Ninth Grozny Municipal Hospital is right nearby. Everyone in Grozny, both soldiers and civilians, knows that the Ninth Hospital is the only one that hasn't stopped working under any circumstances. The nurse has a few yards to go. She puts a foot forward and waits to make sure they don't shoot. Only then does she put the other one forward, her knees bent in fear. It looks like ballet, but it's real life.

In this manner, the nurse crawls rather than walks. The soldiers are obviously amused by this. They curse even harder.

The nurse is completely alone on the road, except for those waiting for her in the armored vehicle, who have already drawn a bead on her, and those behind, who also have their finger on the trigger.

Finally they get bored. "Stop!" comes the bloodcurdling yell from the soldiers behind her. And suddenly, because of this cry, the girl becomes bolder. She straightens her knees, and quickly and decisively goes to the side. She is accompanied by a round of submachine gun shots.

It becomes quiet again on Staropromyslovsky Road. Then a group of about ten women appears. Slowly, groping, they try to move forward in the direction of the Lenin district military command headquarters, whose gates are right across from my peephole. They are mothers, wives, and sisters of men arrested in the night purges. They're going to the command headquarters to find out the ransoms for their men. You have to get there at dawn, before the arrested are taken somewhere else. If that happens, you might never find the person you're looking for at all.

"Get out of here!" The mothers, wives, and sisters are met with a glob of spit from a man in the armored vehicle.

"But those men over there," the women begin to explain, interrupting each other, and pointing in the direction of another armored vehicle. "They told us to come here . . ."

"Get the hell out of here!" the masked men leer like hungry wolves, baring their teeth. "You hear? Get out!"

And more cursing. The women fall into hysterics.

"You're killing us . . . You're taking away our men . . . Thieves . . . Think of your own mothers . . ."

"Shut up, bitch!" howl soldiers from the armored vehicle, heating up with their cursing. "We told you, get out of here! You can't live here. It's our territory."

The women, sobbing, back away. They say:

"Where can we go?"

"Nobody wants us."

A man who appears to be an officer approaches the women. He's been given the role of the good cop who appears after the bad ones. He whispers about something with the women (the ransom), and the women, having been given hope, disperse briskly. Only one continues to argue with the officer, but she leaves in a couple of minutes too. A compromise, apparently, has been reached.

The officer is a financial middleman. There are many such people here, in every military unit, subdivision, and command headquarters. Slave trading of arrested people exists everywhere, and each participant in this financial chain counts on his share. This officer tells the women what ransom they should bring to the command headquarters for their men to be released in the evening. It's an old story: purges with the goal of catching militants end with a primitive trade of goods for money and money for goods.

But not everyone is able to come up with the money, since Chechnya is impoverished. Not everyone makes the deadline set by the officer. And in such cases the arrested men disappear without a trace. Or the middleman announces that the ransom is now for a corpse. And the dead cost more than the living. That's how the military has arranged it, knowing that there is no greater torment for a Chechen than not to observe the funeral rites.

And so the second morning of the blockade comes to an end.

The Only Patient

The blockade afternoon begins. Nothing much changes for Grozny residents. Everything remains closed not just on the citywide level but in every sector, according to the laws of the military mousetrap: you can't drive or even walk from one part of the city to another. You wander around in the ruins as if you were in a labyrinth, following secret paths only to find yourself back at the same sunlit checkpoint. There, a cheerful soldier who is also sick and tired of all this offers to tell you a joke, as compensation for the loss of freedom of those gathered by his cement shed. We on the other side of the barbed wire don't laugh; we just smirk.

"Not funny?" the cheerful soldier asks and suddenly forgets his orders and lets most of the people who are stuck there through. These lucky breaks are key to survival in Chechnya.

I need to get to the Second Children's Hospital, the only emergency center with resuscitation facilities for children in Chechnya today.

March 8th Street is as deserted as the Sahara. The building of the children's hospital resembles a half-destroyed oasis. The windows on the second floor have been knocked out, and the first floor is shocking in its emptiness and total lack of charming children's voices. A big swarthy man with glasses on the edge of his nose sits at the desk in a miserable room trying to read a book. It's the head doctor, Ruslan Ganayev. He is very nervous.

"I'm worried to death. My doctors are taking a boy in critical condition to his home in Argun. His parents wanted it this way. They say if he has to die, let him die at home rather than in Grozny. He's one month old, he's suffering from croup and can't breathe. The doctors will work the respirator for him on the way to Argun, and then they'll come back. Or maybe not."

"Where are the children? And the guards? The administration claims that all hospitals are guarded."

"We've never had any guards here. There are no children either. As soon as the blockade started, the parents grabbed their children and tried to make their way to the villages to hide from the shooting and purges. They even took some kids from resuscitation wards. They simply took out the tubes and carried them away. We had a girl with infantile cerebral paralysis in traction—they took her off it. The only patient we have left in the whole hospital now is a three-month-old, Salavat Khakimov from Alkhan-Kala."

His young mother and aunt stand by the side of the tightly swaddled, sleeping Salavat. They explain why they haven't left with the others. The boy urgently needs an operation, without which he'll die. He has a fistula in his pelvic joint from an injection he got in the maternity hospital. The maternity hospital, like the children's, still does not have running water, so today they are both in essence field stations, with a corresponding level (or more exactly, a lack) of disinfection. The dirty injection resulted in a fistula. The baby's bone is already festering; he has sepsis and a high fever and could die any minute.

The boy was born not long before they started a purge in his native village of Alkhan-Kala, while trying to capture one of the field commanders. The village was then completely blockaded, the way Grozny is now. No one could go in or out, including pregnant women, the sick, and infants carried by their mothers. Everyone was assumed to be a terrorist accomplice. First, the Feds spent a few weeks searching for the bandit in the village, then, after killing him, a few more weeks conducting purges among the residents. It was impossible to take the baby to the Grozny hospital. The village doctor's assistant operated on Salavat three times, right in their home, without anesthesia or antiseptics. Salavat is a real victim of the antiterrorist operation, although he is only three months old and for that reason alone cannot be a terrorist.

"He's having surgery tomorrow," his mother says. "We can't put it off any longer. I'm very grateful to the doctors who will operate despite the blockade."

The boy lies across an adult bed; there are no children's beds here. We sit down near him and fall right through—it turns out that all the beds have holes in their metal nets, and unless you put something underneath the mattress, like an old wooden door, you can't lie or sit on it.

The medical equipment used by the doctors looks very strange too. If not for the sign above the entrance that reads "Second Municipal Children's Hospital," you might think it's a warehouse with some ancient tools waiting their turn to be thrown away. But this junk that the doctors find invaluable has its own war history. Before the attack on Grozny at the beginning of the war, in the winter of 1999–2000, the doctors hid all their equipment in the neighboring basements: if a bomb hit one of them, everything in the other basements would still be intact. In one purge, the Feds discovered a basement with surgery tools and destroyed them all. There were reports on TV that they found a "secret operating room" where wounded militants were treated. The equipment that, by pure chance, remained intact in other basements, is now used to treat the children on March 8th Street, at Dr. Ganayev's hospital.

In the meantime, there is a lot of talk in Moscow about how a "peacetime life is taking shape in Grozny," about convoys with medical equipment sent there by the Ministry of Health, about trucks with medicine. City mayors change all the time. Every mayor makes yet another speech about the "new Chechnya," but doesn't do a thing, just like those before him. The present mayor is Oleg Zhidkov, an FSS colonel, an unpleasant fellow with glassy eyes and the organization's hatred of openness. He hides in his office, and you can't get him out of there. When he was appointed, the generals spoke on TV about their hope that he would revive Grozny. However, the city is as dead as ever, and Mayor Zhidkov has never found the time to visit Ruslan Ganayev at his hospital. Or any other medical institutions. Zhidkov— along with the other gentlemen responsible for the Second Municipal Hospital, the vice prime minister for social affairs, the minister of health, and their many officials—is on the Moscow payroll.

The head doctor takes off his glasses, revealing eternally sad Chekhov eyes. He doesn't want to talk politics.

"This is our duty," he says softly, quietly. "No matter what . . ."

Suddenly, he sees a silhouette in the dark maze of the hall. Going up to him quickly, he firmly embraces the man who has just entered the hospital, as if he hadn't seen him for a long time. This is the pediatrician who risked his life to take the baby with croup from blockaded Grozny to the town of Argun and has now managed to return.

They hold their embrace for a few minutes, as if the man had managed to come back alive from a doomed military reconnaissance operation.

"It's time to leave. It'll be dark soon. They can spot you," the doctors say.

"Who?"

"Both sides. We could fight off ours, but not yours."

We go out, saying good-bye at the entrance, again as if for the last time. This is the most important tradition in contemporary Grozny: no one expects to live until morning. So they don't spare any emotion. What if there is no tomorrow? For you or the other person?

Conversations in the Kitchen

Another day and night of the blockade. Not since the assault in the winter of 2000 has it been as restless in Grozny as it is during this September blockade. But night comes, and you long to talk. Five women ranging from young to old have wound up together at a table by chance. Everyone wants to forget herself, to blather about good times and romance, unhurriedly unwind women's stories, her own and others'. But in the end, it's all about the war, which hits us in the most painful places as soon as we forget ourselves.

Larisa Petrovna was born, grew up, and has spent her whole life in Grozny. She is Russian. And now, with the arrival of Federal troops, she has been forced into the limited space of one of the Grozny yards. And it's been this way for a few months now.

Her story is a hard one. She was held hostage by Chechen bandits at the very beginning of the war. They demanded that she sign her apartment over to the person whose name they provided. When they failed to get her to do so, they simply let her go, unwashed for many months, downtrodden, with her nails overgrown and curving into spirals.

"Well, it's all in the past," Larisa Petrovna interrupts herself. "I don't want to think about it. I survived, and that's all."

There is nowhere for her to go outside of Chechnya. And now the situation has grown worse. Many soldiers have turned into bandits too, or work together with them. Larisa Petrovna chooses never to leave the home of her former Chechen colleagues, who have sheltered her. She is a retired engineer.

"It's not a good life," I say.

"But where can you go?" says Larisa Petrovna. The mother of little Salavat, who has fistula, said the very same thing to me. People live in this city not because it's a normal life, or because anything is changing for the better, but because there's nowhere else to go. "I don't understand how all this happened. We were waiting for the army to bring us relief, but it brought total slavery instead."

The second woman, Fatima, a Chechen, was widowed long ago. She recently went to the commander's headquarters at dawn, along with a crowd of other women, to ransom her son from the district police department. Her son was taken away at five in the morning, right from his bed. They beat him so badly that his insides were damaged, demanding a confession about ties with the Wahhabis. How could he confess, when he comes from a family that has suffered a lot struggling against those long-bearded militants and is being persecuted by them?

At 6 A.M., Fatima already stood at the police barrier with the rest of the crowd. Soon an officer came out and said, "Five hundred dollars, by 3 P.M., or you'll never see your son again."

"So you came up with five hundred dollars?"

"Believe it or not, I did. I never ran so quickly, from house to house."

Her son got his freedom and is now being treated for injured kidneys. The Chechen policeman who helped collect the cursed five hundred dollars was a friend of the family. He had worked for many years as a policeman up to the time of Dudayev and the present wars, and had returned to the police force last year. He was a man with a high rank and position whose heart was sick over what he was now witnessing. The very evening Fatima paid the ransom for her son, he died of a stroke. While dying in the arms of his family, he kept repeating, "How could this happen?" And everyone understood that "this" was about more than just Fatima's son.

The women at the table do not cry, although they would like to. You rarely hear crying in Grozny. They've all cried their eyes out long ago. Whether or not a woman cries indicates how long it's been since she returned to Grozny from the refugee camps.

Outside, it is dark and quiet. Even the dogs haven't been barking for a long time. Somewhere far off, there is a glow from sporadic, noiseless bombing. It resembles thunderstorm lightning a bit. After midnight, the armored vehicles start screeching again. Everyone bends down and hunches over, making herself smaller. Is it coming for you?

In five minutes, there's a feeling of relief. It's not for you. The armored vehicle rumbles past.

"This is what we've come to: we're glad it's for someone else," Fatima concludes.

It's five hours until the next blockade dawn, and we need to survive them. This is a very intimate affair. You survive as you are born, alone. You need to part company, so you can lie down, close your eyes and remain one on one with a world that does not want you.

Viktoria and Aleksandr: Grozny Newlyweds

"You're such a bum, Sasha! Such a bum . . ." Vika coos sweetly, over and over again. She's trying to reach something with her outstretched hand. There's a dark hole behind her that looks like an open refrigerator.

Finally, she finds what she wants and reaches out toward Sasha the bum:

"Here's your comb. We should look decent . . . Comb your hair . . ."

We met yesterday evening. During the past night, two more bullet wounds appeared in their window. However, neither of them pays any attention to these treacherous holes. The action takes place in Grozny.

"They were shooting . . ." they say, indifferently. And they immediately laugh and caress each other, just like the newlyweds they are, inspired by the past night and completely free of any "yesterday," no matter how bad it was. This couple really knows how to live in the moment. After all, it's still a long time—three whole hours— until the new Grozny day will begin, and then they'll have nothing but problems: what to eat, where to get water. Then anger and resentment will come, and awareness of the cage they've been driven into. Eventually, at around three, the chronic lack of food will make itself known.

But now it's time for breakfast. A Grozny wartime breakfast.

"It's best to pretend that we have as much as everyone else in the country," says Vika, offering me some hot liquid that they proudly call "morning tea." "Or else you'll go out of your mind."

"And to forget that there's nothing but tea in the house?" Sasha half asks and half states.

"What are you trying to say?" Vika slants her eyes coquettishly. "That I'm a bad housekeeper? Hmmm?"

Vika and Sasha are Grozny newlyweds. They're from the town of Ivanov, a suburb that has no streets—only house numbers.

More formally, their names are Aleksandr Georgievich and Viktoria Aleksandrovna Jura. They were legally married on April 6, 2001, a few months ago.

"Enough, Vika. No more nonsense! Just read!" orders the freshly combed bum, drinking tea.

Vika continues to flirt and make eyes at her husband, who is putting on a stern air, for a couple of minutes. Then she reaches to the side again and picks up a notebook that she's had during the entire war.

> You understand, but still you cannot feel it:
> Another's pain, though bitter, doesn't hurt.
> Your knowledge that you're just an invalid
> Is piercing; it becomes self-torture, shock . . .
>
> Here you sit, a grasshopper who's stumbled.
> You go five steps, but then sit down again . . .
> And though the wind alone embraces you,
> Your soul strains ever upwards anyway.
>
> How badly nature always seems to mock us,
> How fate continues every day to test us.
> When you're out walking, looking like a freak,
> With all the gazes riveted on you.

it was

"Enough of this wailing," Sasha interrupts. "Don't you have anything more cheerful?"

However, you can see that he likes this poem very much. He just doesn't want to show weakness in front of guests.

Sasha and Vika are invalids of the first category. Vika was hit by a motorcycle when she was ten, and everything that's wrong with her now is the result of heavy skull and brain trauma. Sasha was simply born that way. Their motor functions go on strike together. There are good days, of course, especially for Vika, who can still move about somewhat. But for many months, they spend most of their time in a space of about twenty square feet, in the kitchen of a surviving first floor of a five-floor building (the apartments above them are burned and bombed out), sitting at the table by the window that the bullets are flying through.

Vika Jura is a poet. She writes poems in old school notebooks—hers and other people's. She works very hard on her style, often rewriting poems. And for this reason she sleeps very badly at night.

"Just as a poet should," adds Sasha.

"Imagine," says Vika, picking up on what he says. "When they were shooting at us yesterday through the window, I was sleeping very deeply right then. Because I was able to write a good line in the evening. So I didn't even wake up, even though I'm a terrible coward."

"Just let Vika recite. She's written some good poems about the war."

> What's going on here, what is going on?
> How do you, who give these orders, sleep?
>
> Those who live here get it from both sides—
> The army and the bandits. But what for?
>
> Some people here are desperate for freedom.
> And others—to apply their will by force.
>
> And they're still bombing . . .

Vika has become sad. She silently strokes the "night" holes in the windowpane.

But that's what a husband is for, to drive away sadness. This is Sasha's firm position. And he begins to "treat" his favorite poet.

"Don't think Vika's a crybaby—she's a real rascal. Let's hear the one about the liver."

"Oh, no. She's from Moscow, she wants something about the war, something serious."

"Putting on airs again?"

"Fine! I'm so tired of you!" But even this she says lovingly.

> Once Liver declared:
> You are hurting my shoulder!
> I now want to live
> Independent and free!"
> Then Sole jumped up too:
> He said, "That's right! Hurray!
> I declare that I too
> Want to be independent!
> Decide what to do—
> And walk all by myself!"
> And the little girl Spleen
> In a thin little squeak
> Said, "Your paté is nothing—
> Compared to self-ruling!"
> From all this disorder
> The body decayed.
> The Microbes then shouted:
> "Hey, we're first-class guys!
> We're now most important!
> In chaos we've won!"

Vika is very satisfied with Sasha's reaction—he bursts into laughter.

To comprehend these fragments and glue them together into one whole is very difficult for me. There's the cruel war, the fifth month of the marriage—still the honeymoon—severe disability, poetry. It's all too unbelievably mixed up.

"Vika didn't cry even during the worst of the bombing. She shouted, 'I can't bear it!' But as long as she was shouting, I knew she'd survive," says Sasha.

In life, you strive to get from the superficial to the real. There it is, you think, right around the corner. Oh, no, again you're out of luck, it's just a mirage. And you think that if you dig deeper into yourself, you'll find it. But vanity is vanity, and you're right back, running in circles after new, more vivid sensations and impressions, only to face defeat again.

Here, in the smoldering ruins of Grozny, there's nothing to see except suffering, your own and others'. Yet it is precisely here that life is the most real, even though it's almost like a cave, and the three-by-three patch in the kitchen resembles a stage. And for some reason you keep your comb in the refrigerator. There hasn't been any electricity for a few years now in the town of Ivanov. The refrigerator has turned into a closet, which is suitable only for keeping combs in.

A stove? The family has one of those too. There's no gas, though. And for that reason the pots arranged on it are just symbols of a struggle for a better future, in which there will be gas, and you won't have to make fires in the street to cook.

A sink? Of course! What kind of kitchen would it be without a sink! But unfortunately, there is absolutely no water in the pipes.

And there's a lampshade hanging overhead, but no light!

I'm ashamed to cry in their presence. So I don't. I don't know how to express my feelings—they're all so petty compared with their life. Everything in their kitchen is like a stage prop—the stove, the refrigerator, and the faucets—except for the feelings. And in Moscow kitchens everything is real—the stove, the gas, the hot and cold water from the faucets—except for the feelings. There, it's the feelings that are just props. We're too satiated for a country that's been at war for so long.

"You're such a bum, Sasha!" Vika gets a bit mad. "It's only morning, you know. How many times do I have to tell you not to smoke on an empty stomach. It's bad for you!"

"I can't stop, Vikulya! I've smoked since I was seven."

"Since you were seven? You hear that? I wouldn't have married you if I'd known."

Then—her fresh, ringing, morning laughter. Still not spoiled by anything from the day. And Sasha's bass, always teasing.

When you leave someone's house, you always know whether you'll ever want to come back. I would like to be in this house again. I'd like to sit there and enjoy the company of these people. And feel the life that flows through them, despite the unique wartime apathy that strikes everyone here. There have been so many deaths nearby that the dead lie unburied this whole time, maybe two or three steps away from you. The Juras are all the more likeable for having overcome so much. *They live real life in the trappings of war.* Against the background of their happy smiles, your troubles don't mean a thing. They're just figments of your imagination.

A Village That No Longer Exists

There is no man who would claim that the grief of Khatyn* is greater than the horror of Guernica. You can't use scales or a ruler to measure suffering. Everyone has his or her own pain, and this pain is worst for whoever experiences it. The second Chechen war has added a few new pages to the country's history, comparable to both Guernica and Khatyn in terms of the number of victims, and the ruins, bloodshed, and consequences for the whole world. And it is not at all important that no one has recognized this yet; the time will come when everyone will speak of it.

One of these pages is about Komsomolskoe.

Komsomolskoe used to be a big village in the Urus-Martan district, a little over four miles from the district center. It had thousands of residents, a hospital, a club, stores, lovely hilly, winding streets, and a charming Alpine view of the mountains.

A man named Ruslan Gelayev grew up in this village. And this, in essence, determined the course of the village's history and sealed the fate of its thousands of residents.

At the beginning of February 2000, after field commander Gelayev's detachment had entered Komsomolskoe, the Federal troops completely destroyed the village. The siege lasted for one month, after which both Gelayev and the Feds went "home," leaving behind a monstrous conglomeration of burnt houses, ruins, and new graves at the cemetery.

A Year and a Half Later

If you walk along the former Tsentralnaya Street, a feeling of unreality caused by everything that has taken place here will overwhelm

---

* A town in what is now Belarus that was burned with its inhabitants by Nazi occupation forces in 1943. A memorial to all the towns in Belarus that were similarly destroyed now stands at the site. *Trans.*

you. On the one hand, it is a lifeless desert devoid even of chirping birds, so it doesn't have the natural soundtrack that we are used to. On the other hand, it looks like the setting for a horror film, with voices heard from time to time.

To reach these voices, you have to go uphill. It seems that there was a street here in the good old days; nowadays, you can only see overgrown, untidy bushes sticking out everywhere, bashfully covering some background ruins.

A man in threadbare clothes appears on the well-trodden path. He is as thin as a Buchenwald prisoner. It is probably because of the tuberculosis—there are many cases now in Chechnya.

"Do you live here?"

"Yes. This used to be Rechnaya Street." He waves in the direction of the bushes he came out from. "Who are you looking for?"

"Anyone who lives here."

"That would be me. There's no one else on this street. They say 150 families came back to the village. But they are all homeless."

"Is the head of administration here? The village council?"

"No, we're on our own."

"What do you mean?"

"There just aren't any authorities here. They probably think our village doesn't exist at all. For them, Komsomolskoe has been wiped from the map—otherwise, they'd remember about us, ask how we're doing."

"Could you show me your house then?"

"I already told you, I don't have any."

"So where do you live? It's fall now."

"In a barn."

The man's name is Mohammed Dudushev. It turns out that he was born the same year as me, but he looks like an old man.

Mohammed has a big family—his wife Liza, six kids, and his mother. The family is crammed into a tiny brick hut—a "barn"—they built this past summer. Their house is nearby; it was destroyed by a direct hit. The ruins are lovingly covered with the thick blue plastic that was once dispensed to the village's residents from the United Nations.

"We wish they'd help us with construction materials. We can't build it all by ourselves, not now, not in the near future. Only the poorest families, with a lot of kids, who can't make it even to Ingushetia, are left in the village. So I'm trying to protect my construction site from the rain, wait until things get better. Maybe all this will change." Mohammed coughs, struggling for breath. He has tuberculosis all right.

"What did you have for lunch?"

"Nothing."

"And for breakfast?"

"Some corncakes and tea."

It is scary to look at the Dudushev children up close. They have the same dried-up bodies as their father. They are very dirty: water and heat are scarce in the ruins, and the electric wiring needs fixing. You can't really call it life.

Like most people trying to survive in Chechnya, the Dudushevs are subject to low spirits and unhappy thoughts. They only hope for the future, when corn crops will play a key role. The field begins right by the brick barn. This harvest is the only thing that could change the course of their lives, which have been completely destroyed by the war.

"We'll keep part of the corn for food in the winter," Liza says, "and sell the rest to buy a cow, so we don't starve. Our two cows were killed during the attack. It's been hell since then—there's no food for the kids. Sometimes they bring us some flour from the Danish Council, as if we were in Denmark, and that's it. There's no other humanitarian aid from anyone. We also need to buy shoes for the kids with the corn money—see, they're barefoot."

Liza herself seems to be wearing a fifty-year-old dress.

"All my clothes got burnt," she says catching my gaze. Liza must still be young and pretty, but you can't really see it now.

Naturally, they never received any compensation for their burnt home and belongings that were destroyed in the course of a military operation. The ideology of survival in present-day Chechnya is very simple: live as best as you can, and if you can't, then that's your problem.

What's more, the Dudushevs seem to be the very category of people the high tribunes in Grozny and Moscow are raving about. Officials cite them as a "good example": they did not leave for Ingushetia, demand to be placed into a refugee camp, or ask for regular humanitarian aid. They just go on living on their land. You would think that simply by helping the Dudushevs and those like them, you could entice other families who might be not such a good example to come back to their own country from refugee camps, and you wouldn't have to ask them twice.

The Children

When Mohammed's older son Isa sees a Russian, he stops speaking Russian out of spite, although he can, as his more friendly parents confirm. He angrily shakes his head, demonstrating his utter dislike, and finally runs away, quickly moving his bare feet and muttering something.

"The older kids have no shoes at all," Liza goes on with her topic.

When I saw those contemptuous flashing heels, my first thought was, "He's going for a submachine gun hidden away somewhere." There's a lot of hatred in Isa's look and gestures, even in the stubborn back of his head, and in the way he squats and pointedly turns away. But it's not his fault. The life of today's Chechen teenagers is an endless chain of horrors, and continual participation, year after year, in burials of family and friends, all of whom died an unnatural death. And of course, the adults' everyday conversation is about those who are still alive and those who have been found dead, the way the purge went, and what kind of ransom was paid for whom to the Feds.

Isa comes back, and Liza translates for him. It turns out that he wants to know why Putin announced a moment of silence to honor the victims of the American tragedy while never saying a word about the innocent Chechen victims. Why is there so much talk about the flooded city of Lensk, with Shoigu* personally giving his word to Putin to rebuild it, but no one says a word about ruined Chechnya? Why was the whole country stirred when the Kursk sailors were dying, but when they were shooting people leaving Komsomolskoe right on the field for several days, "you kept silent?"

---

*Sergei Shoigu: The permanent minister of the Ministry for Emergency Situations since its founding in 1991. A protégé of Yeltsin, he is one of the most influential political figures under Putin. Shoigu is the founding father of the hastily assembled Unity Party (now renamed), which brought Putin to power.

"They shot at me—do you understand?" He switches to Russian.

And he runs away again, his heels flashing. Most adults are probably capable of dealing with the nightmare that has enveloped them on their own, and in time of even finding some kind of explanation that brings them peace. But it seems that the young people of Chechnya, whose teenage years have been flooded with the endless tears of their sisters and mothers, are not going to overcome it. The younger generation of Chechens—high school seniors or graduates—is the toughest generation that has ever lived here. Independence Dudayev-style? They've seen it. The first war? They've survived it. The second war? They've been through it. Corpses? More than you can handle. Their goal in life? To hide from the man with the Kalashnikov in time. The value of human life? They've watched it go down to zero.

Isa's fourteen-year-old younger sister Zarema looks like a small, hunted animal who expects nothing but trouble. She was four when Dudayev declared that girls should not go to school at all. She was seven during the first war, and twelve when their village was destroyed. She's seen it all with her own eyes.

It is impossible to deny the state of decay that Chechnya has experienced by the third year of the second war. The only question is, how can you fight it? How can you make your children believe in a better tomorrow? How can you believe in it yourself?

Liza, who is a product of the Soviet system, tries to calm things down. This is a typical Chechen story today: the older generation is much more loyal toward the Russians than the teenagers and young adults are.

But their mother's diplomacy has no effect: the kids are too tough for that. Their grandmother is the only one still smiling. She survived Stalinist repression and exile. She went hungry many times and got used to coming back to life and then looking death in the face again.

The Flowers

It's time to say good-bye. Isa has not returned, with or without a submachine gun. Mohammed, yet another homeless, thoroughly humiliated Chechen man who is unable to do anything for his family, asks:

"Do you want to visit our neighbor, Grandma Savnapi? She lives not far from here, on what used to be Nagornaya Street. We call her Grandma Savnapi. She doesn't have anything except her flowers. But they're very pretty."

Savnapi Dalayeva is not a "grandma" at all. She was born in 1944, and has a gentle, beautiful face and deep gray eyes. But she is toothless, and her skin is covered with wounds. The fence around her house has been shot full of holes. Her house does not even look as good as Mohammed's construction site—there is nothing but a barely standing foundation. But on both sides of it, Savnapi has set up a lovely flower garden, a rockery, as garden books would call it.

"I walked around the deserted village after the attack. I'd pick up a flower from the ashes, bring it here, dig up a hole—and here's my garden . . . I like beautiful things."

Little by little, people gather around. I have never seen such terribly thin people anywhere. They tell me about a family of two invalids, one mentally ill, the other suffering from asthma. There is another family with an invalid child. The third family has had all its men killed . . .

"Does Gelayev help you out now? Is he supporting his village?"

They laugh:

"He's already helped us enough. See how he's supporting us?"

When they stop laughing, the women add:

"Damn him."

Everything will be written down in the history of the second Chechen war. Poverty, hunger, illness, homelessness. General Troshev. President Putin. Everyone who destroyed a living organism and did not even try to fix things later. The Gelayev phenomenon will be there too. Gelayev has abandoned his people in need; he is no longer with them, and the people are not with him, either.

A Lawless Enclave

The young, lame Dr. Sultan Khajiev, head of the septic department of the Ninth Grozny Municipal Hospital, leans his wounded body heavily onto a cane and takes a blanket away from the squeaking cot far off by the window of ward 1. The blanket was covering the body of Aishat Suleimanova, a sixty-two-year-old Grozny resident from Khankalskaya Street.

Aishat's eyes express complete indifference to the world, and it's beyond one's strength to look at her naked body. She's been disemboweled like a chicken. The surgeons have cut into her from above her chest to her groin. The postsurgical incisions are not straight but forked like a family tree. In some places the seams refuse to stay closed, and you see wounds that have been turned inside out. The nurse sticks strips of gauze onto it, as if there were deep, empty holes there, and Aishat doesn't even cry.

"I can't feel anything," she says through her gray lips. But the movement of her lips is not in sync with her words, as if it were a very badly dubbed foreign film.

Two weeks before our conversation, a young fellow in a Russian serviceman's uniform put Aishat on a bed in her own house and shot five 5.45-caliber bullets into her. These bullets, weighted at the edges, have been forbidden by all international conventions as inhumane. After entering a body, they rush through it, tearing apart all the internal organs along the way. Aishat's son, who is sitting next to her, hasn't shaved for a long time—this means that there has been a funeral in their family. He looks at me with an alienated expression of undisguised hatred. And when he is about to say something, he suddenly stops short, as if to say "it's not for you to feel sorry for us." Aishat is the one who wants to talk, and share her suffering, as it is so undeserved and therefore all the more excruciating.

"We had already gone to bed. Suddenly—it must have been about two at night—I heard someone knocking loudly. And knocking was bad news at this time, since it was after curfew. We opened the door. Two soldiers stood there. They said: 'We need beer.' I answered: 'We don't sell beer.' They said: 'Give us beer!' I said: 'We don't allow beer in the house.' 'OK, Grandma,' they said. And they left." Aishat clutches her neck. It's not an onset of suffocation, but a wave of tears and sorrow. She touches the shoulder of her increasingly gloomy son. Reassured by this contact, she continues: "It was probably an hour later when I woke up again, and these two soldiers were already going through our rooms. They were rummaging around and saying, 'This time we're here for a purge.' I understood: we were going to be punished for not giving them any beer. The soldiers looked through our medicine—my husband has asthma. One of them went into the room where our grandchildren of five, a year and a half, and four months were sleeping. I was afraid he'd rape my daughter-in-law. I heard the kids scream. The other took my husband into the kitchen. My husband, Abas, is eighty-six. I heard my husband offering him money. And then, he screamed! The soldier had killed him with a knife. Then the soldier left the kitchen and took me into the bedroom. I felt as though I couldn't move. And he started talking to me so gently, pointing to the bed: 'Sit here, Granny. Let's talk.' And he himself sat down across from me. 'We're not beasts, we're from OMON*—this is our job.' And the children were crying in the other room. I said: 'Don't frighten the children.' 'All right, we won't.' He answered gently. And with these very words, not even getting up, he let me have it with his submachine gun. My daughter-in-law told me not long ago that after the shooting they just closed the door behind them and left."

Aishat couldn't be taken to the hospital until the next morning. It is nearby, but for anyone who isn't a bandit, Grozny has a very strict curfew at night. It's fine to stab a Chechen with a knife, but to ask permission at the checkpoint to take a wounded person to the hospital is almost like asking for your own execution.

"She was bleeding, getting weaker, peritonitis was already starting," the doctors say. "It's a miracle that she survived. Let's go into reception now. They just brought a woman in the exact same condition there. She's a victim of the night banditry. Maybe you'll be able to talk with her before the soldiers show up. And if they do, don't be afraid—we'll get you out of here."

The forty-four-year-old Malika Elmurzayeva is groaning, with her hair scattered loosely on a hospital oilcloth. The doctor is trying to raise her head, but the woman is losing consciousness from the pain. You can see how patches of her thick, beautiful, dark red hair are missing here and there from the parts of her head where they should be, and are hanging by scraps of skin.

Malika lives in Grozny Neighborhood No. 1, on Kirov Street, in a five-story building, in a wing with no men. It was around two o'clock at

---

*Police Special Task Force, military detachments of the Russian Ministry of the Interior. Participated actively in both Chechen wars.

night when they started banging on the door: "Open up, you bitches, this is a purge!"

They opened the door, of course—there was nothing you could do. Just so long as they didn't burst the door open. A group of young men in uniforms and masks and (as became clear from their conversation) a mixture of Chechens and Russians, came to rob the building, which had already been robbed several times.

Three of Malika's female relatives were sleeping in her apartment. One of them was fifteen. The gang acted as if they were going to rape her, and yelled at the others: "If you don't do what we say, we'll rape her to death." They grabbed Malika by her hair and dragged her up the stairs to knock on other people's doors and ask them to open up for a neighbor.

Everything ended in marauding and blood. The women who had spent that night in these apartments were mercilessly beaten on their legs, kidneys, and heads.

"Did they rape anyone?"

Malika is silent. Those who brought her here, the beaten women who opened their doors when she knocked, are also silent. Their silence is too stubborn.

The bandits' bacchanalia on Kirov Street lasted until five in the morning. In Grozny they're used to the marauders leaving the places where they're "partying" by six, before the end of the curfew.

"Look at the numbers!" the doctors say. "From June 1 to September 18, 2001, we received 1,219 patients here at the hospital, including outpatients. Of those, 267 had wounds from firearms or mine explosions. Most of them are victims of these night robberies."

To find out what's going on in the city, you have to go to the hospital. This is where the final acts of all these dramas and tragedies take place. So while those in the administration who are being paid to "construct peace" in Chechnya blabber nonstop about "peacetime" Grozny, new patients "wounded by firearms" are brought every day to the hospital of war-stricken, bandit-ridden Grozny.

The war in this city has depraved everyone weak enough to give in to it. Nighttime criminals attack the ruined homes of people who are already wretched enough as it is. On the one hand, this criminality is led and encouraged by Federal servicemen. Without their consent and support, today no bandit would be capable of wandering the streets during curfew, let alone shooting, robbing, and raping. However, it also requires the active participation of Chechens. By the beginning of the third year of the war, it turns out that the gangs combing the ruins at night are a fraternity of criminals from the Chechen ranks, mixed with servicemen of the same stripe who are here "on duty." And they don't give a damn about their ideological and national differences, or the fact that they belong to opposing sides. I'm sure that even if they announced the end of war operations and the withdrawal of troops tomorrow, Grozny would remain under the heel of criminals, and who knows when it would be able to throw it off. It's easy to start a war, but it's almost impossible to fish out all the monsters that it begets.

"Gross Grozny": that's how residents of Grozny refer to their once beloved city. And these two words reflect more than just pain from the loss of streets and squares that have been turned into ruins. There is also a horror of the future, since the present has sunk into the darkness of the outright banditry that is the main result of the war.

A small but very important observation along the way. Recall the doctor's words, strange at first glance: "We'll get you out of here, if the soldiers show up." This is not just the wartime paranoia that affects everyone to some degree. It is also part of Grozny's reality. The soldiers, rulers of local life, have created a barbaric order in which anyone who knows about the actual conditions of the civilian population can be equated to an enemy spy and has to be dealt with according to wartime laws. And considering that all of Chechnya is now flooded with willing helpers of the FSS from among the Chechens, to fall into the hands of soldiers and not get away is very easy. Therefore, you hear precisely this everywhere from friends: "we'll get you out of here," "we'll hide you." But good Lord, from whom? From those who are fighting on the money of taxpayers like myself? In order to talk with Aishat, and stand in the reception room next to Malika, who has been torn to shreds, you have to behave like a spy from a third side in the camp of enemies who have unexpectedly reached an agreement with one another.

Aishat's criminal case has been initiated in the worst division of internal affairs of Grozny—the October district division—where they both commit and investigate crimes. The same goes for Malika's case. The doctors, like intelligence agents, are quietly moving me to the side, to secret hiding places in the hospital, so that I can sneak past the soldiers. These soldiers, who just came in unexpectedly for an inspection, have not introduced themselves or shown their papers to anyone, not even the head doctor.

"We are a nation of outcasts. And whoever is with us is also an outcast," says Dr. Khajiev as a farewell.

"And what happened to you? Why are you limping?"

The doctor, like his patients, suffers more from the unbridled license of war than from disease. At noon on Russian Independence Day, at the intersection of Pervomaiskaya and Griboedov Streets, an armored vehicle from the Lenin district military command in Grozny crashed into him.

"Why did it crash into you?"

"It just did. It darted out at high speed. I didn't even see what happened. I was just hit really hard. My Zhiguli was totaled. But I lived."

"Then what happened? Do you know the license number of the armored vehicle? Did they open the case?"

"Yes, they did. And that's as far as it got."

"Why?"

Because Chechnya is a zone where some people can do whatever they want, and the others have to accept it.

Russia continues to nurture an enclave where citizens' rights don't exist. It's a very dangerous business. If only the world could see the eyes of Aishat Suleimanova's son! The gaze of a hunted outcast, whose father was killed only because he was an outcast, and whose mother was disfigured for the same reason. At the beginning of the war, most Chechens were still surprised by their new situation and yelled, "We're people just like you! We demand respect!" But now no one yells. Because everyone agrees: they are a nation of outcasts.

Will everyone continue to accept this way of life? Aishat will. But it's not likely that her son will. Here's a tiny bit of national history. At the end of the nineteenth and beginning of the twentieth centuries in Russia, there was a wave of state-sponsored anti-Semitism that differed very little from today's widespread national anti-Chechen frame of mind. The Pale of Settlement zones were developed. Children grew up knowing that they were forbidden to move freely unless they had permission from the police and weren't allowed to study in many educational institutions. This created an inferiority complex and ultimately crowned many Jewish youth as martyrs. They were prepared to avenge their desecrated childhood, because they didn't want their grownup years and old age to be desecrated the way their parents' and grandparents' had been.

The whole world knows the result. Most of the big-name Bolsheviks who carried out the October revolution came from among those shtetl Jews. They did not just want to stop living as outcasts, but also aimed to get revenge on their offenders. And did they ever get revenge. It's strange how yet again we've forgotten what we should never forget under any circumstances. Dr. Khajiev agrees with me. In the third year of the war, we are already meeting too many young Chechens with sparks of hatred in their eyes and one single dream: to punish those who have offended them.

A Nameless Girl from Nowhere

In room 45 on the second floor of the Grozny retirement home, a small, silent child lives side by side with fifty-three old men and women. She could be four, or she could be seven. She keeps her head low, and her eyes are sharp and alert. She moves like a wild cat, always trying to hide deep under one of the home's metal beds. The room is sparse and empty, as is typical of wartime. According to the custom of this war, the windows are covered with plastic, since glass remains the hardest commodity to obtain in Grozny. Her metal bed has nothing but a striped mattress on it. And she resembles a child only in her height.

What has happened with this girl is one of the mysteries of the second Chechen war. The old men and women call her Angela, and they say she is four. But nobody knows for sure.

The girl was brought to the retirement home in the Katayama district of Grozny in the early spring of 2001 by strangers who left right away. They said they were not her family or friends, just passersby who took pity on the orphan. They knew that the retirement home had food and heat again, so they took her by the hand and brought her here.

The child was dirty and unkempt. Her hair was all matted, and she had fleas. She was very thin, hungry, in ragged clothes, and almost barefoot: she wore torn sandals on her skinny feet, not proper footwear for early spring, even in Grozny.

She said her name was Angela, and this was the only thing she ever said. Angela was accompanied by a middle-aged woman—they wandered along the Grozny streets together. But it was difficult to say who accompanied whom or who was helping whom to survive. The woman, who introduced herself as Raisa, was obviously mentally ill, dirty and hungry, of an indeterminate age. It was not even clear if her name was really Raisa. She behaved very strangely: she would talk nonsense and make up scary things like Hitchcock. Before burning Raisa's clothes, the nurse Zinaida Tavgireeva checked all her pockets but did not find any ID, either her own or the girl's. Raisa did claim that she was Angela's relative and that the girl's last name was Zaitseva. The girl was Russian, then. When they washed her, a typical oval Slavic face appeared from under many layers of street dirt, and her hair turned out to be blond.

Later, a few inconsistencies surfaced. Raisa said that Angela was "the daughter of her husband's second wife." Her husband had supposedly died, and his second wife, Angela's mother, followed him shortly. Raisa now considered herself to be the girl's stepmother. As is customary in Chechen families, she took the orphan into her care. If he had two wives, does that mean he was a Chechen? This question Raisa couldn't answer.

So here's what has happened: in the civilized Europe of the twenty-first century, a child appeared from nowhere, and no one knew who this child was. The war that we allowed to happen has deprived this girl of something even orphans have—knowledge of her name, and when and where she was born.

After a month, Angela put on weight and got back some of her color. She let the doctor examine her, and little by little started talking and running around the halls, bringing joy to the lonely old people. But she still could not remember anything about herself. But every time the cooks noisily dropped a big metal ladle on the floor of the home's kitchen, she would hide under the bed. And she would fall down right away wherever she stood, clutching her head tightly in her hands, whenever she heard shooting. All that was left from her past were these automatic movements.

Journalism is a good job. You meet a lot of people, and many are willing to help those you ask them to. That is what happened here too. After about half a year of annoying paperwork and begging the officials, Angela was adopted by a middle-aged couple from the North Osetian town of Mozdok. They were Chechens who had run away from Grozny during the second war and were now unwilling to return. Their only son was killed in the war, without leaving them any grandchildren. I have a picture of Angela with her new parents. A completely different face looks out at me from this picture: bright quick eyes, an open smile, a proud turn of the pretty head. Not a trace of that wild homeless Grozny orphan.

I am not going to visit her, although I'd like to see her happiness after all the terrible things she has been through. I don't want to remind her or her new parents of anything. They have to forget it all—that is the key to their happiness.

The Burning Cross of Tsotsan-Yurt

The government, via the public figure of the Russian president's assistant Sergei Yastrzhembsky, who is responsible for "creating a proper image of the war," pronounced its "special operation" of December 2001 and January 2002 in Chechnya an "obvious success." This figure assured our millions of people that for many months the government had been applying a tactic of driving the militants out of the mountains and several villages into the village of Tsotsan-Yurt. On New Year's Eve, no fewer than one hundred militants were blockaded there. As a result of severe fighting with "massive fire from houses turned into fortresses," a large number of them were caught or killed.

Crappy New Year!

In Tsotsan-Yurt everything started on December 30, when the whole world was about to sit down at the festive table.

"'Happy New Year!' I told the soldier who was the first to come into my yard," a feeble, very old woman says, mumbling and whistling through the two teeth she still has left in her mouth. "And the soldier answered, 'Crappy New Year, Grandma!'"

The camera darts around her house. The old woman explains something, stumbling and muttering. Her speech is very unclear. But no words are needed anymore.

The wardrobe has been knocked down, everything inside it broken.

"Where are your clothes?"

"They took them all. They said I was hiding the bandits, and started robbing right away."

The dishes? All broken and thrown on the floor.

Pillows and mattresses? Cut open.

Sacks of flour? Also cut open with knives. The flour has been spilled on the floor so that nobody can ever bake anything with it.

"I had two hundred sacks of hay in my shed," the old woman's neighbor says. "The soldiers brought a guy from the other end of the village there, put him between the sacks, and burnt it all."

An old man with a long beard, wearing a tall white sheepskin hat, is leaning heavily on his cane. He can barely stand—from old age and sorrow:

"They came in and said, 'Where's your tape recorder certificate?' And my tape recorder is thirty years old. What kind of certificate could I have? But if there's none, they just take it away. You have to pay them if you want to keep it. They took all the potatoes that I've saved up for the winter. If they didn't want a sack with flour, they'd just tear it open and spill the flour. They burnt all my fodder corn for the cattle. I had three pairs of pants—they took all three, and my socks too. They left anyone who paid the ransom of five or six thousand rubles per family alone. There was a smaller ransom of five hundred rubles per person not to be arrested. They didn't touch the militants at all. Then a bus drove up. They forced everyone in, including the children. They put grenades into the children's hands and screamed that they'd blow up the children if the parents didn't give them money. The Feds kept a young woman with a one-year old baby from the Soltalatov family outside while her mother was running from one neighbor to another collecting the ransom that they demanded. They even took the infants' clothes. My daughter-in-law was forced at gunpoint to write a note saying that she was thankful for what they had done and was giving them two sheep as a New Year's present. They promised to come back and burn down the house if she wrote a different note later. They taunted us like this for three days, coming and going. Is this any way to establish order?"

The mosque, of course, is the best building in the village. It has newly repaired walls, and a lovely, freshly painted fence. Soldiers, or maybe officers, came into the mosque. And they took a shit there. First they piled together the carpets, mosque plate, books, and the Koran, and then they shat on top of the whole thing.

"And they call themselves civilized people? And say we're from the Middle Ages or something? Russian mothers, your sons behaved like animals here! And there was no stopping them!" the women in kerchiefs slid askew yelled. Six days after the Tsotsan-Yurt pogrom, these women cleaned up the human shit from the mosque. "Damn you Russians! We'll never forget this! What mothers gave birth to these monsters?"

Boys crowd around, listening. They keep silent. One cannot take it anymore, turns around sharply and leaves. He was taken with the adult men into the "field," to the temporary filtration point, interrogated, and beaten. Another one, nine years of age, is asked by the grownups to tell us what he saw.

"I crawled into a basement from fear. The soldiers beat everyone, came after anyone. So I hid. But there was a dead man down there, and I got scared and ran out."

"Look at me, I'm an old woman," another woman says. She is not at all frail; her voice is strong, her back straight. She's quite brisk, but still an old woman. "And they yell at me, 'Bitch! Whore!'"

"And at us too," other old women nod sadly. They have canes and the bent, gouty legs of people who have worked their whole lives.

"How am I a 'bitch'?" one of them who was silent before cries out. "I worked for forty years as a milkmaid, my cows gave record yields. And this soldier screams at me, 'We'll make things so bad for you, you'll beg to be sent to Siberia.' But I've already been there, and it was better than here."

"I told them, 'Shame on you, boys!'" the first old woman continues. "'What if someone called your grandmother a bitch?' And the soldier says, 'They wouldn't, because she's Russian.'"

Up until January 3, a regular punitive operation was going on in Tsotsan-Yurt, with pogroms, fires, marauding, arrests, and murder.

A Cross in the Snow

The shape of a cross has been burned into the snowy ground. On this spot the Feds burned Buvaisar, a young Tsotsan-Yurtan, after shooting him dead. The old man in the white sheepskin hat says:

"The soldiers didn't even let us say the prayer for him. They started burning him right after they shot him."

There is nothing left of Buvaisar but this cross.

According to Memorial, a human rights center, representatives of the Federal forces cruelly tortured several men to death during the purge in the village of Tsotsan-Yurt (December 30, 2001, through January 3, 2002). Idris Zakriev, born 1965, was taken from his house on Stepnaya Street in armored vehicle A-611 at 7:45 A.M. on December 30. Musa Ismailov, born 1964, the father of five children, the oldest of whom is fourteen, was also taken by the Feds from his home. Also, on January 7, after the purge had ended and the blockade had been removed, the Tsotsan-Yurtans found the remains of at least three men at the outskirts of the village—their bodies had been blown up. They managed to identify the remains of Alkazur Saidselimov, born in 1978.

And what about Buvaisar's burnt remains?

Alas, there aren't even any bones left, and his death cannot be verified.

"In fact, the list is not complete," the Memorial members claim. "It includes only those we double-checked."

"The soldiers took dozens of people away from the families that couldn't collect a ransom," the Tsotsan-Yurtans testify. "But we'll keep silent as long as there's a chance to get them back. If we name them, they'll surely be killed and buried somewhere secretly."

The Authorities

According to official reports, the following forces took part in the "special operation":

- soldiers of the Russian Ministry of the Interior and the FSS (permanently deployed in Khankala, the head military base in Chechnya);
- members of special units of the Main Intelligence Department of the Russian Ministry of Defense (so-called flying detachments or death squads);

- representatives of the Kurchaloi District Military Command and provisional district departments of the Ministry of the Interior;
- Lieutenant General Vladimir Moltensky, commander of the United Group of Armies, in person.

Interestingly, there is an official record of the presence in Tsotsan-Yurt of the representatives of the prosecutor's office, in compliance with the order of the attorney general of Russia. But in this case, the prosecutors only gave their blessing to the military craze and pogroms, like army chaplains, without opposing anything.

But there is another side to the "authorities," the one the Tsotsan-Yurtan elderly talked about. Where was Kadyrov, the head of administration of the Chechen Republic? Where did Taramov, the head of the Kurchaloi district administration, go?

Throughout the New Year celebration, everyone who has any kind of civil authority in Chechnya has left the republic for vacation. The civil authorities have abandoned their people, leaving them to be eaten alive by the military. I do not believe that they didn't know about the upcoming New Year special operation. Or that they didn't at least learn about it on December 30. If they did, they haven't come back to defend the people they abandoned. Later, after the holidays, Kadyrov was seen by his people on TV, against the background of the Kremlin, heartily shaking Putin's hand.

In conclusion, a few more details.

First, about the salaries and pensions that were given out right before the New Year holidays. During the Tsotsan-Yurt purge, the Feds destroyed all the grain that the collective farm workers had received as their payment for the summer. They also expropriated all the old people's pensions, including the allowances for invalids dispensed right before that. They destroyed all the equipment of the furniture factory that had been recently set up in the village. Second, the Tsotsan-Yurt events did not happen by chance, but were a result of systematic ideological policies of the military establishment. The Tsotsan-Yurt measures were later applied in Argun, where the purgers moved to conduct the special operation from January 3 through 9. For example, the soldiers tore down a sugar refinery that had also been up and running. Now, of course, the refinery does not function anymore, since the soldiers have taken away the machine tools. The stolen product—sacks of sugar—was later being sold in neighboring villages at 180 rubles per sack, while the market price for sugar in Chechnya is three times higher. And those who saw this could not get their phone calls through to the prosecutor's office, to get them to arrest the sellers of the stolen goods.

I am intentionally not giving out the names of the Tsotsan-Yurtans who agreed to testify about what has happened in their village. All too often, the Feds exterminate those who dare open their mouths.

Starye Atagi: The Twentieth Purge

What is a "purge"? This word has been introduced into our vocabulary by the second Chechen war or, more precisely, by the generals of the Northern Caucasus United Group of Armies. TV reports about their so-called antiterrorist operation are broadcast from Khankala, the group headquarters near Grozny. The citizens are assured that a purge is nothing but a "verification of legal residence." So what is it actually?

The end of 2001 and the beginning of 2002 proved to be the cruelest period of this war. The purges swept all over Chechnya, destroying everything in their path—people, cows, furniture, gold jewelry, household items . . . They came to Shali, Kurchaloi, Tsotsan-Yurt, Bachi-Yurt, Urus-Martan, Grozny, then back again to Shali, Kurchaloi, Argun, and Chiri-Yurt. Blockades lasting many days, crying women, families doing everything possible to take their teenage sons anywhere away from Chechnya. Group Commander General Moltensky, decorated with orders and stars, shows up on TV—always against the background of the corpses of those who resisted the purge—as the main hero of the current phase of the Chechen conquest. After every new purge, he reports significant progress in the search for militants.

From January 28 through February 5, 2002, a purge took place in the village of Starye Atagi, twelve miles from Grozny and six from the mouth of the Argun valley, or the Wolf Gates. This was the twentieth purge in the village since the beginning of the second Chechen war, and the second this year. For the twentieth time, fifteen thousand residents (Starye Atagi is one of the biggest villages in Chechnya) found themselves blockaded inside several rings of armored vehicles, not only around the village, but also around each block, street, and house. What was going on inside?

Fire at the Boy!

"I was glad when they took us to be shot." Mohammed Idigov, a sixteen-year-old tenth-grader at the village's High School No. 2, has the eyes of a grown-up man. Combined with his teenage angular build and awkwardness, this looks strange. As does the calm way in which he is talking about what happened. During the twentieth purge, they tortured him with electric shocks at the "temporary filtration point" set up at the edge of the village, along with adult men. On the morning of February 1, the worst day of the purge in terms of its consequences, Mohammed was arrested at his home on Nagornaya Street, thrown into a military KAMAZ truck like a log, and then tortured while the commanding generals watched. General Moltensky himself seemed to loom nearby—at least, that's what Mohammed thought.

"How come you were glad? What about your parents? Did you think about them?"

He furrows his eyebrows like a child, fighting back his tears:

"Other kids get killed too."

A pause. The boy's father, a retired Soviet Army officer, stands nearby. He spreads his hands the whole time, repeating, "How can this be? I myself—I was in the army. How can they do this?"

"It was cold," Mohammed continues. "They made us stand facing the wall for several hours, with our hands raised and our legs apart. They unbuttoned my coat, pulled up my sweater and started to cut my clothes with a knife from behind, down to my body."

"Why?"

"So that I'd be even colder. They beat us all the time. Whoever passed by would hit us with anything he had. Then they separated me from the others, put me on the ground and dragged me around in the dirt by my throat."

"Why?"

"No reason. Then they brought sheep dogs and started siccing them on me."

"Why?"

"To humiliate me, I think. Then they took me to be interrogated. There were three men asking questions. They didn't introduce them- selves. They showed me a list and asked, 'Do you know which of these are militants? Who's treating them? Who's the doctor? Where are they staying for the night?'"

"And what did you say?"

"I said I didn't know."

"And what did they do?"

"They asked, 'Do you need some help?' And they started to torture me with electric shock—that's what they meant by 'help.' They attach the wires to you and turn the handle. They probably made this device themselves, from a telephone. The more they turn it, the stronger the shock. During the torture they asked me where my Wahhabi brother was."

"Is he really a Wahhabi?"

"No. He's just my older brother. He's eighteen, and my father sent him away so they wouldn't kill him the way they kill a lot of young guys in the village."

"And what did you tell them?"

"I kept silent."

"And what did they do?"

"They gave me more shocks."

"Did it hurt?"

His head on his thin neck slumps below his shoulders, down to his angular knees, as he crouches on the floor. He doesn't want to answer. But I need his answer, so I insist:

"Did it really hurt?"

"Yes." Mohammed doesn't raise his head, speaking almost in whis- per. His father is nearby, and the boy doesn't want to appear weak in front of him.

"That's why you were happy when they took you to be shot?"

He shudders as if he had a high fever. Behind his back I can see a bunch of medicine bottles with droppers, syringes, cotton swabs, and tubes.

"Whose are those things?"

"Mine. They beat me so hard, they damaged my kidneys and lungs."

Mohammed's father Isa, a thin man with a face all plowed with deep wrinkles, joins the conversation:

"In the previous purges they took my older son, beat him, and let him go. So I decided to send him away, to stay with friends. In this purge, they crippled my middle son. My youngest one is eleven. Will they take him next? None of my sons shoots, smokes, or drinks. How can we go on living?"

I don't know. Nor do I know why our country, along with Europe and America, has allowed children to be tortured in the beginning of the twenty-first century in one of the modern European ghettos, mistakenly called "an antiterrorist operation zone." The children of this ghetto will never forget.

"Give Us Everything of Value!"

On the evening of January 28, several rows of soldiers and armored vehicles formed rings surrounding the village. At dawn, all the streets were covered with armored vehicles with dirt smeared over the numbers. Under the threat of being shot on the spot, people were forbidden to leave their homes and yards. Helicopters flew very low over the village, as if they were stopping to land, and shingles flew from the roofs like maple leaves in an autumn wind, leaving them uncovered. You can make an innocent face and continue to call this a purge, but it's plain as day that a real war operation was being carried out in Starye Atagi.

"I was at home," says seventy-year-old Imran Dagayev. "I knew that the gate had to be open, otherwise they'd smash it with a tank or an armored vehicle. At six-thirty in the morning, the soldiers burst into our yard. They pointed a submachine gun at me. I immediately showed them my passport, but they didn't even look at it. The other members of my family also weren't asked for their passports. The first demand of the soldier who seemed to be the superior was: 'Give us your money and gold jewelry! Give us everything of value.' I answered: 'I don't have any money or gold. I'm retired, and all eleven of us live on my pension.' He said: 'I don't care how you live. Give it to us!' They split up and looked through the rooms, started to turn the place upside down. Nobody was allowed to move. They threw the wardrobe with clothes on the floor, and it broke instantly. They rummaged through the dishes, and found a gold ring and a chain belonging to my oldest daughter-in-law in a vase. One of the soldiers took them. The others started to take dishes. They had plastic bags prepared, and they put the set of dishes into it. One of them took my new shoes and shoved one of them into each of his jacket pockets. The sideboard with the remaining dishes was tossed to the floor, and all the dishes broke. They knocked over the chairs and couch, and cut them open with their knives to look for hidden money. But they didn't find anything else of value. Running through the rooms in search of valuable items, they asked, 'Where are your sons?' I answered that my son had died, and I didn't have any others."

Old Dagayev really did just bury his thirty-year-old son Alkhazur. At the request of the village administration, Alkhazur, together with the others, went to Khankala, to the main military base, for the body of a fellow villager who had first been detained at the time of the previous purge and then killed there, in Khankala. A serviceman who introduced himself as an FSS official, Sergei Koshelev, acted as the go-between for the ransom for the corpse. He demanded a lamb, a video camera, and a Zhiguli. But after he received everything, he still didn't give back the body. At the same time, everyone who brought the ransom to Khankala disappeared without a trace. This happened on December 22, 2001. On the fourteenth day, the bodies of everyone who had disappeared were found not far from Khankala, in a ditch. One of Alkhazur Dagayev's eyes had been cut out, and the body was black from being beaten. He was killed by a pistol shot at close range in the left temple.

"You have no more sons?" the soldiers laughed, and they went into Tatiana Matsieva's house on neighboring Maisky Street. They weren't interested in anyone's passport there either, but they did steal from her home: "(1) a medal 'For Labor Achievements,' (2) a TV and VCR, (3) soft pillows and furniture of an East German make, (4) a dresser with a mirror from Hungary, (5) four tapestries, (6) thirty-five movie videos, (7) a sack of potatoes, (8) a one-hundred pound sack of sugar, (9) men's shoes (two pairs of boots and one pair of sneakers), (10) . . ."

Passions reached a fever pitch in blockaded Starye Atagi. Day by day, the harassment by the soldiers, who had camped out around the edges, became more and more irrational.

On the morning of January 29, Liza Iushayeva, in her last month of pregnancy, began to give birth. This often happens unexpectedly, and does not depend at all on the purge deadlines set by General Moltensky. Liza's relatives ran to ask the soldiers standing at the cordon to let a woman in labor into the hospital, but the soldiers took a long time to reach a decision. The women reproached them loudly, asking them, don't you have mothers, wives, sisters. And they answered that they had no family and were from orphanages. And also that they had come here to kill the living, not help those being born.

When the soldiers took pity, Iushayeva could not walk the three hundred steps to the hospital. The relatives started to make arrangements again, this time about a car. Finally, Liza was driven to the hospital. But a completely different cordon was standing there, and different soldiers. Without going into details, they stood both the driver and Liza against the wall, as they always do, in the pose of a captured militant with their hands up and legs spread apart. Liza held this pose for some time, but then began to sink down. Soon the baby appeared, stillborn.

It's possible to understand a lot, but what could the soldiers have been thinking at that moment, seeing a woman in labor before them with an enormous stomach dangling down to her knees, half unconscious but in the required pose, legs spread apart?

The old man Turluev suddenly died on February 1. He was very old, and he died because his time had come. He needed to be buried. Men had to be gathered to wash his body, read the prayers, and take him to the cemetery.

The soldiers forbade the old man to be buried in the Muslim cemetery. Why? Because of the purge. They cited an instruction about transportation being forbidden, including funeral processions. Never mind the fact that the purge itself, and all the instructions involved in it, was completely illegal.

However, on that very day, the Feds themselves dropped in on the cemetery. Everyone knows that there is no place dearer to Chechens than this one. What can you rob a cemetery for? There is nothing around the graves except for a little prayer house, a kind of shed where the burial tools are stored and where they read the last prayer.

So the soldiers took away the special wooden crate for the washing of the dead, burned the burial stretchers, stole the shovels for digging the graves, and took the window frames, doors, rugs, and the Korans to boot. What for? They burned it all, including the Korans, to warm themselves up.

The next stop was a house not far from the cemetery. Malkan, a grandmother, lives there. The soldiers chased her to the basement, asking her to "get out some cucumbers." After this, they locked the trapdoor and wouldn't let her out until her relatives brought a five hundred–ruble ransom.

The policeman Ramsan Sagipov, a junior sergeant of the patrol service, had been wounded in Grozny at the end of December while guarding the New Year tree. On the morning of February 1, he was lying in bed, recovering at his home in Starye Atagi, on Nagornaya Street. His arm was in a cast, and the stumps of his ripped-off fingers were bleeding.

Hearing shots on the street, Ramsan ran out of the house. It's shameful for a policeman to sit it out when people need to be helped, even if he's wounded. Soldiers grabbed Sagipov right then, took away his service revolver, and set about beating him, purposely trying to hurt him where he was bandaged.

"Did you tell them you were a policeman?"

"Of course."

"And what did they do?"

"They said, 'You're all from the same gang! We'll shoot everyone!' Then they threw me into a KAMAZ truck. When I tried to look up, they kicked me and beat me on the head again, with a rifle butt."

Attracted by the noise, Vakha Gadayev, head of the village administration, and eight of the eleven village policemen, ran up. The soldiers yelled at them too: "You're sheltering militants!" They hit Gadayev with a rifle butt and disarmed the police, bound them and threw them in the same KAMAZ the others were lying in. In this way, all the local power in the village was paralyzed.

The Poultry Farm

Those arrested were taken to an old, abandoned poultry farm at the edge of the village. The soldiers had set up their temporary headquarters and a filtration point here. Since this was the twentieth purge, a special term had been established for a long time in Starye Atagi. The filtration point was called the "poultry farm." If you were dragged in there, it meant that you would be tortured in the best-case scenario, and killed in the worst.

The official name for the "poultry farms" is "temporary filtration points," or TFPs. TFPs are one of the biggest problems today in Chechnya, which is plagued by large-scale purges. The Feds put them at the outskirts of the villages that they "check," on farms, or simply in the field. TFPs fulfill the role of temporary holding cells, which they are not, however, from the legal point of view. If you ask public prosecutors, they merely spread their hands. The purge is over, and in place of filtration points, where people have been tortured and interrogated, there is only a clear field or some kind of ruins, and all charges of illegal detention or confinement collapse. You can't build a case out of thin air.

However, there are people around who have gone through these illegal poultry farms. They will never forgive and forget.

"At first we had to run the gauntlet." This is the policeman Ramsan Sagipov again. "The soldiers arranged themselves by the truck in rows opposite each other, and we were thrown out of the truck at their feet. Each of them beat us as much as he wanted. Then they lined everyone up against the wall. I was bandaged, and one of them came up to me, turned me to him and said, 'He's wounded.' And he immediately struck me on the head with his club. Then others took the bandages off my arms and started to press down on them."

"How?"

"With their feet. I was thrown onto the ground. Blood was spurting out everywhere. Then they dragged me into some kind of car. They crammed me in and drove off. To be shot, I thought. But they just drove around and brought me back."

"Were you interrogated?"

"Yes. But the interrogation lasted only about five minutes, no more. And I was let go the same evening."

"And that was it?"

"Yes. But now I'll need an operation on my arms."

"Do you understand why you were arrested and held?"

"Yes, so I could be harassed."

"But you are one of them, a certified official of the Ministry of the Interior, with epaulettes. You serve the same government they do."

"Of course. But when the purge begins, I'm just a Chechen in their eyes, not a policeman."

Said-Amin Apayev, from Nagornaya Street, is a tall, strong, young father of a family. If Ramsan is crushed by everything that's happened, Said-Amin doesn't hide his deep scorn for the Feds. A disgusted smirk appears on his face every time he begins to talk about the purge.

He is a neighbor of the Idigovs. On February 1, around eleven in the morning, he stopped by their place to watch the TV news. And right then, the masked men burst into the house and forced him and the sixteen-year-old Mohammed face down on the floor. And from there to the KAMAZ truck, and from the KAMAZ to the poultry farm.

"We all begged them not to touch the kid," says Said-Amin. "We begged them really hard. But the soldiers answered that schoolboys make good bombers. In the poultry farm, we were lined against the wall with raised hands, spread legs, and lowered heads. We weren't allowed to talk or even stir. If you did, you'd get a blow from behind. They beat us with fists, legs, rifle butts—whatever they wanted. We stood there like that for six to eight hours. At night we were locked in a prisoner van. On the morning of February 2, we were led to the wall again and kept in the same position until the evening. At twilight we were brought in to an investigator to be questioned. He demanded that we give the time and itinerary of the militants' movements, their secret meeting places and addresses. On the morning of February 3, we were lined up against the wall again, and then three of us were taken for some reason to Novye Atagi, where a purge was also going on. In the evening we were returned to the poultry farm, forced to sign in some book, given our passports and set free. I didn't understand why we were selected. What was the purpose?"

During those days all the TV channels in the country showed Said-Amin from Starye Atagi. There was General Moltensky, doing an interview and standing right in the middle of the poultry farm, with the arrested men—including Said-Amin—in the background. The general announced that they had detained bandits with weapons, and that the local police were defending them.

"Lies," says Said-Amin. "We didn't have any weapons at all. We were at home. The police were also released, because they only tried to stick up for us."

"What about the Wahhabis? Your Starye Atagi bandits?"

As usual, the real bandits were taking cover in their homes.

Dollars and Rubles

We live in gloomy times. The air is poisoned with the lies of the military higher ranks, the lawlessness of the lower ranks, and the rotten stench of money that the soldiers take as compensation for their leaders' deceit. That's the way the Chechen system works.

"Twenty or so soldiers burst into our house and took my son's passport," Raisa Arsamerzayeva from Shkolnaya Street says. "They wanted to take my son to the poultry farm. I gave them a hundred dollars. They made me write a note saying that I don't have any claims on the military. Then they left, taking the power generator and my daughters' lingerie with them."

This time, commerce ruled in Starye Atagi. The soldiers took mostly those who could not pay the ransom to the poultry farm. They entered the houses and demanded money for the men right away. If you gave them the money, there was no filtration for you, no suspicion that you might be connected with the militant units. If you didn't, you got both filtration and suspicion. Ransom for living goods ranged from five hundred to three or four thousand rubles, depending on the age—the younger, the pricier—and on the soldiers' visual appraisal of the home.

This time they also took money for women in Starye Atagi. As is customary in these places, prices for women were much lower than for men. And you paid for something different too: to avoid rape. The Feds took three hundred rubles from one family not to rape their young daughter, and five hundred rubles from another. They also took earrings and necklaces.

Finally, the residents went out into the streets, lit fires, and stayed there every night. They hoped that being among other people could save them from death and rape. It did not save everyone.

Final Details

By February 4, Starye Atagi presented a huge canvas of robbery performed by the members of legalized bandit units conducting "operations to capture members of the illegal bandit units."

People sat by fires everywhere in the streets. On the last day, the Feds blew up Mahmud Esambayev's empty house. The famous dancer was born in this village and, according to tradition, built a lovely mansion for his family here. Another wealthy house, which belonged to the Kadyrovs, got the same TNT treatment. It was first robbed clean, then blown up. Its owner has lived in Germany for a long time now.

What else? The soldiers also performed the trick of shitting in the mosque, a staple of recent purges.

"They left Starye Atagi on February 5," Imadi Demelkhanov says. "They were in a hurry. Two masked soldiers rushed into my yard demanding a thousand rubles for my KAMAZ truck."

It was the fourth time during this purge that soldiers had asked for money not to blow up his KAMAZ. Twice Imadi gave them five hundred rubles. Then he ran out of money and gave them two chickens as payment. On February 5, he offered chickens again, or a calf. But the soldiers wanted the money.

"I refused to go borrow from my neighbors, I was too ashamed. Then they made me face the wall, shot my right wrist and said, 'Now you'll go borrow the money.' And then they left."

On February 5, at dawn, it started raining hard. Armored vehicles left the village roaring and squelching, and the water from the sky showed the people a small truth about those who had harassed them for eight days in a row. They saw license number E403 on the last armored vehicle in the column. The vehicle drove up to the Kadyrovs' former house, now blown up, and the masked soldiers jumped out and told the residents to be careful: "There might be mines inside." "So some of them are normal people," the residents said to one another. But then they saw the E403 soldiers stop by some other empty houses and take a few more things from them.

The only thing the methods of this war accomplish is to recruit new terrorists and resistance fighters, and to rouse hatred, calling for bloody revenge.

And what about the Wahhabis? They stayed right where they were in Starye Atagi after the purges. What's more, their street patrols make the curfew unnecessary, which seems almost unbelievable if you come here, for example, from Grozny or from the mountains. It means that order, which the Federal generals have raved so long about, really does exist in Starye Atagi. But it's the same old order that existed here before the war. And the years of bloodshed—thousands of dead on all sides, wounded, crippled, and tortured—were all in vain, and things are just as they were before the war, except there are more ruins, and new faces in the government. The houses have been robbed clean, and half a million people have turned into beasts. And the country is now one more bloody war older.

The military in Chechnya hates prosecutors: it victimizes and intimidates them, and doesn't let them go anywhere. Nevertheless, prosecutors managed to visit Starye Atagi, and were very proud of being able to initiate several criminal investigations—there were TV reports and public speeches about that.

Here is a document worthy of Saltykov-Shchedrin:* ". . . these facts were subject to prosecutorial examination during the period when the special operation took place . . ."

In other words, prosecutors were present at the site of cruel, shameless war crimes. They witnessed them without interfering. And they have the nerve to call it "prosecutorial examination during the period when the special operation took place."

V-Day

An old man sits on a wobbly stool with bullet holes, barely holding his uncooperative body in balance. He is exhausted, pale and gray, almost blind. His skin looks like a rag—he's obviously starving. His legs are visible through his shabby pajama trousers with faded hospital stripes, which provide very little warmth. His thick lenses in a silly pink ladies' frame are tied together above his nose and to his ears by strings. Big buttons on his ladies' coat, of the same pink color, complete the image of a crushed man struggling not to fall off his stool.

---

*Mikhail Evgrafovich Saltykov-Shchedrin: a nineteenth-century Russian novelist and satirist. *Trans.*

"And that's the way he li-ives, the bravest Russian he-ero," an old Soviet song flashes through my mind, a totally useless song in today's Grozny, but persistent in its trembling melody. "The he-ero who has fought for Mo-otherla-and . . ."

The old man in pink glasses mumbles this song. His name is Pyotr Grigorevich Baturintsev, a retired border guard captain and a veteran of World War II. He has survived two Chechen wars in this ruined house at 142 Ugolnaya Street, in the Staropromyslovsky district of Grozny. Now, sitting on his stool, which has been brought outside into blossoming nature, he meets the eighty-sixth spring of his life and the fifty-seventh after what everyone considered the final victory over fascism for a long time.

"How's life treating you, Pyotr Grigorevich?" This is a stupid question in Chechnya today, but somehow I blurt it out.

The old man raises his head from the top of his cane with difficulty and starts crying.

"Uncle Petya has almost nothing left of his own. All he has is from the ruins. His glasses, and his coat," someone behind him says while he struggles with his silent crying spasms. "From the dead, I think."

"I don't have a life . . . I used to have one . . . A long time ago . . .," the old man finally says.

Pyotr Baturintsev fought for three years, from 1942 to 1945, as an officer of the northern group of the Caucasian district. Grozny was among the cities that they liberated. His life after the war was clear and simple: he came back to the city, soon got married, and started to work at the Electric Device Factory, where he stayed until his retirement. He was invited to meetings by Young Pioneers, and would put on his medals for the holidays.

"I used to have a life," he keeps on saying. His body trembles as he tries to wipe his tears. He pokes at his face, missing the spots where his tears flow.

A woman wearing men's sandals and a torn blue blouse comes by noisily, staring at the strangers with eyes that are wild but not angry.

"I'm his wife. My name is Nadezhda Ilyinichna. I'm seventy-six, ten years younger than him. That's why I can still walk, as you see." The woman invites me into their home. "We've sat through two wars here. We never went outside, just to the basement. That was the only way to keep the apartment. And we bought it too!"

Nadezhda Ilyinichna proudly shows me the ruins that she owns. It was raining for a long time the day before, and the apartment looks soaked. There is a big hole in the ceiling, which is covered with hothouse plastic.

"Sometimes it seems to me that we live in paradise." But her voice belies the idea that it's a paradise. She realizes that she is actually in hell. "We live well. Many people don't even have any walls left around them," she goes on, and it becomes clear why her voice is so stubbornly metallic. She does all she can to stay within the limits of the philosophy she adopted a long time ago: be happy with what little you have.

"We all respect our old ones," quietly sings a Chechen neighbor. He is the only person who looks after the veteran Uncle Petya these days, taking him to the bathroom, washing him, bringing water from some distant place, and keeping the Baturintsevs from dying of hunger.

"Does anyone from the military ever come here? From the City Military Committee, perhaps?"

For the first time, a smile unexpectedly appears on Pyotr Grigorevich's worn-out face. He is surprised that someone does not know that the military visits you here only for purges.

Nadezhda Ilyinichna caresses a small girl who runs up to her. It is obvious that she is sad and lonely without her family—her children and relatives.

"Her name is Aishat. She's the daughter of our neighbors, the Elmurzayevs. I feel so good around her. We're friends. Pyotr Grigorevich and I have granddaughters too: Larisa is twenty-five, and Olenka is twenty-three. They're great girls."

"And where are these girls?" The awkward question comes out as if on its own; I should have put it more mildly.

"They're very busy." Such short answers are usually used to close a topic that has turned tragic.

But now Pyotr Grigorevich wants to speak, to defend his distant great girls.

"They live in Pyatigorsk, in the student dormitory. Larisa's looking for a job, and Olenka's still a student at the medical school. You see, they can't take us in there, and it's impossible for them to come here, either."

The old man even tries to get up from his stool in agitation, but he cannot; his knees are too shaky.

"What about their parents?"

Nadezhda Ilyinichna switches to an angry whisper:

"Our son lives in Blagodarnoe, in the Stavropolsky region, and he has his own problems. Let's not talk about this in front of Pyotr Grigorevich."

We step away, to spare the old man a difficult subject.

"Should I call your son or write to him? Tell him how you're doing . . .?"

"No, you shouldn't." It turns out that Pyotr Grigorevich has heard every word. He is not crying anymore, although the Parkinson's disease in his hands is growing visibly worse. Now he is as stern, firm, and determined as his wife. His behavior shows that there is some old family dispute, and not even the war, poverty, or the Baturintsevs' hunger and illness in Grozny can resolve it.

I have seen so many tragic stories like this of the Russian elderly living in Grozny during this war. Their Russian relatives (that's what they call them in Chechnya) don't want to take their family out of the war region. As you travel around this horrible city, you see many forgotten people. For example, here's the home of an old Russian woman whose Tyumen relatives refuse to take her in. She is still alive. And on that street an old Russian man used to live in the ruins (he died three months ago from hunger), forgotten by his two sons and three daughters, who are scattered around in different regions and cities. And here we turn from Staropromyslovsky Road toward Beryozka, one of the city neighborhoods. There is a retirement home nearby. Last Easter, Maria Sergeevna Levchenko died here. She had come to the home not long before, in November, with her older sister Tamara Sergeevna, both suffering from extreme emaciation. Having lost their homes, they lived for more than a year in basements, in terrible conditions, not washing for months, and not seeing so much as a piece of bread for weeks. In the fall of 2000, Tamara Sergeevna lost her mind in a basement from all the suffering and starvation. Maria Sergeevna couldn't take it anymore, and, putting her older sister in a cart, walked wherever her feet would take her—nothing could be worse than this. Seeing this horrifying procession, some good people told her where the retirement home was. Having fulfilled her task of finding a free warm place, food, and medicine for her sister, Maria Sergeevna soon died of a fulminant cancer.

Would this tragic event have occurred if their brother and numerous nephews, who live in a southern Russian city not too far from Chechnya, had taken the sisters into their home at the beginning of the war? Of course not. But their family did not want to take them in. Although they knew about what was going on in the Grozny retirement home, neither the brother nor the nephews came to Maria Sergeevna's funeral, and now they are in no hurry to come and get the lonely Tamara Sergeevna. The healthy Russians don't want the sick Russians, and although the stories of the Levchenkos and Baturintsevs are family tragedies, they are also a modern Russian national tragedy, thrown into bold relief by the war. Wherever cruelty is a norm of life, no one can expect compassion and mercy, not even the weakest. No one thought about taking Pyotr Baturintsev, a war veteran and invalid who received no help from his family, away from the bombing and shooting before the attack of the winter of 1999–2000 that destroyed most of Grozny. Not a single military official visited him, a retired army officer, to see if he was alive after the attack, if he was hungry. They would not have had to walk very far, either; his house is only six hundred feet away from the Military Command.

This is real fascism, like Hitler's infamous idea of destroying and discarding the weak and sick as ballast on the road toward a better future. It is a kind of state fascism that has successfully taken root in family relations: the very type of fascism that Pyotr Grigorevich spent his younger and healthier years fighting against.

I am often asked by Grozny Chechens, "Why do you treat your own people so badly?" The Chechens from Ugolnaya Street put the question more broadly: "How can we believe that the new government is here to help us, if even an old Russian man, a retired officer, is even worse off under the newly established 'Russian power' than he was under Dudayev and Maskhadov?" Nothing similar to what happened with Pyotr Grigorevich could ever happen to an elderly Chechen.

Not a single Chechen family, except those regarded with the utmost disrespect and contempt, would treat an old man like that!

Eighty-two-year-old Umar Akhmatkhanov lives at 259 Klyuchevaya Street, not too far from the Baturintsevs. Umar is an invalid of the second category from World War II. His legs are very weak, and he is almost blind. Like Pyotr Grigorevich, he spent both Chechen wars at home, in the basement, not wanting to leave because of the bombing.

However, there is a huge difference between the life of the veteran Baturintsev and that of the veteran Akhmatkhanov, a participant in the Battle of Stalingrad. Umar's house is well kept, though it shows traces of the war. His floors and clothes are clean, his granddaughters bring him everything he asks for right away, his sons (all college graduates) and his daughters-in-law help him out. As an old man, he is the center of the family life, according to Chechen tradition. If you are an old man, then all the younger family members are indebted to you. They will never abandon you; they will feed you even if they have to go hungry. It is impossible to imagine what circumstance would make Chechens "forget" about their old man. There would always be someone, even a very distant relative, who would come up to take care of the sick person. Otherwise, it would be a disgrace for the whole family.

"You know, World War II was a good war," Nadezhda Ilyinichna Baturintseva says in parting, and you realize how full of despair a person must be to call a war that took millions of lives "good." "And this is a bad war," she concludes. "You can't understand who it's for and who it's against. It's not for us, that's for sure."

The Chechen Choice: From the Carpet to the Conveyer Belt
The Tactic of Carpet Bombing at the Beginning of the War Has Been Replaced with a Strategy of Conveyer Belt Destruction of People

During the three years of the Chechen war, the government has hinted several times that once Khattab and Basayev are killed, the war they call an antiterrorist operation will be over. And then, finally, a disproportionately large military contingent of nearly one hundred thousand, opposing the Chechen population of six hundred thousand and the two thousand militants (according to official figures), will leave the republic. Then, the murders, torture, and kidnapping by gentlemen in epaulettes, and the massive war marauding that is inevitable under occupation, will also come to an end.

But despite the solemnly announced death of Khattab "after a long and serious illness," and that of Basayev too, supposedly, the troops are still there. And there have been no changes in their methods of carrying out the war. The purges continue, the commerce in living and dead bodies by soldiers as the principal military operation in Chechnya hasn't ended, and thousands of people search for their kidnapped relatives and, in the best case, ransom their corpses from those who defend the Motherland from terrorism.

Tall

Imran Janbekov, from Goity village of the Urus-Martan district, was very tall. And he was only twenty-two. It was these circumstances that sealed his fate. In accordance with the new Chechen traditions, Imran was taken away at night, and that was it. Just the way it happened with many others.

"Now I get up every morning and go looking for my son," says Imran's mother Zainap, a former beauty. Her head is bent so that only her high forehead and her hair are visible. Her limp fingers hopelessly outline circles on the tablecloth.

"Where do you go?"

"Wherever my feet take me. To the Urus-Martan command headquarters, the Ministry of the Interior in Grozny, the republic FSS . . . I show them a photograph, and ask if anyone saw him. Not long ago, in one of these institutions, I was shown the report of another fellow's arrest. And I read the 'reason for arrest' line: 'tall.'"

"That can't be!"

"That's what I thought at first too, but . . . there it was, right before my eyes. There was no reason to take away my Imran either, except for his being 'tall.'"

In recent years, Imran almost never left the house, at his parents' insistence.

"Why not?" I ask.

"We wanted to protect him," Zainap cries. "He was one of these 'tall' ones: six feet three and a half. And when it became clear that the first people the Feds would arrest were the physically strong, well-built men, we didn't even let him go to his college. They were too strict at the checkpoints. And then we thought it over and decided that he needed to study, so my husband and I took turns driving with him to Grozny, waiting there, and accompanying him home."

They accompanied a twenty-two-year-old, like a kindergartner? But that's what today's Chechen life is like.

"But we weren't able to protect our firstborn." Zainap looks straight ahead, as though at a funeral. "We accompanied him by day, but they came at night. At exactly 12:05. All of them were in masks. There were two armored vehicles and a military UAZ van outside. My son was put in the armored vehicle. I ran after the car, screaming 'Imran! Imran!' Then I ran up to the exit checkpoint on the road leading to Grozny. And they yelled from there, 'Stop! We'll shoot!' I shouted, 'Go ahead and shoot! Murderers! They've kidnapped my son! They've crammed him right into that armored vehicle you just let go by without checking!'"

The soldiers guarding the checkpoint lowered their automatic weapons, not wanting to shoot a mother. The only thing she saw was the number "02" on the back of the vehicle. Everyone in Chechnya knows what "02" means: that the vehicle belongs to Ministry of the Interior units.

Nobody now knows where the kidnapped tall fellow is. *All* of the governmental and military institutions of Urus-Martan and all other regions, and even the corresponding republic departments have announced that they didn't arrest him. The Janbekovs wrote complaints to all the public prosecutor offices and heads of administrations—from Yasayev, head of the Urus-Martan region, and Akhmad-Khaji Kadyrov, leader of Chechnya, to Putin. Letters, complaints, petitions . . . Everything turned out to be in vain.

Throughout the world, mothers live on hope. This is their life's credo, on which the future of the planet depends. If their children are sick, there is the hope that they will get well. If they stumble, that they'll get back on their feet. If they're missing, that they'll be found. And that's how it is with Zainap.

"People say that if the corpse isn't thrown out in five to seven days, this is a good sign." Zainap passes along one of today's Chechen myths. "It means that he survived the tortures of the first days and was sent to

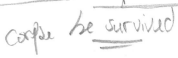

Khankala. He's strong, he'll make it. Only I dreamed that he couldn't stand, they beat him so hard."

A mother's heart wants to believe in this myth. But then there is Chechen reality, which is the very opposite. If a person isn't rescued from the Federal jails in five to seven days, look for a corpse.

"There are many parents in our position in Chechnya," continues Zainap. "Hundreds, thousands. We often stand at the beginning of the road leading to the Khankala military base until curfew."

"Why do you stand there? What are you waiting for?"

"Information about our loved ones. Often go-between officers come up to us from there, tell us the price for those who are still alive. Or for corpses."

That's how Zainap and Adlan Janbekov spend their days. At night they go over everything, like in thousands of other sleepless Chechen homes, trying to understand what they did wrong, how they displeased the Feds, what their son could be guilty of.

The Janbekovs can conclude only this: Imran knew Turkish well. He had studied at an Istanbul college for two years. And someone may have denounced him for this.

"But it's a good thing to know a language," I say.

"For you, yes. But not for us. The Feds might have thought that he got corrupted in Turkey." His parents explain how they understand life around them. "When I remembered that Imran knew Turkish," says Zainap, "everywhere I looked for him, I started explaining that our boys had been sent to Turkey at the Russian government's decree, to study! The vice premier himself, Lobov, oversaw this exchange. And Imran, who was fifteen or sixteen then, shouldn't have to answer for that now! But there's no one we can tell this to. Nobody listens. No matter how I sort over my son's life, I can't find anything dangerous about him. I'm very certain, since he was with us the whole time."

What Are the Rules of the Game?

I'm at another Goity house, in the evening. The corpse of a person kidnapped by soldiers has just been handed over to them. I'm speaking with the twenty-year-old Salambek, a nephew of the dead. We're talking about what to do now, the meaning of everything that has happened, and what young Chechens think about all this. Life has taught Salambek to be silent—always, under any circumstances. And he's as taciturn as a concentration camp prisoner of many years.

"What do young people in Goity do these days, besides hiding from the Feds? Eighteen- to twenty-five-year-old guys can't stay at home for three years in a row every day just so everyone knows that they're not militants, can they?" I ask.

"What can we do besides dying?" answers Salambek.

I hope that Salambek is just joking. But he isn't. In general, young people here rarely laugh—they've gotten out of the habit. Look how many fresh graves there are in the Goity cemetery. Salambek is perfectly serious. His impassive, motionless face shows a grimace of tortured hopelessness, and his large eyes, above wide, frozen cheekbones, stare stubbornly and reproachfully.

Most of the people in Chechnya who have survived up to this moment are full of despair. They live in this despair, this sheer hell, like in a dreary starless night. This is the main result of the total lawlessness imposed on the population in the course of the second Chechen war. You take your life into your hands if you leave the village, or even if you just walk around the village. Either way, you could be arrested. The Federal "broom" sweeps young people away every day. Visiting Urus-Martan is even more out of the question; the road is filled with checkpoints, and any one of them can become the last in your life. Examples abound.

Before the war, approximately forty thousand people lived in Goity. Now there are no more than fifteen thousand. Everyone left if they could, to save their children. And there's nothing here for those who remained, except for the infamous Chechen "package": Federal raids, night purges, marauding, morning discussions of who was taken away this time and what was stolen along with them, regular burials, stories about the ways those who survived were tortured, and whose corpses looked like what.

There is no library or movie theater, although the buildings remain.

"When was the last time a movie was shown here?"

"When I was little, before the first war."

Imran Janbekov's mother is worn out and ravaged by grief. With what little decisiveness she has left, she bursts out:

"Russia has turned us into cattle. It is driving our youth into the arms of whoever comes along first and says, 'Go with us.' I even think like this now: I'd rather the bearded ones, the Wahhabis, beat us with sticks for vodka. A stick is still better than an exploding bullet. Sticks and stones won't break your bones. Most of all now, we want to know the rules of the game. We want to understand which of us you don't like. And why? What should we be tortured for? What are the reasons you've been commanded to kill? To kidnap? Right now we don't understand anything, and everyone is being destroyed in turn—those who were with the Wahhabis and those who were against them. And most of all, those in the middle, who weren't with anyone. Like our Imran."

There is nothing I can say. Because the time of Putin is the time of silence about what's most important in this country.

Ruslan Aushev: "Nobody Guarantees Life in Chechnya Today"

Ingushetia, a small republic neighboring Chechnya, used to be part of a unified Chechen-Ingush Autonomous Soviet Socialist Republic with its capital in Grozny in Soviet times. From the very beginning of the war, Ingushetia distinguished itself in relation to the politics of the Federal center, defying its methods of so-called antiterrorist operations.

When the bombings of Grozny and most of the villages started in September 1999, Ingushetia opened up all of its borders to the many thousands of refugees flooding in, by order of its president, Ruslan Aushev. Very quickly, two hundred thousand refugees turned up on Ingush soil. In the best case, they were settled in hastily constructed camps and tents; in the worst case, in electric generator sheds, gas stations, garages, deserted farms, and even cemetery sheds. One should bear in mind that Ingushetia's own population was scarcely more than three hundred thousand, with a corresponding capacity to provide water, electricity, and food. Ingushetia was the only republic to act this way, in contrast to its neighbors. The model example of pro-Kremlin behavior of the territories surrounding Chechnya was Kabardino-Balkaria. In September 1999, protective cordons were put out on the borders of the Republic of Kabardino-Balkaria, at the orders of its president, Valery Kokov, who was completely under Moscow's control. And the tired, hungry people, out of their minds from everything they had experienced, with infants and the elderly in their care, urgently needing medical help, were forced to turn back. But where? There was no going back to Chechnya, so the refugees all went to Ingushetia, which bore the brunt of the Chechen exodus. Ingushetia went on performing this feat as best as it could. It took care of the refugees for nearly three years, despite attacks from the Kremlin-controlled media and the unprecedented pressure and blackmail from Moscow that President Aushev was exposed to the whole time. This would ultimately lead to his retirement in January 2002, the special presidential elections, a succession of difficult ordeals, and the establishment in April 2002 of FSS General Murat Zyazikov, a protégé of the Kremlin and Putin, as president. It also resulted in the increased power of the national secret services, which by that time had taken root in all government nooks and crannies of the country, just like in the Soviet era.

Right now, though, it's the end of February 2000. It's still a long way from Aushev's dismissal, and we're talking in Magas, the recently rebuilt capital of Ingushetia, in the presidential palace. Our conversation takes place against the background of the stream of Kremlin ravings pouring in from the press about how "the end of the war is coming" now, after the storming of Grozny and the departure from there of the militants, with Maskhadov and Basayev at their head. As everyone now knows, there has still, to this very day, been no end to the war. But we didn't know this at the time.

"So is this the end of the war, or not?"

"Of course not. Everything's only beginning. The military actions are continuing along the entire perimeter. There are militants in Grozny, and also in the villages. But where are the terrorists? The way I see things, antiterrorist operations can end only with hostages being released and terrorists arrested, punished, or killed."

"But haven't some of the hostages already been freed? The military shows them on television."

"Those were the ones who could be released from captivity without large-scale military action. Actually, I think that without the war they would have been released even sooner."

"So what would you call this stage of the war?"

"I don't know, because in general I don't consider it any sort of stage. The bases of terrorism haven't been destroyed. They're still everywhere in Chechen territory. The guerilla warfare that has been announced continues."

"But the Kremlin assures us that peacetime conditions are taking shape in parts of Chechnya."

"Where? Show me! We have more than two hundred thousand refugees in Ingushetia, just as before! Everyone from the southern districts is here. And from Grozny too. Why are people so eager to leave Chechnya and come here? Why is it that instead of people returning, there are new streams of refugees? For me personally, this is the main sign that the situation is unstable. Recall the first war. Then too, when the intensive bombings of Samashki, Achkhoi-Martan, and Grozny were going on, thousands of people fled to Ingushetia. But this took place only for a short time; we didn't even put up tents then. And as soon as the fighting ended, people moved back to their homes. We didn't expel them; they themselves wanted to go back, because they sensed some kind of basic stability at the time. People believed that even if things were bad, you could still get by. Now things are different. People have no hope for the future, and for that reason they remain in Ingushetia. What's more, some of them tried to return, but ran into bombings and purges and came back to us again. The second reason refugees don't return to Chechnya is that there is no actual government there. Who guarantees life in Chechnya? This is a person's principal constitutional demand on a government! And nobody guarantees it! Who is answerable if a militant comes and kills you? Nobody. Or if a mercenary shows up and robs you? Nobody. That's why people plan on staying in Ingushetia to the end, since it has stability and government. If someone insults or hurts you, the whole power structure comes into play—the police, public prosecutors, courts."

"Nevertheless, handouts of soup and free bread have ceased in refugee camps in Ingush territory," I said.

"Things are very difficult for us, it's true. Though most of the refugees are still located in Ingushetia, we aren't receiving the means for their subsistence from the Federal budget. And Moscow knows what's going on: our debt for refugee support is four hundred and fifty million rubles! Where did it come from? In order to feed the hungry people fleeing to us, we bought groceries, baked bread, etc. on loan (and how else could we have done this?). As a result, we're in debt to our own bread factories, to the cooks who prepare the meals, to the grocery suppliers. We couldn't continue this way. If it weren't for the help of humanitarian organizations, I don't know what we'd do now. Also, I don't think the majority of Ingush living in Chechnya before the war will ever return there. Many Chechens and Russians will also stay here. And we have to provide them with permanent residence! But who will pay?"

"It's common knowledge that the Federal center sees only one way out of the refugee crisis: forceful resettling of people back home."

"Create the proper conditions, and if people want to move back, they will. That's my position. And the main words here are 'create the proper conditions.' However, the overwhelming majority of officials don't want to hear about such a policy, and forceful methods won't accomplish anything. I posed the following task to our Ingush government: determine a realistic picture of which refugees in the camps want to go where, and report it to me. If it turns out, for example, that forty thousand people plan to stay in Ingushetia as permanent residents, that means we would need to build new cities and villages and finance it with money for the restoration of Chechnya after the antiterrorist operations. Or let's say it turns out that twenty thousand have decided to relocate to other regions of Russia. In that case, depending upon where they want to go, that region would have to receive the means to supply them with housing. That would only be fair."

"What do you think—when will the war end?"

"Strong-arm tactics won't solve the Chechen problem. We need to look for a purely political solution. And it's the same as it always was: making an agreement with Maskhadov. But what do we hear? He's not legitimate, so they initiated criminal prosecution, and submitted his case to Interpol. That puts a nail in the coffin of the political process, and then all we can do is fight to the end, lose soldiers, officers, and civilians. As a result we'll pay three times as much for the war."

"All right, let's say they're at the negotiating table. What do they talk about?"

"First about a cease-fire. Then about terrorist bases, illegal military units, etc."

"But isn't it unlikely that Maskhadov will agree to this?"

"Why do you think so? This was Maskhadov's position from the very beginning."

"Whatever negotiations there are, one thing is clear: Maskhadov won't be president of Chechnya. The people don't want him."

"You're right. But that is a question of political dialogue, secondary to the military question. If the Chechen people don't want Maskhadov, let them choose someone else for themselves, and Moscow will deal with this new person. However, since the Chechens have chosen Maskhadov for now, we need to sit at the table with him. It's not out of the question that after everything that's happened, Maskhadov himself might make some kind of decision. But let him do that with dignity."

"Could peace negotiations take place with anyone else, besides Maskhadov?"

"No. Not while he's president of the republic."

"Of a republic that for all intents and purposes doesn't exist?"

"Whether there is actually a republic or not, he is the president, a legal entity. Whether he's good, bad, or weak, the most important person for negotiations is Maskhadov. Let's not replicate our Russian nuthouse, with its contempt for law. Imagine that you go to a factory, and it's in ruins, no one's getting paid, everyone's stealing. Who would you talk to?"

"The manager."

"There you go! Maskhadov has the state seal, the flag, and everything else. What other power do you hope to find in Chechnya? Of course you could bring in some other Chechen from Moscow and put him behind the desk, but he wouldn't be legitimate."

"There's a lot of talk about March 26, 2000, the Russian presidential elections, as the turning point of a new time period. What will this date mean for Chechnya?"

"Absolutely nothing. No more than the 27th, or the 28th, or April 1. It will get warm and sunny, which means the military activity will double or triple."

"That's your theory?"

"No, it's a lesson from 1996. At that time, there were no more than three thousand militants in all of Chechnya. Eight hundred Federal troops went to Grozny and resolved the whole problem. Before the present war, if you listen to the military, there were twenty-five to twenty-six thousand militants in gangs. If five thousand of them have been destroyed (though my statistics tell me it's less), where have the other twenty thousand gotten to?"

"They've scattered."

"That's right. They're waiting for their hour to strike."

"But you can't fight empty-handed. Where do they get their ammunition?"

"They are assisted."

"By whom? Everything is blockaded. That's what they said on TV."

"Go ahead and listen to what they say on TV, but the reality is that it's not completely blockaded. They can get everything they need. They have weapons and ammunition."

"What do you think about the Feds' unprecedented cruelty to the civilian population?"

"The hatred on both sides in this war is simply ferocious, staggering. The soldiers fiercely hate the Chechens, and do whatever they want given the opportunity. The Chechens hate the Federal soldiers just as much. I can't imagine how they will ever talk with one another."

"But they need to live next to one another, right?"

"I'm convinced that that's a question for tomorrow. As long as they're fighting, the hatred will only increase. There's only one way to turn the tide now, and that's to end the killing and stop talking about Chechens on TV as if they're all bandits. No more insulting the people as a whole! And no more tricking your own people, either. If antiterrorist operations haven't succeeded in the course of a month, if the objectives haven't been fulfilled, then that's that! You can't just continue conducting antiterrorist operations for seven months."

"You are part of the country's political establishment. Do you know anyone in the Russian political elite who exercises sound judgment on the Chechen question?"

"Only Yavlinsky* talks at all sensibly about it. Everyone else is in a nationalistic frenzy. This includes the people who say 'bomb them.' As far as Ingushetia goes, we won't let Chechens starve. But I still think the main thing is to persuade the government that no military solution is possible in Chechnya."

---

*Grigory Yavlinsky: Russian politician whose Apple Party advocates granting Chechnya full independence if the people choose that in a referendum; as an economic adviser to Gorbachev he called for a market economy. *Trans.*

Everything that Aushev predicted then came true, with one exception: he is no longer president. And in May 2002, after Moscow failed to deal with the refugee problem, and the barrier in the form of Aushev was removed once and for all with the establishment of Zyazikov as the new president in Ingushetia, it began to simply resettle the refugees back in Chechnya by force, to the ruins, where they are subject to purges, kidnappings, and illegal executions.

A Pogrom

"They forced us to crawl naked across the floor from room to room ..."

"They walked on our beds with their boots on ... "

"They called us monkeys, black monsters ... "

"They spat in our faces ... "

"They beat us over the head with the book *The Fate of the Chechen-Ingush People ...* "

"They ripped our hair out ... "

"And what did you do?"

"Me personally? I am Truffaldino* from Bergamo. That's my role now. And in general I'm 'the Beast.' Beslan Gaitukayev, group monitor. I'm from Grozny."

"And did you crawl on the floor too?"

"Yes. They shouted at me: 'Backwards! Crawl to the room!' And I did ... Then: 'Enough! Go back to the hall.' And so I did ... "

On March 28, 2001, all the students from the national Chechen theater studio Nakhi, which was formed by the Moscow State University of Culture and Art to train a nucleus for a future Grozny theater troupe, missed class for the first time ever. The studio consisted of six girls, nineteen guys, the artistic director, Professor Mimalt Soltsayev, People's Artist of Russia, and academic supervisor, Professor Alikhan Didigov, Distinguished Artist of the Kabardino-Balkarian and Chechen-Ingush Autonomous Republics.

This was not a strike. At 5:30 A.M., a detachment of strong, armed, masked men with dogs, wielding sledgehammers for breaking down

---

*The clown, a stock character in commedia dell'arte. Also the main character in Carlo Goldoni's play *The Servant of Two Masters* or, as it was also called, *Truffaldino from Bergamo*. Trans.

doors and locks, burst into the fifth floor of the dormitory where the students all lived together with their teachers in the Moscow suburb of Khimki, without knocking or ringing. As adroitly as if they were storming a plane captured by terrorists, the gang quickly spread out among the rooms, and in just seconds they had a submachine gun or a pistol at the temple of everyone sleeping.

The next act followed without an intermission. They set about dragging the half-sleeping student actors from their beds by the hair, beating them up, kicking them, and howling all sorts of unprintable obscenities.

Beslan-Truffaldino came to his senses first, but that only infuriated the captors even more. Lying on the floor in just his underwear, the group monitor merely asked, "Could I get dressed?" He received, first, a sound smack in the mouth, and second, a flowery rebuff, with some choice curses, which could be translated as 'Should I bring you some tea too?' After which a strapping fellow in camouflage swung open the balcony door.

For over three hours, the students, spread out along the floor in nothing but underwear, "cooled off" in the early spring morning draft, while the Chechen pogrom went on.

"They insulted us, called us mujahideen who should be killed. They said that Chechens tended sheep their whole lives, and they were going to send us back to a pastoral life. They howled that since we were Chechens, that meant we were guilty of everything," recalled Shuddi Zairayev, an elegant youth with the manners of a romantic hero. He is Silvio from "Truffaldino."

What is shocking is that there is no trace of amazement in his story. Only a statement of fact. Their emotions have been spent back in Chechnya. Students for the Nakhi studio have been chosen from refugee camps in Grozny, and unique people live there, people who are more accustomed to genocide than to breakfast.

The youngest in the studio is Timur Lalayev. He just turned seventeen. He's very thin, smiling, agile, and he laughs a lot.

On March 28, they sicced dogs on him. Timur speaks sparingly of his own ordeal. He says of others:

"Shuddi got it worse than anyone else. They asked us, 'Is anyone here from the Staropromyslovsky district?' Shuddi answered, 'I am.'"

And that's when it began! 'We stopped by Staropromyslovsky in 1995. So many of our guys died there.'"

The residence listed on Shuddi-Silvio's passport really is a street in the Staropromyslovsky district of Grozny. They beat him up to their heart's content. Then they told him they'd take him into the forest, shoot him, and bury him in a pit.

"What were you thinking about then? That they were just trying to scare you?"

"No. I decided that it was the end for me. They weren't joking with the others either. They ripped out clumps of Timur Batayev and Ortsa Zukhairayev's hair."

On March 28 in Khimki, the Moscow Regional Department for Organized Crime Control (RDOCC)* waged this cruel operation. It was not their first such exploit, either. This time the detachment was united with the similarly minded Moscow District Special Emergency Detachments.† The pretext for the punitive actions was to check on an anonymous call to the police about a possible hiding place for TNT. But the actual goal was to have fun. And the real grounds for this measure was the students' nationality.

"Did you understand exactly what they wanted?"

"No, absolutely not. They beat us, smashed everything around. And that was it."

In the course of the purge it became clear that most of the masked men had just returned from military assignments to Chechnya. Naturally, they hadn't undergone any rehabilitation after battle. And this is the result: they were trigger happy, mentally on edge, full of pent-up emotions and demanding an excursion for a purge, the way a drug addict craves a needle.

"We realized that they just had to go off at someone," says Anzor Khadashev, from Grozny.

---

*One of the regional subdivisions of the Russian Ministry of the Interior. The task of these subdivisions is to investigate circumstances of kidnappings and to search for victims. They were active in Chechen territory not just in the first and second wars, but also between the wars, cooperating with field commanders and leaders of terrorist detachments.

†Subdivisions of the Russian Ministry of the Interior. Their ostensible main task is to free hostages. They have taken part in both Chechen wars, along with regular army units.

"In Chechnya they're the bosses. They came here, and they want to be the bosses here too. We're the best material for that," continues Anzor. "And to be serious, they're simply nuts. Why did they take my family pictures? What do they need them for? Why did they take a phone card from another of our students? And they also took the student money collected for food. We eat like most students, on pooled resources. I notice that they're afraid of everything. When we were being picked up off the floor to be taken to the Regional Department of Organized Crime Control for questioning, I saw that as soon as you look them in the eye, they shout, 'Don't look! Want to remember me? Turn around!' They're afraid even when they're in masks. Is this any way to live in your own home?"

Tamerlan Didigov is the son of Alikhan Didigov and a graduate of Moscow State Law Academy. He lives together with his father right here, in the dormitory, in room 37. On the morning of the pogrom the Didigov father and son got it worse than anyone. Maybe it was because Tamerlan wasn't sleeping at the moment the men in camouflage broke in. He had already gotten up so he could unhurriedly dress for the state exam. Tamerlan was supposed to take his civil rights test that morning. And as soon as they tried to knock him down to the floor, he simply said, "Look at my papers! What kind of militant am I? I have a civil rights exam now!" Who could imagine that this would make the bandits so angry? "Oh, you're studying civil rights too, you monkey! You should be in the mountains. Go there!" Then they started to beat his father, a fifty-five-year-old professor, until he lost consciousness, kicking him and hitting him with their rifle butts. They spat in his face, and stomped on his back. They tore off his clothes and twisted his fingers. When Tamerlan pleaded for them to have mercy on his father, they put handcuffs on him, and started to twist his wrists around with a submachine gun.

"We had bundles of issues of the newspaper *The State News*. My father is friends with State Legislature deputy Aslanbek Aslakhanov.*

---

*Currently a deputy of the Russian Federation State Duma (the lower house of Parliament) from Chechnya. Elected under military pressure in August 2000. Retired major general of the Ministry of the Interior, scholar and author of books on the mafia and corruption in Russia. He was chairman of the Committee for Legal Questions, Law and Order, and Crime Fighting of the Russian Federation Supreme Council at the beginning of the first Chechen war (1994).

The State News is issued with Aslakhanov's help, and also with the assistance and support of the Federation Council and the State Legislature. The paper's credo is the ideology of the pro-Putin Unity Party and faction. Aslakhanov sometimes gives us issues of *The State News*, and we pass them out among our friends. So when the masked men saw these bundles, they yelled: 'What's this?! You're spreading anti-Russian propaganda here!' Really uneducated people—they don't know, understand, or read anything."

When Professor Didigov lost consciousness from his beating, they stuck a pistol under his pillow right in front of Tamerlan's eyes. Then they asked, 'Where's your father's coat?' The son showed them, and then they put the silencer from the pistol into the coat pocket.

They threw the shoes from the balcony. They ripped up all the posters with pictures of Deputy Aslakhanov, took all the documents of the Nakhi studio, and nine hundred rubles. And also the professor's wife's perfume. They swept everything that they found into their pockets: socks, pens, small change from on top of the refrigerator, instant coffee, boxing gloves ... Because they were used to doing that in Chechnya. They'd go into a house and take whatever they wanted.

That's how things went until noon. Then the soldiers started to get ready to leave. They lined all the Chechen students up in single file and started to lead them downstairs, room by room, to the cars. There wasn't enough room for everybody there, of course. So they were beaten and humiliated again. The interrogations at the RDOCC lasted until evening. However, the students had the impression that they didn't really have anything to ask them about. The series of questions went something like this: Are your parents fighting? Where is the hexogen? Have you ever seen any militants? How do you feel about the army? ...

The law enforcement officials—government employees by their status, acting in the name of the Law and the Constitution—conducted a genuine national pogrom in Khimki. And nobody stopped them—no public prosecutors rushed to uphold the law.

This means that the men in epaulettes are not just igniting international discord—a crime that automatically entails criminal punishment. They are initiating monoethnicity in the country, that is, its future breakup into national compartments: separatism. The very same kind that President Putin, whose employ the RDOCC officials are in, is supposedly struggling with.

In conclusion, something about the artistic intelligentsia. It's very meek, as usual. During the Khimki pogrom, the theatrical community reacted so apathetically that it was as if an army of influential actors and directors holding liberal views didn't live in Moscow.

Only the students' professors came to their assistance.

"I've worked at the Institute of Culture for twenty-five years. I teach Russian. Right now I have some guys from the Chechen studio in my class. They're very hard-working and enormously motivated to learn. What happened to them simply made me sick." The voice of Svetlana Nikolayevna Dymova, an instructor at the Moscow State University of Culture and Art, is trembling. "The first thing I said to them was, 'You know, they were bandits; they could come after me too. Don't despair. We professors very much want you to study with us!' I realize that no one will find the bandits, no one will bring them to justice. The scariest thing they said then was, 'We won't let you study in Russia!'"

The finale of the pogrom turned out to be in much the same style as the rest of it. In the evening the entire male contingent of the Nakhi studio was simply released to go wherever they wanted, without being charged with anything. The students said some of the RDOCC officers even tried to apologize, assuring them that it was the men from the Special Emergency Detachments who were "bad": "they're like torpedoes—they shoot first, think later."

"We forgave them," said Timur Lalayev. "Because they're sick."

Half a year later, Andron Konchalovsky came to the exam at Nakhi. He invited students for roles in his new film. They debuted and were noticed.

The investigator of the RDOCC, who was especially ferocious with the Chechen students on March 28, 2001, took to drink, was fired, and now works as a stock boy in a Khimki department store. When he's drunk and sees Chechens, he yells, "Hey! Remember me?" And he tells his drinking buddies how he used to beat them back then. "You see, they moved up in the world," he adds.

And the Chechens pass by silently.

Five Hundred Rubles for Your Wife: The Chechnya Special Operation
Ruins the Country

On June 14, 2001 there was a meeting in the Ingush village of Orjonikidzevskaya on the Chechen-Ingush border. The participants were refugees from Chechnya living in Ingushetia as well as those citizens of our country whose passports have that line, so unpleasant today, about residence in the belligerent republic. This acts like a red flag before a bull on any Russian policeman and forbids them to work legally or have medical insurance or a place for their children in school. The nervous crowd of about two thousand adopted the following appeal to world society: "Conduct an examination and analysis of the situation in the Chechen Republic on the basis of international law, declare the rights of Chechen citizens to self-defense in the event of lawless conduct of servicemen and in the absence of legal defense from the Russian leadership."

And further: "Call on U.S. President Bush, as the head of a government that plays one of the key roles in world politics, to appeal to the Russian leadership (President Putin) ... " (the rest is the same as in the first text).

And also: "Call on the heads of the 'Big Seven' in the forthcoming summit to influence President Putin ... " (also continuing as in the first text).

In translation from official to normal language, this appeal to the American president and the chief world leaders would read: "Help us survive! Appease the army and Putin! Be a third arbiter! We don't know how to fight military lawlessness! Tell us whether we still have any rights! Or should we accept that we're nobody?" It's a howl of despair by people who have been driven into a corner.

However, the appeal of the Orjonikidzevskaya meeting provoked the worst possible reaction from Russian society. For the umpteenth time, the Chechens were charged with anti-Russian behavior, separatism, and the desire to slander Putin in the eyes of the world.

Why do we turn a deaf ear? Is it because the war has completely ceased being personal and has turned into several talking-head generals on the TV screen?

There are familiar faces in the crowd at the meeting. Here is a stern-looking woman with cold eyes, a typical wartime Chechen. She is from the mountain village Makhkety in Vedeno district. Her situation is tragic: her fourteen-year-old son was "flushed down the toilet."* Just plain "flushed," in the literal sense, by the direct hit of a shell into a village outhouse when the kid was doing his business. This woman's home is almost at the edge of the village, so the Feds could see from their posts who was going where around the yard. They understood why the boy was going down the path to the far corner of the yard, and they fired a shot. Just for fun, but at the same time, fulfilling the direct order of their president.

And off to the side is a father whose unmarried grown-up daughter went through the filtration camp in Urus-Martan, where... But in this case it's better to be silent. Just one detail about her incarceration: she was forced to crawl up and down steps on all fours, like a dog, holding a pail of excrement in her teeth.

Neither the mother from Makhkety nor the father from Urus-Martan is in the mood to play political games. They don't give a damn about separatism—they're faced with their own sorrow. They're enemies until their dying day with both Maskhadov and Putin. And if they cry out for help at the meeting, appealing to world leaders, you'd better believe them.

June 5, 2001, in Grozny, at Theater Square (there used to be theaters here). There is such a thing here—once there were theaters. People came to a protest meeting. They were holding signs in their hands: "Give me back my mother!" These are from children whose mothers, arrested in a purge, have disappeared to no one knows where. And also: "Give us back our children's corpses!" That's from mothers whose children have disappeared without a trace in the purges. A couple of armored vehicles puff along the road past the meeting. Middle-aged men, probably mercenaries, not soldiers, are on top of the car. They are cheerful and vigorous, with strong, healthy teeth. They're wearing masks and bandannas, with automatic weapons and grenade launchers pointed at the crowd. They're convulsed with laughter, leaning against the armor in ecstasy, and that's why their rows of powerful fangs can be seen through the holes in their masks. They point fingers

---

*In a 1999 press conference on the problem of Chechen militants, Putin announced that "we will flush the bandits down the toilet." He used the word *mochit*, which literally means "to make wet," but is also criminal jargon for "to kill." *Trans.*

in cut-off gloves, mostly at those with the "Give me back my mother!" signs. And to top it off, they demonstrate with rude gestures what they plan to do to both the protestors' moms' and their sons' corpses.

Nearby is an officer, the superior of the group. He behaves the same way.

Of course all of this is details—rude gestures, flushed down the toilet. But it is from just these details that we find out what life is about. As if it weren't bad enough that your mother or child has been taken away and their bodies haven't been returned—they also have to mock your pain! Who can stop this? Putin? The minister of defense? The attorney general? No. These gentlemen aren't trained to think about details. Only the West is the people's big advocate. Therefore they appeal to the West for the sake of survival.

I'm ashamed to look into the eyes of an exhausted Chechen named Shomsu, whom I've known for a few weeks now. I can't help him in any way. Since January 8, Shomsu has been looking everywhere for his nephew Umar Aslakhajiev and his friends Nur-Mohammed Bambatgiriev and Turpal-Ali Naibov. All three were driving around the village of Kurchaloi on that day. A purge started there early in the morning. And at ten, they too were purged, along with their dark green Zhiguli, and that was the end. There hasn't been any news about them to this day. For the past half year, Shomsu has combed all of Chechnya, many times, far and wide. And now he doesn't know what else to do. I don't know either, and don't understand the basic things: where is the Zhiguli, for example? What is it guilty of, even if there were some basis to assume the guilt of its owners? And who exactly expropriated it? And having stolen it, why didn't they answer for the crime? And why is it that to this day the arrested men have not been charged with anything or released? How much time does the government need to write up the indictments, half a century? The way it happened in the past with "illegally repressed" people? And why are the big shots in our country loudly discussing, at the initiative of the generals, the possibility of introducing public executions for the militant leaders, if executions without trial for ordinary Chechens are already taking place?

There are tons of questions, but not a single answer. And if an answer actually is given, it's as if they think we're idiots. Here's how it usually happens in Chechnya: a relative of someone who has disappeared goes to the necessary military official. The officers around him usually prompt you helpfully: "He's the one you need." And "he" says:

"I am Sasha."

"What? Just Sasha?"

"Yes, just Sasha."

This "Sasha" doesn't reveal his last name, title, or position. He feeds you with promises for a couple of months: just wait a bit, I'll find them tomorrow, or at least their grave.

"And while I'm working on it," hints "Sasha," "I just saw a very nice suit for two hundred dollars at the fair in Khasavyurt."

"Yes, yes," the family of the kidnapped person catches the hint. "A suit, of course, a suit... We'll go to Khasavyurt on Saturday."

On Sunday, "Sasha" already has a new outfit. But he asks for a banya too, for his various bodily needs. You're adults, you know what this involves. And it's arranged. And "Sasha" announces, as a sign of gratitude, that the three men and the car who are being searched for are at the 33d Ministry of the Interior forces brigade base. Soon this turns out to be a big lie: neither the three unfortunates nor the Zhiguli are at the 33rd. And "Sasha" himself disappears, having squeezed everything that he needed out of the suffering families. "Sasha" was already planning to leave Chechnya; he was approaching the end of his military assignment and wanted to get a new outfit.

Who will stop these "Sashas"? Their supreme commander-in-chief Putin? No, he's shown no such desire—he'd rather just hand out awards.

What else can you try? Another call to the West for help?

But Shomsu continues. He shows me official answers to his inquiries about the missing men. And this is another type of activity of the officers searching for those who have disappeared in the purges— statements, with signatures of supposedly responsible parties underneath. But in fact, they're false. The officers in Chechnya, like the undercover intelligence agents, have three or four IDs with different last names. And there's no one you can hold responsible.

The right granted to the soldiers to hide their actual last names, "so that militants won't take revenge on their families," has gradually become one of the major causes of the crimes and monstrosities in Chechnya.

But how can Shomsu and others like him find their way through this maze of deceit? How can they get on the track of the law? It's impossible to do it. Shomsu has papers signed by Police Colonel Oleg Melnik (whose name probably isn't really Melnik at all), Lieutenant Colonel Yury Solovei (who might not be Solovei), and also Colonel Smolyaninov. The last, on the one hand, is Nikolai Aleksandrovich, but on the other hand, answers more readily to the nickname "Mikhalych." Besides this group, there's also a "Yurich," a man who calls himself the deputy of the head of the Kurchaloi FSS regional department. His multiweek participation in the matter of the search for Aslakhajiev, Bambatgiriev, and Naibov consisted of actively leading the family by the nose, such as by advising them to stay out of it and to give up, because the Main Intelligence Agency has something to do with it. And why would the Main Intelligence Agency be involved if Shomsu's nephew were just an ordinary person, a peasant?

Having thus advised them, Yurich takes off for his native Belgorod. Or maybe not for Belgorod. And maybe he's not Yurich either. Maybe he's the one who killed the people Shomsu is looking for and is now covering his tracks.

This vicious cycle of widespread lies has been maintained by people who call themselves officers. After this unrestrained lawlessness, they leave for their homes, all over the country. Chechnya as a mode of thinking, feeling and acting, spreads everywhere like gangrenous cells and turns into a nationwide tragedy, infecting all strata of society.

Here's another example. Two years after the beginning of the second Chechen war, which has become, among other things, an arena for unruly marauding, it is clear that Chechens everywhere have been robbed blind, and that the robbers have turned on their own. Zhenya Zhuravlev is a soldier in the motorized rifle company of the third special assignment brigade of the Ministry of the Interior forces. His unit, 3724, was deployed at the village of Dachnoe, near Vladikavkaz. From there, he was sent to Chechnya, where he stayed for eight months on some mountain without ever going down. He couldn't send or receive letters. Zhenya's mother, Valentina Ivanovna Zhuravleva, a widow and kindergarten teacher in Lugovaya village of the Tugulymsky region in Sverdlovsk, waited in vain for some news from him and cried her eyes out as she sent him registered letters.

Finally an answer came. Zhenya, whose term of service had already ended in April, pleaded with her to come and take him away from Vladikavkaz. The village collected some money, and Valentina Ivanovna, along with Zhenya's aunt, a retired railway worker named Vassa Nikandrovna Zubareva, turned up at Dachnoe.

At first the officers didn't present Zhenya at all—they were clearly hiding something. Then the soldiers whispered that Zhenya had only been brought from Chechnya yesterday, and straight to the hospital. They secretly took his mother to the ward in the evening. Zhenya was lying there with his legs festering up to the knees. He said he hadn't washed himself for a few months on the mountain, and he always wore high boots. This was the result. His mother went to the officers and pleaded with them to give her back her son to be treated somehow in the village. They said, let's take his "war" money, for participating in the antiterrorist operations, and divide it up fifty-fifty, and you'll get your son.

Zhenya categorically forbade Valentina Ivanovna to divide up his money, and so he wasn't able to go home. He spent a long time in Dachnoe, and Valentina Ivanovna was nearby, together with other mothers to whom the officers had not returned their sons, demanding to split the money in exchange for demobilization. All of these unfortunate victims of the second Chechen war sent Vassa Nikandrovna, the aunt, to Moscow, and she went to one official after another. And only then did things move forward. The soldiers were allowed to go home. But the officers weren't jailed.

Here is the story of one young Muscovite, who begged me to keep his name secret, fearing revenge. On his day off, at midnight, he was driving with friends to a dance club. Some policemen with their sleeves rolled up above the elbows and bandannas on their shaven heads stopped the car and said, "We're taking the girl." The "girl" was the wife of one of the passengers; she was going dancing with her husband for the first time since giving birth to their first child. "We're taking her, and we won't give her back," shouted the law enforcers. The husband's friends held him back and tried to persuade the cops: "She'll need to feed the baby soon." "What do we care?" The only thing the young mother had done wrong was to leave her passport at home. Since she didn't have her passport, they couldn't see whether she was a lawful resident of Moscow. They agreed to let the husband pay five hundred rubles for his wife, and then they could move on.

It turned out that the patrolmen had been on an assignment to Chechnya not long ago. After leaving the zone, they had continued their military tactics in peacetime life.

"It's a good thing the patrolmen didn't shoot, since they are 'Chechens,'" everyone said when they were told this story. They said so seriously, not surprised by anything.

The "Chechnya" special operation has infected the whole country, which is becoming more and more beastly and idiotic. The value of human life was already very low in Russia, and now it has slipped to almost nothing. We have all reached the depths, like the unrescued *Kursk*. And there's no order for rescue.

Chechnya's Unique Islam
Unwanted Mullahs

When you wander around Chechnya for a while during the current war and listen to the stories people tell about what they've experienced, you notice with surprise that there's almost no place for mullahs in these mournful tales. Only now and then does anyone make the following quick comment: "I went to the mosque, and the mullah helped me gather ransom money for the Feds." February 2002 is the only time I can remember in these three war years when the clergy of the distant Shatoi mountain region wrote a petition screaming out with pain and outrage, addressed to a former mullah there, now serving as the Chechen mufti. This mullah had been given an office next to that of the pro-Moscow head of the republic, Akhmad-Khaji Kadyrov (also a former mufti), and, after becoming a bureaucrat, quickly forgot about the people's suffering. The petition described extraordinary circumstances: the murder and incineration in January 2002 of six Shatoi residents, including a pregnant woman and an elderly director of a village school whom everyone respected, by ten soldiers of an elite subdivision of the Russian Federation General Staff, and the equally extraordinary indifference of the muftis to these tragic events. The mullahs wrote that they were ashamed of this indifference.

And here's a completely different example. Many people go to see the old, very wise local mullah in the tiny, well-kept village of

Isti-Su (not far from Gudermes), military situation permitting, of course. They go to him for advice, and simply to talk. Surprisingly, this popular Chechen mullah turns out to be a German. More precisely, he is a former German prisoner of war, who had fought for the Nazis in World War II. After he was captured, he wound up doing forced labor restoring Grozny, married a Chechen, converted to Islam, and raised half-German, half-Chechen children, who during Gorbachev's perestroika were able to emigrate safely to their father's homeland. He himself, at that time, was an unofficial spiritual leader of a certain part of the Chechen population. Although they fully recognized that he was not "one of them," it didn't make any difference anymore; he couldn't abandon his people to poverty and suffering. He is living out his complicated, contradictory life in Chechnya, which has been drowning in bloody wars since Gorbachev's departure. And near him there are dozens of mullahs of pure Chechen origin, who are unwanted and have nothing to do, because no one goes to them.

Everything that is happening today with Chechen Islam is a consequence of both Chechen history as a whole and the current political experiments on Chechnya.

But first, some historical information. Chechen Islam is very young. Specialists disagree on the exact dates of the Islamization of the Vainakh* tribes. Most likely, Islam became the official religion in the first half of the eighteenth century. Also, it remains an intricate mix of Muslim traditions and ancient adats—the rules of Chechen life of the pre-Islamic period—which tend to preach family, neighborly, and communal values.

The Chechens are Sufis, and they unite many Sufi virds (brotherhoods, or in the exact translation from the Arabic "vird," a short prayer). The vird in Chechnya is like a community of murids (students) of a certain shaikh (an ustaz, or teacher), where the murid learns everything from the ustaz, who in turn has taken all his spiritual knowledge from his own teacher. According to the Sufi interpretation, the "I" is nothing. The "I" should be subservient to the whole as determined by the teacher. Zikrs are Sufi collective prayers

*A general name for the Chechens and Ingush, who are ethnically very close. "Vainakh" means "our people."

or incantations (running in a circle in a communal group), which are supposed to free the "I" of a zikrist from fear and evil desires. Typical Sufi poses include crouching with crossed legs and holding the right wrist in the left hand—this also allows for control over one's body.

Chechnya has its own virds. They are strengthened first and foremost by close family bonds within each vird. The most influential vird in Chechnya is the Kuntakhajin. The particular moral unity of this brotherhood played a major role, for example, during the last presidential election campaign in April 2002 in Ingushetia, where many Chechen Kuntakhajins moved during Maskhadov's presidency between the two wars, away from the Saudi-influenced Wahhabi domination. The Kuntakhajins even had their own presidential candidate in Ingushetia. Kunta-Khaji, the founder of the vird, is one of 356 Muslim saints. His followers believe that he is still alive, that he is a defender of the people, and that he comes to them at their times of greatest danger. For example, in the present Chechen war, many people talk of Kunta-Khaji appearing before them in the form of a white-bearded elder at the moment of their miraculous rescue from seemingly inevitable death.

The Chinmirzoev vird is also very strong. Its founder, Chin-Mirza, united the poorest peasant families in East Chechnya after the Caucasian war of the nineteenth century. He preached peasant labor ideals and everyday asceticism, rejecting war and robbery.

The Viskhajin vird was founded by a man named Vis-Khaji during World War II among Chechens who had been deported to Kazakhstan. He united around himself women who were widowed with children.

The Deniarsanov vird, founded by Deni Arsanov in the 1920s, was highly respected in Chechnya for preserving holy secrets and prophesying the fate of the nation. Many educated people of the Soviet period who found themselves in positions of leadership came from this vird. Currently, it is in a prolonged, bloody conflict of revenge with the influential field commander Ruslan Gelayev, in connection with the treacherous 2000 murder in the Kurchaloi district center of twenty Deniarsanovians by a company of twenty of Gelayev's soldiers. Therefore, the vird participates very little in external political life.

Virds are much more influential in Chechnya than mullahs and official muftis. They're closer and more understandable to the

Chechens as structures of a family type, and are more traditional than jamaats (communities).

It's possible that things wouldn't have worked out this way, but for the help of the Communists. Soviet power sent young Chechen Islam into the underground. After the return of the people who had been deported from 1944 to 1957, they were forbidden to erect mosques, unlike other north Caucasian peoples. This brought things to a point where in Chechnya, there was almost no clergy to be controlled by the KGB, and this was actually a plus. Viable, free Muslim religious communities emerged. In every village, if there was a mullah, he was exclusively their own, a self-made man who answered to the village and was appointed by it. And if there was no mullah, that was fine; the elders were respected much more and a brotherhood existed in the vird. Therefore, Chechens reacted to the subsequent establishment of a muftiate either indifferently ("we'll keep living the way we always have") or with anger ("they're tied to the KGB").

As a result, a completely unique Islam emerged in Chechnya by the end of the Soviet era. This Islam was free, with many conflicting Sufist virds and individual interpretations of Islam, where all individuals were their own bosses, even in matters of faith.

Perestroika began and Doku Zavgayev became the first Chechen to be appointed first secretary of the Chechen-Ingush republic party committee (earlier they had always been Russian). Then, a Clerical Department of Muslims of Chechnya-Ingushetia was finally created (a muftiate, a council of ulems). At the end of the 1980s, hundreds of mosques were built, and two Islamic schools were opened, in Kurchaloi and Nazrani (now the capital of Ingushetia, which separated from Chechnya). Thousands of Chechens and Ingush made pilgrimages to sacred Islamic sites for the first time. But for all that, the Chechens lived the way they were used to living.

Then the wars began. On the one hand, the number of believing Muslims increased, youth began to visit the mosques, and many turned to prayer. But on the other hand, the problems of Chechen Islam only became more serious. First, so-called "Kadyrovism" (after Akhmad-Khaji Kadyrov) brought discord to their community. Second, Chechnya was penetrated by "Saudi Wahhabism" (a religious current of Sunni Islam, whose followers affirm that theirs is the "pure" Islam, and all the others are not, thus rejecting Sufism). A religious schism was taking place within families. Fathers were cursing their sons for following Wahhabism. And sons disowned their fathers for their unclean, non-Wahhabi Islam, which had been unthinkable before.

Kadyrovism

Akhmad-Khaji Kadyrov has traveled a twisted path in life. He is now a completely secular figure, the administrative head of the Chechen Republic, having been appointed to this position in July 2000 by President Putin, who also gave him the title of Colonel of the Russian Army. But before this, he was a mullah with a shady financial past. He organized the first Chechen pilgrimage to Mecca, and in doing so stole money from his people. The king of Saudi Arabia footed the bill for this first pilgrimage, but Kadyrov never returned the money he had collected to anyone, which people have recalled once in a while to this day. Later he was a field commander during the first Chechen war, one of the people closest to Dzhokhar Dudayev. And in 1995, he became the mufti of Chechnya with the title of "field mufti," because he was named to this post not by the Chechen spiritual leaders, but by a group of field commanders of the first Chechen war who at the time were looking for a clergyman capable of announcing a holy war against Russia. Everybody but Kadyrov refused.

Chechens know that Kadyrov will never endanger his own financial interests. Even now, he participates in an illegal oil business. I've never met a Chechen who would say, "I respect Kadyrov." It is surprising and frightening that this head of a republic has zero authority. Everyone says something like "He's a traitor, he'll end badly." They're referring to how Kadyrov ran from Maskhadov to Putin at the beginning of the second Chechen war. What's most striking is that both opponents of the Kremlin and pro-Russian Chechens, members of the former opposition to Dudayev, Ichkeria,* and Maskhadov, speak of Kadyrov in this way. In 2001 and 2002, Kadyrov has again done nothing to gain the respect of his people. He became infamous in Chechnya, since he

---

*The official name of Chechnya is "The Chechen Republic of Ichkeria." "Ichkeria" was added in 1994 by the decree of then-president Dzhokhar Dudayev. *Trans.*

did not in any way oppose the purges. In connection with this, most say that he betrayed his people, and this is of course much worse than to have betrayed Maskhadov and independent Ichkeria.

My meeting with Kadyrov in his office in April 2002 was disturbing. He just glowered unkindly at me, and talked a great deal about himself, about how he was Maskhadov's spiritual mentor, and how he shaped him as a person and as the leader of a nation responsible for the fate of his people. He described himself as categorically opposed to any peaceful negotiations with his former comrades in arms, and said that he hoped to restore NKVD night methods of destroying people in Chechnya.

Here's an excerpt from our conversation:

"The main problem at this stage of the war is the purges, an inadequate and unjustifiable application of power against the civilian population—marauding, torture, and the selling of arrested people and corpses. When people disappear and no one says where they are, and then relatives find the bodies, it spawns at least ten new militants. For this reason the number of militants never decreases. It was fifteen hundred then, and it's fifteen hundred now. President Putin came out strongly on my side on this topic."

"How do you plan to fight these purges, which are spawning new militants?"

"I am hoping for a firm stand by Putin. I said to him, why doesn't a single general answer for what's been going on during the purges? And the president demanded that they be stopped! Although of course this is not the first order from the president about Chechnya that has not been obeyed."

"How can you, as head of the republic, help the people?"

"I tell the president about everything. The people continue to suffer. We need honest officials, and these are hard to find. I mean administrative workers of towns and villages. They are afraid to come out openly against the bandits, because they have no backing. I raised this question with Commander Moltensky and the president. We are trying, but it's not simple. It's easier for you—you just ask questions."

"Still, what do you have the power to do? What can you personally do to oppose military despotism in Chechnya?"

"I have no authority against the military. I have asked Putin for such rights."

"Do you think someone should be ruling Chechnya single-handedly?"

"Yes, so that one person would answer for everything, including the power structures. A dictator is needed here, in the literal sense of the word."

"Suppose you were that dictator. And there was a purge in Argun. What would you do?"

"If I were the dictator of Chechnya, I wouldn't conduct purges. To find a bandit, I would quietly gather information and appear at his door at two or three at night, shake his hand, and say hello. After such a visit, this bandit would disappear. With three or four other such operations, everyone would be clear on everything. That's just what happened when the NKVD was operating. One knock at the door, and the person would never be heard from again. People knew this and were afraid of it. That's how things were then, otherwise there would have been no order."

The Chechen's new wave of increasing disrespect for their muftis, who were not particularly influential before, is connected precisely with the name and activities of Kadyrov, who is never called anything but a "traitor." The Chechens are also quite cold toward the mufti Shamayev, whom Kadyrov dragged into this post. As a rule, they express their opinion of Shamayev very simply: "This one sold out too, and he doesn't speak up for his people to Putin and the generals."

The Chechens value those who are genuinely wise and courageous. If such a man happens to be a mullah, great, but if not, that's fine too. It is more important to belong to a vird. The Chechens also struggle, using teip (clan) and vird forces, with religious extremism in their ranks, with the Wahhabis (who are called "the bearded ones" here). The Wahhabis are very unpopular. It would be a mistake to suggest that they have any serious influence or play any kind of role in Chechnya. Their role and influence actually boil down to weapons, which they do possess. They are feared, just like the Feds, who also only have force to count on. But as history has shown, all conquests eventually end.

Executions of Reporters

Musa Muradov is a member of the Chechen elite, the editor in chief of the *Grozny Worker*, the only independent Chechen newspaper. He is a superbly educated, fearless man who has been through both the first and second wars. If you were to tally up his services to the Chechen people, Musa would already have earned a monument in his lifetime. But in the beginning of fall 2001, Musa, instead of a monument, received an anonymous letter stating that he, as well as the entire male contingent of the paper (Abuezid Kushaliev, Alkhazur Mutsurayev, and Lema Turpalov) were required to repent for their collaboration with "occupation forces" and for receiving "monetary handouts" from "the Jew Soros," signed by the "Supreme Shariat Court and the General Command"—Shura, the militants' religious and military organ—about which they say, "It is Basayev alone, no one else." If they didn't repent, they would be executed. The sentence would be carried out by "the emirs and district judges."

This means that wherever Musa appeared, he'd be killed.

Musa threw everything aside and took his family to Moscow. When we met there, he asked me, "What do you think I should do next?" We were both aware that the threats were for real.

The *Grozny Worker* never interrupted its publication for long, not during the days of Maskhadov or in wartime. And it never wanted to be under someone's control. Several times, the participants in the Chechen conflict (both the Feds and Maskhadov) offered their "sponsorship," but Muradov refused them. Given the circumstances—war, secret service games—Musa found a much better way for the paper to survive. He didn't take money from either side (although this would have been the simplest way out). Instead, he applied for a grant from the Soros Fund, going through the complex selection system, and managed to receive the means for publishing the paper from someone who did not make any political demands of him.

I'm not too crazy about Soros or his politics, but if his fund allows reporters to be independent in wartime conditions, then it's good as far as I'm concerned.

Since the summer, the militants' headquarters—no matter how much they try to deny it—has been virtual, and their "Resistance" becomes reality only when the war demands it. You can "communicate" with this "Resistance" using Caucasus Center, a site on the Internet. This site is how the world generally finds out what Aslan Maskhadov thinks about what is going on in his country. Often these thoughts seem too unsound and propagandistic, confirming that Caucasus Center is simply Yastrzhembsky the other way around.

That's where I turned for an explanation of the threats received by the *Grozny Worker*. I quickly received an answer from the site by its editor in chief Yusuf Ibrahim, who announced that "we still don't have any information," although "in such cases we usually find out the Shariat Court's decisions quickly. We think that this misinformation was initiated by the Secret Service, and that Musa Muradov's life is in danger. He could be killed by Russian secret servicemen, so they can then shout out to the world that mujahideen kill reporters."

Movladi Udugov,* the "father" of Caucasus Center, who fled from Chechnya a long time ago but pretends to maintain constant contact with Shura and its commanders, could not shed any light on this either.

I began to insist: tell me who is now the head of the Supreme Shariat Court, capable of confirming or denying the Muradov ruling? Who is the district emir (Musa is from a Grozny district village; earlier, Field Commander Arbi Barayev† was the emir there) that would carry out the sentence, if it really exists?

The answer was a long, deep silence. That's exactly what I thought: there is no head of the Supreme Shariat Court, and there's no district emir either, except for Barayev, who has died. Aslan Maskhadov didn't voice his opinion of the "sentence" either. I tried to look for him, and so did Muradov, a reporter to whom Maskhadov is extremely indebted, by the way, since it was only through his efforts that the world knew what Maskhadov thought of this or that issue over the course of many months.

Then I turned to the other side, to the FSS. After all, the FSS has the responsibility of leading the so-called antiterrorist operation. What's

---

*The most treacherous person in Dudayev and Maskhadov's governments. Responsible for the Ichkerian ideology. Was the Chechen minister of information. A liar and political manipulator. Fled from Chechnya when the second Chechen war started; now lives in Qatar and runs the pro-Basayev, anti-Maskhadov Web site Caucasus.

† Barayev was allegedly responsible for numerous kidnappings and murders, including the decapitation of four Western telecom engineers in 1998. *Trans.*

more, it's officially the FSS's task to defend citizens' constitutional rights, of which the most important is life.

The FSS gets away with some indistinct mumbling: "This was done by militants." And they don't say anything more about "the case of Muradov and the *Grozny Worker* reporters" than Caucasus Center and virtual Maskhadov.

Silence does not bode well. That's what the war has taught us. Muradov and the *Grozny Worker* are a thorn in the side of everyone in the conflict: since Muradov doesn't serve anyone, he's an enemy. And the letter? It's a sign, a signal: "We'll let you live only if you will be under someone's control, and if you remain your own man, you'll die." That's the sentence that was really passed on Muradov and the other three reporters in a country that continues to establish a type of democracy in which absolutely no one wants independent reporters, and it's easier to destroy them and blame competing secret services than to accept their existence.

Who wanted to remove Musa and his three colleagues? The answer is obvious: those who want to continue the war. And it's not important whether their name is Ivan Petrov of the FSS or Shamil Basayev of Shura; they are carrying out a joint special operation.

This is a double betrayal. It fully corresponds with the type of politics that is being established in Russian society in connection with the current president's previous profession. If in Yeltsin's times we lived from one of his diseases to the next, we now live from one special operation to the next. As soon as a campaign to destroy Viktor Popkov, an independent reporter and human rights advocate who was fatally wounded in Chechnya, was completed, another campaign was launched to destroy Muradov. Neither side of the Chechen conflict can act on its own, without the support of the other side, its supposed opponent.

In conclusion, a few words about Chechen civil society. Where are the ordinary Chechens, who would profit a great deal from the work of Musa Muradov and his colleagues, uniquely important people for this society? Have they flooded all the Moscow papers, the Putin administration, the FSS, the Ministry of the Interior, the attorney general, Basayev, Maskhadov, and Caucasus Center with letters of protest and indignation?

Not at all. And this isn't the first time, by the way, that the Chechens have sat it out, including those who have benefited constantly from the *Grozny Worker*'s help. The very people for whose benefit Muradov was working.

The secret services' destructive operation was successful. Half a year after the events I've described, the *Grozny Worker* has ceased to exist. Musa doesn't like Moscow, but he can't leave it. The threats come in an endless torrent, and there is no one to defend him. The male reporters of the editorial staff have scattered for their lives in various directions, with their families.

Occasionally, and with great difficulty, Chechen female reporters, who have taken the burden of the war onto their shoulders, issue this newspaper. Are these Chechen women simply not afraid of anything? This is what many people ask, including the soldiers robbing, mocking, and raping them. Yes, the Chechen women aren't afraid of anything— because they're afraid of everything.

Russia's Secret Heroes

The essence of the ruling regime of a country is how it designates heroes. Who are the "Chechen" heroes? And what do we want in Chechnya? What are we doing there? What is our goal? Who are we rewarding for what? And what are we trying to encourge?

There

The tea got cold long ago. We're drinking it in a café at Magas Airport in Ingushetia. I'm ashamed to look Colonel Mohammed Yandiev, an officer of the Ingush Ministry of the Interior, in the eye. It's the third year in a row that I'm ashamed.

As a result of a criminal blunder of the Moscow bureaucracy during the storming of Grozny in December 1999, someone had to risk his life to save eighty-nine elderly people from a Grozny retirement home that was abandoned under the bombing. No one wanted to brave the firing for their sake. Colonel Yandiev was the only one of the hundreds of Russian colonels and generals gathered on this small area near Grozny to say "yes." And with six of his officers whom he had personally asked about this, he crawled for three days—this was the only possible way—along the streets of Grozny to the neighborhood of Katayama, to Borodin Street, where the lonely, hungry elderly were dying in the care of a government that had forgotten its duty to them.

Yandiev rescued all these old people from Grozny. The losses turned out to be minimal. Only one old woman died along the way; her heart couldn't take it. But the colonel was able to save all of the others from bullets and shells flying from both sides of the crazed battle, as if each of them were his own mother or father.

"To this day, they send me letters on holidays. I don't even remember their names. But they remember me. And they write," Yandiev says, very quietly. And I have to drag these words from him, otherwise he would have been silent. "They thank me, and that's the best kind of gratitude," Yandiev insists, continuing to stir the sugar he already stirred long ago in the cold tea. "I don't need anything else."

But I need for there to be something else. I am a citizen, and for this reason I want to know why the colonel still has not received the title of Hero of Russia that he was nominated for early in 2000 for his deed, for the true courage he showed in saving eighty-nine citizens of his country. What do you need to do in Russia, the way things are now, to not only be a hero, but to be officially acknowledged as one?

Here

The path to answers to these questions turned out to be quite treacherous. The babbling of the high-ranking officers responsible for moving the applications higher and higher in the capital of our Motherland, toward the president's signature, boiled down to two arguments against Colonel Yandiev's candidacy as a Hero.

First of all, he is "one of them." In translation from their Moscow bureaucratic language, that means that Yandiev is an Ingush, and Ingush in the army aren't trusted much, like Chechens. Yandiev, I was told, is "practically a Chechen," and "who knows just what was going on in Grozny then—he might have made arrangements with militants."

And what if he did? For the sake of eighty-nine lives?

But there's a second reason too, and this argument doesn't only concern Vainakhs. It turns out that we are only supposed to give the title of Hero if the person "killed a bandit."

"And if they saved someone's life?"

"That's not quite what we're looking for."

"So do you give it for rescues or not?"

"Who would admit that they don't?"

Alas, I gave my word that I would withhold the names of those who agreed to give inside information on this matter. These people, though they have big stars on their epaulettes and orders on their chests, are merely gofers in the grand scheme of things, obeying a higher authority. They know which documents the president *won't sign*. And Putin *won't sign for rescues*. Just a detail, you think? By no means. We've all observed how the word "mercy" has been swept out of the government vocabulary. The government relies on cruelty in relation to its citizens. Destruction is encouraged. The logic of *murder* is a logic that is understood by the government and propagated by it. The way things are, *you need to kill to become a Hero*.

This is Putin's modern ideology. When capitalists can't get it done, comrades take over again. We know very well that they never forget to line their own pockets. That's how things stand: at the end of the seventh year of the war, and in the third year of the second campaign, Chechnya has been turned into a genuine cash cow. Here, military careers are speedily forged, long lists of awards are compiled, and ranks and titles are handed out ahead of time. And all you have to do is kill a Chechen and submit the corpse.

So here I am, sitting across from Mohammed Yandiev. A normal hero in an abnormal country. He hasn't robbed anyone, hasn't raped anyone, and hasn't stuffed any stolen women's lingerie inside his camouflage jacket. He has simply saved lives. And therefore he's not a general. And his Hero application is rotting in Moscow vaults.

A Perplexed Afterword

I called the Information Department of the Russian presidential administration. The head is Igor Porshnev, but it's generally better known as the department of Sergei Yastrzhembsky, an assistant of Putin's who is responsible for "information support for the antiterrorism operation." I had two very simple questions. The first was, How many soldiers have received state awards for their participation in the second Chechen war? And the second was, How many of them earned the Hero of Russia title?

The Information Department sent me to the Putin administration's Department of Government Awards, whose head is Nina Alekseevna Sivova.

"That information is classified," the assistants firmly stated, categorically refusing me any chance to talk with the bosses of their departments. "It's not subject to disclosure."

"But that's absurd!" I objected.

Finally, in Yastrzhembsky's department, which is responsible for the formation of a "proper image of the war," they took pity and at least agreed to "examine an official inquiry on this subject," albeit without guaranteeing a positive answer (of two numbers!) or a date by which they'd examine it (and indeed, an answer never came!).

A conversation with Nina Sivova from the Award Department soon took place. And she affirmed: "This information is in fact confidential, for official use only."

Maybe some people remember this term from Soviet times. Wherever you looked, everything was "for official use only."

"Why are the Hero of Russia and other awards confidential?" I tried to find out from Nina Alekseevna.

"For the protection of those who receive these awards," came yet another cryptic response.

"But I'm not even asking for their last names."

"Call back . . . "

"Tomorrow, again?"

"Yes, tomorrow. Maybe . . . "

Or maybe not. A country in which the number of heroes is information for official use only of those bureaucrats who handed out the awards, and where real heroes don't receive the Hero title, is hopeless. It will lose all wars. Because it never encourages the right people.

Killed by His Own

"One gunshot wound straight through the head and neck," wrote Major Igor Matyukhov, expert of the 632d military court medical laboratory of the North Caucasus Military District, in an official report of yet another autopsy he performed. He added: "Massive loss of blood. Rupture of the left carotid artery." This is a description of the cause of death resulting from "one gunshot wound" that took place on February 5, 2001, at Khankala. Court medical expert Matyukhov also indicated where the "trauma" that proved to be fatal for the soldier Danila Vypov took place: "deployment of a separate subdivision, Military Unit 20004."

Khankala is the holiest of holies for the generals waging war in the North Caucasus. It is the head military base, where the main headquarters of the group is posted, and it is guarded in several circles and along all its perimeters by barbed wire, nets of checkpoints, minefields, and so on. You might ask: what kinds of mines are there, inside?

Officers of unit 20004 (the Ministry of the Interior Kamyshin regiment) told the family of Danila, who didn't live to twenty, something completely different: that their son and brother was blown up on a mine, his body ripped to shreds, and he needed to be buried in a soldered coffin.

And when Danila's older brothers demanded further explanation, and one of them went to the military morgue at Rostov-on-the-Don, he clearly saw an entrance hole from a bullet above Danila's upper lip. It couldn't have been from a mine fragment. And there was no body ripped to shreds. On February 20, Danila's brothers, who were living in Saint Petersburg, wrote the appropriate inquiries to the chief military prosecutor, the Saint Petersburg garrison military prosecutor, the Saint Petersburg Military District Command, and the Chechen military prosecutor posted in Khankala. They also told officials of the human rights organization Saint Petersburg Soldiers' Mothers about everything.

And what happened? Nothing! Silence. Danila's body was brought to Saint Petersburg. The generals prohibited an independent civil court medical examination, on which Danila's family placed their hopes for an explanation of the circumstances surrounding his death. They did this so that no one could ever say that Danila was shot by "his own."

On February 22, when Private Vypov's dead body was brought from the Rostov-on-the-Don military morgue to the one in Saint Petersburg, I flew by helicopter from the 119th paratroop regiment in the Vedeno district to the Khankala military base. On the floor of the helicopter lay the body of yet another young soldier killed in the Chechen war, wrapped in a camouflage shroud. He was fatally wounded this morning in the regiment territory, and died a few minutes before the helicopter took off.

The soldier was born in 1982, in Chelyabinsk. Our paths crossed completely by chance. And it was also by chance that I could see with my own eyes how an FSS officer, together with the chief of staff of the 119th regiment, shouted at his soldiers, who were bringing yet another body killed by "gunshot wounds," to take the bullets out of their automatic weapons for examination. It always happens that way, when soldiers are suspected of shooting their own comrade.

I was the only one surprised by this procedure, although there were about twenty officers standing near me. They seemed used to all this.

Sometimes it happens with the Americans, whom we Russians curse for all we're worth, that during their military exercises, a shell falls straight from their plane onto the territory of their military base. But the whole world shouts about this, and the generals mourn, and when the U.S. president finds out about the tragedy, he honors the memory of the killed soldiers and officers with a moment of silence at the first public opportunity and orders an investigation.

It works differently with us. Soldiers are killed. Bullets shot by their comrades are taken out of their bodies. What for? So that no one else can see the bullets. Then the military command hides both the bullets and the body from the relatives, wishing to bury the soldier secretly, along with the reasons for his death. If people find out some details later anyway, then it's purely by accident. In any case, if the truth seeps out somewhere, nothing follows. Neither headline TV news, nor newspaper reports, nor investigations. The families are guaranteed a total lack of information. Society couldn't care less. The president acts as if nothing had happened—he's not the American president, after all—he goes skiing in some nice Siberian village. The members of the Duma don't even think of raising their fat behinds out of their cushy Parliament chairs in memory of yet another soldier killed by his own fellows in Chechnya. The government doesn't take off their hats, but simply continues to divide the budget money among themselves, not the least bit concerned that just one of its monthly infusions into Chechnya for conducting "war operations" is fully sufficient to restore the ruins there. The General Staff doctors its weekly data about losses in the North Caucasus in the usual fashion. Yastrzhembsky travels to the West and talks about the militants' atrocities... A dead end. The nation has completely forgotten how to blush and experience any kind of discomfort before mothers whose sons have returned from Chechnya in zinc coffins. They've forgotten that such a country is very easy to defeat.

What else can I say? That Russia became Danila Vypov's second homeland when he was a child? The boy was born and grew up in Uzbekistan, but his family relocated to their historical motherland because of the impossibility for Russians to live any longer in the town of Shirin of the Syrdarin district. Danila grew into a young man in Volgograd, and was taken to defend his new motherland. And you already know the rest.

It's Hard to Get Cartridges in Mozhaisk

Unit 63354. Private Alyosha Klenin joined the army in fall 1999. He was one of the untested soldiers who were the first to go into battle in October, to Dagestan and Chechnya.

Alyosha was able to write a few pages home from there, and was then "forgotten" by his trustworthy commanders on a lonely mountain road next to a broken armored vehicle, with an absolutely predictable result. No one has seen the soldier Klenin since February 2000; he disappeared without a trace.

I have death certificate number 1151 in the name of Aleksei Vladimirovich Klenin. The date of issuance is September 10, 2001, nineteen months after Alyosha's grandfather Vladimir Alekseevich Shurupov, a resident of the Moscow suburban town of Mozhaisk, began his torturous path through the national bureaucratic hell. All he wanted was an answer to a simple question: Where was his grandson? The one he sent, alive and well, to the system that is called the army?

These nineteen months contained everything that you could imagine in the Fatherland. Tons of letters and complaints to all military and public prosecutor offices, including general and military offices, and to all conceivable government organizations, right up to the presidential administration.

The answer was mocking idiocy. It turned out that *no one* in the whole world noticed the soldier's disappearance except for his grandfather. For several months, the military unit regularly received allowances and uniforms for him, the private's name remained in the lists, and everything went on as though he were still in the column for the morning and evening roll calls.

Only after his grandfather's appeals, reinforced by inspections of the main military prosecutor's office and the presidential administration, did the nation's military bureaucratic machine, albeit with reluctant screeching, begin to move forward.

The burial of the remains sent to Vladimir Alekseevich Shurupov took place on September 11, on the day of the bombings in America. The corpse wasn't the one that had already been shown to him once at the 124th military court medical laboratory in Rostov-on-the-Don, for identification. Then there had been one bullet hole in the skull; now the grandfather found two.

"So what did you decide to do? Demand another medical examination?"

"No," he answered. "What's the use. I can't do it, I don't want to. I buried him as if it were Alyosha."

And he cried, quietly, silently, hopelessly.

I often meet loved ones of those who have died in the present Caucasus war—Chechens, Russians, Ukrainians, soldiers, officers, children, and adults. It's a whole orphaned army. They all have identical eyes, like Vladimir Alekseevich's right now—killed not just by grief over a loved one who will never return home, but also by an absolute disbelief that their nation cares about its citizens.

The grandfather continues: "I thought that everything would be done solemnly in the military fashion. The military committee would send a band, an honor guard company to fire a salute over the fresh grave. Nothing like that happened. They explained to me that cartridges and a band were allowed only for officers. Not for privates."

A Death in the Epoch of War Banditry; or, the Case of Colonel Budanov

All nations that have waged wars stumble painfully over the problem of war crimes and war criminals. What do you call these people who have been sent by their country to kill and who have exceeded their authority? Criminals or heroes? And does war justify everything?

*Russia has its own Calley.** His name is Yury Budanov. He's a colonel, commander of the 160th tank regiment of the Ministry of Defense, who holds two Orders for Bravery from the first and second Chechen wars, a representative of the Russian military elite. In the opinion of most, he's a fighter and martyr, persecuted for his "patriotic beliefs." From the point of view of a minority in the nation, he's a murderer, marauder, kidnapper, and rapist. The trial of Colonel Budanov shook the whole country. It turned out to be a graphic demonstration of the worst sides of our society, which is radically split by the second Chechen war. It's plagued by the unbelievable cynicism and lies of the Putin bureaucracy, the complete dependence of the court system on the Kremlin, and most important of all, the striking neo-Soviet renaissance.*

Colonel Budanov started fighting shortly after the beginning of the second Chechen war in September 1999. His regiment was thrown into the heaviest fighting, the storming of Grozny and Komsomolskoe. During the fierce siege of the village Duba-Yurt, Budanov lost many of his officers. And in February 2000, when the regiment was redeployed "for a break" to the edge of the village Tangi-Chu in the Urus-Martan district, the commander, who had taken these losses very hard, was sent home on leave to his family in the Baikal region. However, he didn't stay there for long. His wife found him to be a changed man, unbearable and even dangerous. He nearly threw his oldest son from the balcony, thinking that he had caused a bloody scratch on his little sister's hand. Only his wife hanging onto him from behind prevented infanticide. Cutting short his leave, Budanov returned to Chechnya, telling his surprised comrades in arms that "things were going badly" at home.

March 26, 2000 (the day of Putin's election victory) was also the second birthday of the colonel's favorite daughter, and the commander invited the officers to celebrate it. Toward evening everyone was rather drunk and eager to let off some steam. First they decided to

---

*Lieutenant William Calley led the platoon that killed between one hundred and three hundred people in the Vietnamese village of My Lai in 1968. Calley was sentenced to life at hard labor in 1971. His sentence was reduced first to twenty years, then to ten. He was released on bond in 1974 and paroled in 1975, after having been imprisoned for only three and a half years. *Trans.*

shoot at Tangi-Chu with heavy cannons, but the on-duty officer of the regiment, the commander of the reconnaissance company, Senior Lieutenant Roman Bagreev, refused to follow a criminal order. For that he was badly beaten up by Budanov, who, after knocking down the senior lieutenant, kicked his face with his boots. Budanov's chief of staff Lieutenant Colonel Ivan Fyodorov also joined in the beating. Then, at Budanov's command, they put Bagreev in a pit dug on the regiment base for arrested Chechens with his hands and feet bound and sprinkled lime on him from above, after which Fyodorov also urinated on him.

Around midnight, Budanov decided to go to Tangi-Chu. Later, during the interrogation, he said that he went there "to check information he had on the possible whereabouts of people who were members of illegal armed units," and made up a completely cock-and-bull story about his good friend Major Razmakhnin, supposedly killed by a "female sniper," whose picture he kept in his breast pocket. Elsa Kungayeva of Tangi-Chu was supposedly the one in the picture. So he went there to "arrest" her, to "pass her along to law enforcement officials." But no one has seen this picture—neither investigators, nor anyone in the trial later on. It isn't in his file.

So why did the drunken Budanov go to the village at night? "For a broad." That's how it's put, simply. He took military infantry car number 391 and orderlies Grigorev, Egorov, and Li-en-chou. The four of them drove right up to the Kungayevs' home. The day before, an informant had pointed it out to Budanov as a home with a beautiful woman in it. This informant had kidnapped people for ransom (he has now been convicted of that). The soldiers grabbed the eighteen-year-old Elsa, the eldest daughter of the Kungayevs, and wrapped her in a blanket right there in front of her four younger brothers and sisters. She screamed, but they loaded her into the landing compartment of the military infantry car, and took her to the regiment. There, they unloaded the blanket—Elsa's long hair was dragging along the ground— took her to Budanov's trailer, the mobile home where the colonel lived, and put her on the floor. Budanov ordered them to guard the trailer until he said otherwise. Other soldiers saw all this from the windows of their neighboring tents. Later, during the investigation, one of them, Viktor Koltsov, said the following: "On the night of March 26, 2000,

I was standing guard. When we changed shifts and I stopped by my tent, I saw Makarshanov, the stoker of the chief of staff. He said that 'the commander brought a girl again.'" It wasn't the first time, then?

Then the execution took place. Here is the objective description of it by the military prosecutors who wrote the indictment: "The girl began to scream, bite, and try to break loose... Budanov began to beat Kungayeva, punching and kicking her face and other parts of her body many times... After dragging her to the far corner of the trailer, he pushed her onto a bunk and started to strangle her with his right hand. She put up resistance, and as a result of the struggle, he tore up her clothes. These intentional actions by Budanov resulted in a broken bone under Kungayeva's tongue. She calmed down in about ten minutes; he checked her pulse, and there wasn't any... Budanov called Grigorev, Egorov, and Li-en-chou. They came in and saw the naked woman they had brought over in the far corner. Her face was blue. The bedspread they had wrapped the girl in when they took her from her home was lying on the floor. Her clothing lay in a pile on this bedspread. Budanov ordered them to take the body to the forest, in the area of the tank battalion, and secretly bury it... "

The soldiers Igor Grigorev, Artem Li-en-chou, and Aleksandr Egorov of the 160th regiment were the main witnesses in the Budanov case. They were orderlies of the colonel who served him, tidied his trailer, and accompanied him. On March 27, at dawn, they fulfilled this command too. They buried poor Elsa's body, which had been ripped to shreds, carefully covering the grave with sod. In summer 2000, the military prosecutor would make the decision to acquit these three soldiers as participants in a murder and kidnapping in exchange for evidence against themselves and therefore "in favor of" Budanov on the crucial question: "Was there a rape?" This case is muddled and in part illogical. The officers serving in Chechnya, from the highest to the lowest, supported Budanov en masse, but with the following reservation, which I heard several times in Chechnya: "That he killed her, we understand... She was a Chechen, which means a militant... But why would he 'dirty himself,' rape her?" Budanov understood these attitudes very well. Throughout the entire inquiry, Budanov, wishing to "save face," would categorically deny that it was he who dishonored the girl before he killed her. However, here's where things get difficult. In the criminal case, the report of the very first medical exam done after the opening of the secret grave showed all the signs of rape, either immediately before or right after the girl's death. Therefore, it wasn't clear what would be "better" for the officer's image: to be a rapist or a necrophiliac.

Thus both Budanov and the investigators needed evidence that could make two parallel lines meet. And then, one of the soldiers, Egorov, told the investigator that it was he who raped the Chechen before burying her, committing the outrage with "the handle of a sapper shovel" that he used later to dig the pit for the body. He was given amnesty for this. And it went on this way for two years. But by May 2002, several nuances of the political process (Putin's friends in the international antiterrorist alliance started pressuring him about the unrestrained, lawless officers in Chechnya), as well as previous serious mistakes Putin's circle made trying to clear Budanov suddenly came out into the open. This happened when a very talented twenty-eight-year-old Moscow lawyer named Stanislav Markelov, who tried the first cases in Russia on terrorism and political extremism, joined the proceedings. As a result, the military circuit court of the North Caucasus military district, presided over by the judge Viktor Kostin, switched sides completely, and decided to probe into details that it had not allowed itself to look into before. And then Egorov, who had returned home to the Irkutsk region long ago, couldn't stand it any longer. He was a man, not a machine, and he tormented himself over his lie, and everything he had seen in Chechnya as an eighteen- or nineteen-year-old. In June 2002, he publicly stated that he did not rape the girl with the sapper shovel, and that he had given that evidence under pressure. And if that is the case, then the rapist is an elite officer of the Russian army, crowned with glory and the most prestigious awards of his country.

However, back to March 27, 2000. The most surprising aspect of the Budanov case is that they even decided to arrest him. There are many such stories in the second Chechen war, but very few arrested officers. And Budanov would have come out smelling like a rose if it hadn't been for the absence from Chechnya on March 27 of his immediate supervisor, General Vladimir Shamanov, one of the toughest, cruelest commanders of the second Chechen war, who led the "Western" group of armies. According to army regulations, only a higher commander can give (or deny, if he chooses) permission for one of his officers to be arrested or for a military prosecutor to work on his base. On March 27, Shamanov, Budanov's friend and comrade in arms, was on leave, and his duties were being performed by Valery Gerasimov, a man who had managed to behave in a manner befitting an officer even under the circumstances of the second Chechen war. When the events from the previous night were reported to him, the general himself went to the regiment, let the officials from the prosecutor's office enter the base, and allowed Budanov to be arrested. Budanov tried to put up an armed resistance, but then shot himself in the foot and gave in. One of the investigators, Captain Aleksei Simukhin, who accompanied the arrested Budanov on his flight to the main military headquarters in Khankala, said that during the flight, the colonel kept asking him what he should do and say.

On March 28, Elsa Kungayeva's body was dug up, washed, and given back to her family. Budanov was already in jail. Soon a team of psychiatric experts pronounced him mentally competent and therefore subject to criminal investigation.

Then the whitewashing started. That's how the Kremlin wanted it. They realized that the "dictatorship of law" went too far in this case, and that if they didn't stop it, society would find out the truth about the war.

They decided to take the old, tried and true path of Soviet times. A second psychiatric examination was assigned for the colonel in the Serbsky Institute of Forensic Psychiatry in Moscow, infamous for its activity—fulfilling KGB orders—during the time of the struggle with dissidents. The chair of the Budanov commission was Tamara Pavlovna Pechernikova, a psychiatry professor with fifty-two years of experience. She was the one who signed the schizophrenic sentences for the most famous Soviet dissidents from the 1960s to the 1980s. These included people like Natalya Gorbanevskaya, the founder and first editor of the samizdat bulletin of human rights advocates *Chronicle of Current Events*, who wound up in a psychiatric prison for forced treatment from 1969 to 1972 following Pechernikova's diagnosis. She emigrated in 1975. Vyacheslav Igrunov was pronounced "mentally unsound" by Pechernikova and spent many years in forced treatment for distributing *The Gulag Archipelago*. He's been a deputy of the Duma for many years now, an associate of Grigory Yavlinsky's Apple Party, and director of the International Institute for Humanitarian Political Research. In addition, Pechernikova is fondly remembered by Vladimir Bukovsky, one of the most well-known Soviet dissidents, a political prisoner, journalist, writer, with a doctorate in biology. From 1963 to 1976, he found himself intermittently confined in prisons, camps, and special psychiatric hospitals for publishing documents with facts about "the activities of Pechernikova"—her misuse of psychiatry for political purposes—in the West. He was exchanged in 1976 for Luis Corvalán, the leader of the Chilean communists, and now lives in Great Britain. Pechernikova also testified for the prosecution (the KGB) in the trial against Aleksandr Ginzburg, a journalist and a member of the Moscow-Helsinki group, publisher of the samizdat poetry anthology *Sintaksis,* and the first director of the Public Foundation for the Support of Political Prisoners in the USSR and Their Families, set up by Solzhenitsyn with an honorarium from the publication of *The Gulag Archipelago.* He was given four terms for dissident activity, and in 1979 was exiled from the USSR in exchange for Soviet spies. He died in July 2002, in France.

And so today, as in the past, the commission under Pechernikova's leadership pronounced Budanov not responsible for his actions. And only for the moment of his perpetration of the crimes, which means he couldn't be punished for them. However, he was declared fully competent before and after it, which means that he has the right to return to military service. Of course, this was the only way to clear Budanov, and the government (the president, his administration, and the Ministry of Defense took interest in the trial) made full use of it.

However, this called forth a wave of public outrage, at least in Moscow and the European capitals. It became obvious that the repressive Soviet KGB psychiatric system had been retained and successfully adapted for democratic service. How could this be? Questions rained down on Putin. France and the German Bundestag were especially insistent. Was Pechernikova's appearance in the case of Budanov really by chance so many years after the fall of the communist system?

Then, the court in Rostov-on-the-Don, which seemed about to conclude with a not guilty verdict, suddenly fully altered the course of the choreographed trial in July 2002, at the Kremlin's orders. It canceled the reading of the sentence, expressed doubts about the veracity of Pechernikova's psychiatric report, ordered another, and left Budanov in custody.

The fact that Budanov is still not free is the most important event of our times. First, it is important for the army itself, which has clearly turned into a politically repressive institution in Chechnya. The army was waiting to see whether a precedent would be set in the trial at Rostov-on-the-Don. That is, "Could we do what Budanov did?" At the end of May 2002 (right when the report acquitting the colonel was made public), there was another series of kidnappings of young women followed by murder in the zone of the antiterrorist operation. At dawn of May 22 in Argun, for example, Svetlana Mudarova, a twenty-six-year-old teacher of the lower grades whom the soldiers found good-looking, was taken from her home at 125 Shalinskaya Street. Like Elsa Kungayeva, Budanov's victim, she was stuffed into an armored vehicle in her robe and slippers. For two days, the soldiers did everything they could to hide the place where they were holding the kidnapped teacher. On May 31, her disfigured corpse was thrown into the ruins of an Argun house.

Second, it is also crucial for the people of Chechnya, who eagerly await the outcome of the Budanov case. If the colonel wins, and not justice, it means that there is no hope that Chechnya will ever become a territory where Russian laws operate. It will remain a land under the heel of bandits.

WHO WANTS THIS WAR?

It may seem strange to some, but in the final analysis, the war has proved profitable for all participants. Everyone has found a niche. The mercenaries at the checkpoints get bribes of ten to twenty rubles around the clock. The generals in Moscow and Khankala use their war budget for personal gain. Officers of the middle ranks collect ransom for temporary hostages and corpses. Junior officers get to go marauding during the purges.

And as a team (soldiers and some of the militants), they take part in illegal oil and weapon trade.

And there are also ranks, awards, careers ...

An Oligarchy of Generals

We all know that generals steal from time to time and that oligarchs get rich on budgetary funds. The second Chechen war is unique in that the generals and the oligarchs are one and the same people.

What happens to businesses that lose billions? Very simple: they stop operating.

What happens to the Ministry of Defense if one of its subdivisions incurs billions in losses? The answer is surprising: absolutely nothing. Not only that, but its superiors cite its work as exemplary.

Here is a document that proves this. It came into being when the Ministry of Defense tallied up its results for 2001.

DECISION OF THE ECONOMIC COUNCIL UNDER THE HEAD OF CONSTRUCTION AND BILLETING OF TROOPS AND DEPUTY MINISTER OF DEFENSE OF THE RUSSIAN FEDERATION ABOUT THE BALANCE COMMISSION REPORT: On the results of the financial and economic activity of enterprises and organizations of the Main Department of Special Construction (MDSC) of the Russian Ministry of Defense for 2000.

Here are a few quotes from it:

According to the report from the head of the Main Department of
Special Construction of the Russian Ministry of Defense,
Lieutenant General A. V. Grebenyuk, and an analysis of the
bookkeeping accounts and materials, the Economic Council states
that . . . indicators of the effectiveness of financial and economic
activity are lower than the permissible rates. The structure of the
monetary balance of enterprises and organizations remains
unsatisfactory, and its solvency has decreased. A loss of 1,116
million rubles was incurred for the period covered . . .

The Economic Council has decided the following:

1. To recognize the financial and economic activity of the state
   unitary enterprises of the MDSC of the Russian Ministry of
   Defense for 2000 as satisfactory.
2. To recommend that the leadership of the MDSC of the Russian
   Ministry of Defense conduct special training courses at Base
   766 of the Department of Industrial Technological Supplies to
   spread the successful example in the organization of financial
   and economic work . . .

The indicators of financial-economic activity are "lower than the
permissible rates," yet they are conducting training courses to "spread
the successful example"?

Here some preliminary explanations are needed.

Once the army had what were called construction troops, but now,
after the 1997 army reform, they're simply military construction units.
At that time, four powerful main departments in the Ministry of
Defense were eliminated, leaving just one: the Russian Military Construction Complex (MCC). Its head is Aleksandr Davydovich Kosovan.
By rank, he's a colonel general. By experience, he's a rear officer
who has served in that field for his whole commissioned career. By
duty, he's a deputy minister of defense and head of construction and
billeting for troops and supervisor of the economic council, whose
strange decision inspired my desire to find out what is going on in the
MCC.

What is the MDSC, which incurred such unbelievable losses? Structurally, under Colonel General Kosovan, it is Department No. 1 and in general the best-known in the sphere of military construction.

The domain of the MDSC includes space centers, rocket silos, and secret military sites. However, there is much more. The head of the MDSC is Lieutenant General Anatoly Grebenyuk, Colonel General Kosovan's second in command in the MCC. The chain of command in the MCC works so that Kosovan assigns the main role in all affairs to the MDSC, and the MDSC under Grebenyuk's leadership is fully controlled by Kosovan.

This means that all financial streams to and from the MCC obey the signature of just one man: Colonel General Kosovan. And the primary recipient of these financial streams is the MDSC.

The Kosovan-Grebenyuk partnership controls all budget operations. Besides the MDSC, Kosovan commands the Main Billeting and Management Department (MBMD), which occupies a subordinate position but is also very important in the overall scheme. Let's examine this scheme as an example of the fulfillment of extremely profitable, sought-after state defense orders of 2000 that Kosovan's departments received. It is an order for construction work in Chechnya, which is under the control of the highest government officials, is paid for correspondingly, and is therefore lucrative. It includes construction of permanent garrisons and sites for troop deployment in the Khankala military headquarters, billeting for the 42d motorized rifle division, building of mobile barracks, and so on.

Kosovan designated the MBMD as a distributor of Chechen work and, naturally, a budget recipient of the state defense orders in Chechnya. And the MDSC is the executor. So the money goes from the MBMD to the MDSC. Both departments are self-sufficient judicial entities, so-called state unitary enterprises, which are a serious deformity of our transitional economy. State unitary enterprises, many of which are attached to various government departments and official structures, function today like commercial entities, but they get their profits using basic state funds, in this case from the Ministry of Defense.

However, the money does not stop at the MDSC. According to Colonel General Kosovan's decision—and remember, all financial streams of the MCC are controlled by him—most of the "Chechen" money is sent to another department: the Main Department of Construction Industry (MDCI), a private firm. It is a shareholder's company. And until 1997, when, you will recall, there was a reform of the armed forces, it was simply one of the construction departments of the Ministry of Defense. It became a private company in 1997, but didn't wander far from home (the ministry); it still lives off the fat of the land.

As everyone knows, the success of Russian-style business depends on its ability to suck money from the budget. In fact, this is a portrait of today's MDCI. It is successful because it works in concord with the plans of the official budget receiver, performing an important function of the budget rotation. Successful for itself, naturally.

The giant, unbelievable losses, our starting point, are generated by the MDCI in the following manner: Colonel General Kosovan decided to involve the department in buying up construction materials, equipment, and property for "Chechen" military construction. According to the testimony of enraged military economists of the MBMD, deprived of funding as a result of such decisions of Kosovan, the MDCI buys all materials at inflated prices from certain firms. For example, instead of getting sand for construction from the nearby Stavropol district, they ship it in from Moscow suburbs, inflating the prices. Concrete comes from territories very far from the North Caucasus, such as Perm. Toilets are allegedly from Italy, ceramic tiles from Spain.

But don't imagine that Italian toilets are installed in the Chechen village of Kalinovskaya, where the 42d division headquarters were erected by Kosovan's people. The toilets are still local. Only the price is Italian.

The situation is the same with concrete slabs, sand, and cement. And even the smallest jacking up of prices of construction materials— up to 10 percent—yields an exorbitant loss, more than 25 percent. The profit goes to the MDCI, and the beloved Motherland is saddled with the losses.

Today, in the military-construction complex, everything revolves around Deputy Minister of Defense Kosovan. "With the aim of controlling expenditures of budgetary resources," he signs all financial documents himself. He also heads the control commission, supervising the trinity of the MDCI, the MDSC, and the MBMD. He is the one who makes the decisions, spends the money, and writes the reports. That's how it works: over a billion in losses, but the work is declared satisfactory.

The MDSC and the MDCI do not merely flood the Ministry of Defense with their costly services. Today in Chechnya, they erect barracks and headquarters for units of Ministry of the Interior troops and border troops. This means that Colonel General Kosovan and the "judicial entities" accompanying him monopolize the "Chechen" military construction market, carrying out a transfer of budgetary money, allocated to the Ministry of Defense, the Ministry of the Interior, and the Federal Border Services, directly to commercial structures, and also to someone's pockets.

Once again, the oligarchs are getting rich. And this is the result: the continuation of the Chechen war and the "blowing up" by militants of newly erected sites is extraordinarily profitable both to these oligarchs and to the generals of the national military construction elite. For something so profitable, they will fight as long as they can in Chechnya, until the treasury collapses.

Let's get into the specifics. What percentage of these losses is artificial, from inflating prices? And what percentage is real?

Colonel Fyodor Koraban, Colonel General Kosovan's deputy for economic questions, expressed the MCC position unequivocally. The losses don't depend on their department; they are all fines and penalties for nonpayments to the budget, arising in connection with budget debts to the MDSC for unpaid work they have done. And what else could the colonel say?

However, military economists working in the MBMD and feeling left out (money for Chechnya only passes through them to the semi-commercial MDSC and the fully commercial MDCI) are sure that the losses are artificial, the result of intentional actions by Deputy Minister Kosovan.

Who could resist the chance to be a general, wear fancy epaulettes, accumulate years of service, receive field money, and operate a business at the same time? Not on the side, but right at your workplace! The businessman serves his business interests, and the most important thing for him is to attain a surplus. A successful businessman is willing to make many transgressions in the interest of higher profits. An officer, though, serves the interests of his nation. But what if you're both an officer and a businessman? Who do you serve then? After all, the interests of a private business and a nation quite often don't coincide.

By allowing government officials, and high-ranking officers at that, to constantly change their personae, one of which is completely commercial, the government signed its budget's death warrant. Basic government funds in this case are used in such a way as to necessarily cause losses. Profits go into the pockets of private individuals, further exposing the evil nature of this economic scheme.

Miracle Fields

Whenever a conversation touches upon the reason for the Chechen war, most people say it's about oil. His Royal Majesty the Chechen Pipe and Their Royal Majesties the Chechen Wells have been the unquestioned rulers of hundreds of thousands of people for the past ten years. In Chechnya, whoever owns a well is in the right. Those who fought for Dudayev later received wells from him as a present. Those who were loyal to Maskhadov own the wells that he gave them, which is still a tradition today. This Chechen pie is being greedily divided under supervision of the conquerors, the Federal forces.

On the far edge of Argun, about three miles from the road to Grozny, is the modest entrance to the local collective farm. An inconspicuous road leads to the fields. There is a tractor in the distance, to divert the curious. Someone is even gathering something. Not a single soldier or checkpoint in sight.

A man who looks like a farm guard raises and lowers a rope with red flags on it. Near his shabby hut a simple, red beaten-up Zhiguli is parked. There is nothing unusual about all this, except that our car is being silently followed by four attentive pairs of eyes belonging to the people in the Zhiguli.

We know too that we're not going to a picnic. The former collective farm road through old pear trees leads right to the local "gold mines." The Argun miracle oil fields are located a little over a mile down this bad road. The dug-up main oil pipe, known simply as "the Pipe," is all studded with illegal cuts. Chechen oil flows nonstop from holes of various caliber, from tiny ones, probably made by bullets, and from bigger ones. It is collected in natural pits of various widths and indeterminable depths: "barns," as the locals call them. This is where the initial decontamination and refining of the stolen oil takes place.

One can witness the whole robbery procedure on the farm's miracle field. There are old barns, now dry and resting. In the distance are newly dug pits, also empty for now. It looks like someone was digging here last night. The new barns need a few days for the earth to harden before they will be included in the general chain. And here are the main pits, filled with bright green oil. This means the oil is all "finished," and soon an oil truck will arrive to take it away. But we won't be here to witness that. The farm guard has given us only ten minutes to tour the fields. The silence of the wilderness that surrounds the mysterious pits is broken by helicopters. They fly back and forth over the exposed Pipe, and our knowledgeable guides advise us to leave. The helicopter will just shoot, without asking why we are examining the well. Too much money is involved in this game, and it is easier to kill than to ask questions.

We drive a few hundred feet before passing the local "caretakers," so-called Chechen policemen in a white Jeep without a license plate, but of course armed with automatic weapons. The car doors are already open, and the soldiers are ready to shoot. They were, no doubt, summoned by the guard, who sent the red Zhiguli to fetch them quickly.

Thankfully, the "police" miraculously let us go, and we speed past the guard, who is staring at as, wondering how on earth we can still be alive.

Such miracle fields are scattered all over Chechnya, covering half of its territory. The modern history of the Chechen oil is, first and foremost, the history of oil robbery. You can take as much oil as you want, as much as you are capable of dealing with from the Pipe "on the side." Illegal oil production and refining are flourishing.

However, the main battle is fought not for the miracle fields but for the wells. Perhaps this was why they did not kill us for our tour of the Argun collective farm. All this is just peanuts, the property of the lower classes.

According to official records, the Fuel and Energy Complex of the Republic (FEC) consists of nine branches belonging to the state:

Oil and Gas Production

Oil and Chemical Refining

Oil Production Support

Oil Transportation

Gas Industry (gasification, transportation, use)

The Energy Branch

Ecological Technologies

Solid Fuel

The Research Institute for Oil and Gas.

The main thing about this list is that from the point of view of the state treasury the FEC does not exist at all. But at the same time, everything works. This means that the entire FEC has turned illegal. The Pipe has been divided among numerous criminal groups whose interests are defended by the Chechen police and the Feds.

Those in charge of guarding the nonfunctioning FEC enterprises are also getting richer, by robbing it at a rapid clip. Although all the oil refineries in Chechnya are half-destroyed, there is still a lot left to be robbed. Massive dismantling of the equipment by factory guards is constantly taking place. It usually happens during the night, after curfew, when the checkpoints have orders to shoot at every moving object without warning. Civilian KAMAZ trucks with Chechen license plates, loaded with what was left of the refineries' equipment, move toward Osetia and the Stavropol region. The columns carrying goods stolen from the state are usually guarded by Federal mercenaries, who do not care how they make their living.

These synergies are well organized: the Feds and the Chechen thieves have formed solid criminal gangs. Neither the representatives of the Chechen administration responsible for the FEC nor the soldiers of other military departments dare challenge these new bandit units. For example, the companies of the Grozny City Military Command that are supposed to guard all enterprises on their territory are afraid of being accidentally shot, which has already happened a few times.

Naturally, the Chechen officials have tried to launch the industry and make it work within the framework of the law. But this turned out to be so difficult that the government quickly gave up and put the whole thing off until the war approaches its end. But the end hasn't come.

The Tsotsan-Yurt Fire

Although on paper all wells in Chechnya today belong to the state, they actually belong to someone else. Depending on their real owner, the wells can be of two types: burning and normal. Some wells suddenly start to burn or stop burning, and others are always stable.

If nothing bad happens to a well, that means that its owner is a rich, respected man who keeps his own set of guards, and no one challenges his ownership. Other wells are a subject of fierce fighting, involving firearms.

If you went from Gudermes east toward the Kurchaloi region, Kadyrov's birthplace, you would understand right away where the real capital of the local oil market is. Generally, there is no road anyway in Chechnya where you can't buy some kind of self-made gas, but in the Kurchaloi region literally every house and every bend in the road sports an oil stand. The oil carriers are parked in practically every yard.

I'm driving along an empty road toward a raging fire ahead. This is what they officially call Well Seven, on the outskirts of the village of Tsotsan-Yurt. The closer I get to the well, the more oil sellers I see along the road in the regional center Kurchaloi, and in the mountain village of Novaya Zhizn. It is obvious that the market everywhere is flooded with oil products and that the supply is many times greater than the demand.

Finally, the noise, comparable to the roar of a jet, becomes unbearable. Any reasonable person would agree that you can't live nearby. Yet the neighboring houses are occupied by families with kids. They are poor and have nowhere to move to, even temporarily.

Burning wells are the domain of bandit units that cannot control a well by themselves. When it becomes obvious that a well owner is not strong enough (meaning he doesn't have enough guards), he lights up his well himself (not literally, of course) so that no one can take it from him. Nobody here is bothered by the fact that there are people living nearby whose health could be affected by the fire or that kids grow up just hundreds of feet away.

Usually, the owners pay the Feds to blow up the wells. This is a good arrangement, because the Feds won't capture "their own." The neighboring villagers see how it is done, how the Feds work for the Chechen criminals they supposedly came to exterminate. After the deed is done, the owner sets up a new miracle field a few hundred feet from the fire, like the one we saw in Argun. If official firefighters show up to put out the fire, the local residents know that the well has a new owner, another bandit who has taken or bought it from the old one and summoned the firefighters, which in the local market costs much more than to arrange an explosion.

According to statistics, in October and November of 1999, during the fierce fighting, there were only three burning wells in Chechnya. But when the front moved into the mountains and it was time to divide the property, there were eleven and then eighteen burning wells. By the summer of 2000, the number rose to thirty-four. Then it went down a little and froze somewhere between twenty-two and twenty-five—a sign of stability and good working relations among the partners in the illegal market. Every day, the burning wells release up to six thousand tons of oil into the atmosphere, worth a total of about a million dollars. You can only imagine how many dozens or maybe hundreds of millions of dollars go into the pockets of criminals, if they do not care about losing this million. The excess profits of the illegal Chechen oil business are also clear from the fact that all the wells and self-made small oil refineries are surrounded by fields of burnt black oil. After gas extraction, the black oil remaining in cisterns costs three thousand rubles a ton. But in Chechnya, nobody is interested in black oil. They either pitilessly pour it down into the ground or burn it. Naturally, the thieves do not care about the ecological damage—that's not their style.

The road leading from Well Seven is littered with huge home-refining devices consisting of two cisterns, a fire under one of them, and a few pipes. The soldiers regularly attack the villagers' shaky oil refineries. They shoot, explode, and destroy them. If the owner gives them money, they leave. The ransom stands at five to ten thousand rubles.

And in the meantime, positive reports are submitted to the general staff in Moscow about yet another operation against an illegal oil business in Chechnya. The military ministers inform the public about the latest success in their struggle against international terrorism.

But what is really going on? Even while destroying the refineries, the Feds don't touch the source of the criminal activities, the wells. They fight the result but not the cause. Perhaps this is because they want it to remain there? Because someone is making money on it too?

If the soldiers were given a firm order to set up checkpoints around each well and let in only Grozny Oil Industry employees, believe me, that would be the case. The oil interests of the military are also evident from the fact that there were never any battles at villages near wells. These villages do not lie in ruins. They are protected by both sides, the militants and the Feds. The latter come here with purges only when residents start protesting en masse against the barbaric ways of the criminal oil groups.

For example, there was a time when Ali Abuev, the former head of the Tsotsan-Yurt administration, was considered the leader of the anticriminal movement in the village. He was taken during the last purge. Before he was arrested, the village men he led sealed the well with a cistern sawed in half. Ali was not a Wahhabi or a militant; he was not for Russia or for Kadyrov. He was his own man, a defender of his village's right to lead a normal life, a brave, decent man.

But if you listen to the Feds, they will tell you that Ali was "Khattab's friend" and an enemy of Moscow. Therefore, he will stay in jail for as long as the Chechen war lasts. When you ask for proof, they tell you they have their special agents' reports. That is, the reports of the bastards who opposed Ali's struggle.

After Ali was arrested, the well was set on fire, cuts were made in the Pipe, pits were dug around it, and oil refineries were set up. Life in Tsotsan-Yurt went back to its illegal ways.

Step Right Up, Don't Be Stingy

The final link in the illegal chain of the Chechen FEC is the famous oil exchange. It was set up near the Islam Café at the Tsotsan-Yurt exit back in the prewar Maskhadov days and is still in business. This is a trading point, where they bring oil and oil products to sell to wholesalers. Everything happens right in front of the checkpoint, a few hundred feet away from the exchange.

Its existence would normally be the sign of a well-developed market economy. However, given the present situation in Chechnya, it is more a symptom of a well-structured illegal business. The jack-of-all-trades who produced, refined, and sold oil is a thing of the past. Now there are people who control the Pipe cuts, collect oil in the barn, and then take it away. Someone else brings the oil to the exchange for sale. A third party takes it from there to the refineries. A fourth is concerned only with refining. Finally, there are wholesalers of the final product. Some of them prefer to do their business under the close watch of a nearby checkpoint; others bring the oil for sale to small traders. This is a profitable but dangerous business, since every village has its own racketeers who do not necessarily all belong to one gang, which means you have to pay them all separately.

As a rule, this involves greasing the palms of at least three groups of people: those at the checkpoint at the entrance to the village, the interior village criminals who live off the wholesalers, and the soldiers of different units guarding the exit checkpoint. The amount of the customs tax varies, depending on how close the village is to the battle site, and how big it is (i.e., how many potential sellers it could house).

Who Is Getting Rich?

One of the newly appointed Chechen officials, who demanded that I not reveal his name under any circumstances, or better yet, just forget the whole thing, said that "every night thousands of tons of oil and oil products are being taken out of Chechnya, but we can't afford to buy office supplies."

Chechnya is currently involved in a never-ending bloody division of oil wells and miracle fields, but they aren't making the republic one kopeck. It lacks the means to do anything: restore its industries, build new housing for the homeless. Its oil serves everyone but the republic itself. The crisis becomes even worse because the economic chaos in Chechnya was artificially created and is now being carefully promoted by Moscow. There are still no commercial banks here, no legal sources of financing. All the oil money is kept inside the mattress or outside Chechnya. All efforts to establish a legal financial system are cut short by the open sabotage of higher Federal officials. It is in Moscow's interests for banks, tax inspections, and properly functioning courts and civil prosecutors' offices to be absent in Chechnya for as long as possible. They want the oil dividends to go in the direction most profitable for Moscow and for there to be no state barriers that could alter this direction in favor of the treasury.

Clearly, the situation described above requires two conditions to exist. First, there needs be a protective umbrella (this is provided by the Feds). Second, the officially appointed organs for oil management in Chechnya must be prevented from functioning (this is also arranged).

If you are told that the illegal oil business is rooted in the temporary problems of the change in power and the strengthening of a new Chechen government, do not believe it. The root of the problem is sabotage, the stubborn unwillingness of Moscow—the government, the high state officials, and the general staff—to put things in order.

The only thing Moscow demands of Chechnya is to maintain the lack of order. The bedlam here is commercially profitable, since controlled chaos brings much higher dividends.

That is why oil carriers drive on day and night, with soldiers at the checkpoints saluting them. This is what the whole war is about. Thousands of lives have already been sacrificed in the struggle for ownership of oil wells and the Pipe. Still more will die in the course of the Chechen oil revolution. The price of this problem stands at millions of dollars.

Boys and Girls

On the surface, everything looks good. A train route from Gudermes to Moscow has been launched. The railway hospital has opened a fully equipped surgical ward for the first time since the beginning of the war. New tractors have been purchased for the spring field work—this hadn't happened since 1994. Chechnya has received its own budget, just like all the other Russian regions; this too is for the first time in ten years. The first commercial bank has been registered—it is not functioning yet, but at least it is registered. Moscow has allocated funds for "budget" salaries for 2000 and 2001. The new Chechen government has a whole list of achievements to its credit, aiming at peace for its war-weary people.

And yet, all this progress is not so much due to as in spite of the situation. Often, the real saboteurs of peaceful living are none other than the army of new Chechen officials of the regional and city administrations, who got their positions via personal connections and do not want to work. They openly desire that the war's disorder continue as long as possible. The essence of their life is fraud, deceit, and selling everything for profit, even what should never be sold.

According to reports, the Kurchaloi foster home for orphans has been open since April 15, 2001. If it is open, then orphans should live here, right?

On April 20, 2001, the doors of the former kindergarten on Lenin Street in Kurchaloi, where the foster home is located, were closed. The people who answered our knock sent someone to get Ibrahim Yakhyayev, whom they called the director. Supposedly, he is a highly qualified person, with twenty-three years of teaching experience. Soon Yakhyayev appears. We introduce ourselves and engage in a very strange conversation that sounds as if it were between a deaf person and a mute.

"Where are the children?"

"In their homes."

"Why do they need a foster home if they have their own homes?"

The director blinks and keeps silent, as if he does not understand what I'm asking him.

"Could you please show me the list of orphans who have been living here since April 15?"

"Here it is."

"But it doesn't have any of the kids' current addresses."

"Why do you need addresses?"

"I want to meet the orphans who are in the care of the state."

The director blinks again, staring at the ceiling like a failing student who can't wait for the bell to ring and the class to end, and is trying to make the time pass somehow. He looks at his assistants, and they start singing the same old tune: "You'd better leave right now—you're not safe. There are bandits here. The Feds come all the time. They might kill you."

"Could you please find some of the kids from this list now and bring them here?"

"What for?"

"I need to see them!"

After a long wait, they finally bring three very young girls. At first, the director tries to tell me that they don't speak any Russian. But the girls are too small and naïve to lie like adults, and it turns out very quickly that they do speak Russian. I hesitate, not knowing how to ask the orphans what happened with their moms and dads. I don't want to open up old wounds. When I finally ask, the girls start smiling happily. It turns out that their mothers are alive and well.

"Where do you live?"

"At home. With our grandma and grandpa."

Yakhyayev doesn't even bat an eye, as if this is exactly the way it should be.

"Don't you think this is strange?"

He silently shrugs his shoulders.

"And where is the equipment paid from the state budget and allocated to you, as the forms say, on February 10 and 13?"

"At the warehouse."

"Let's go there and have a look."

"It's at my home."

"The warehouse is at your home?"

"It's safer that way, no one will steal it."

"All right, let's go to your home."

At this moment a completely out-of-place, content smile appears on the director's face.

"Impossible!" he says happily, feeling that he has won and that the pesky people will have to leave now empty-handed.

But I insist. It turns out that the director's home is quite far from here, in the village of Geldeken, where a purge is going on now, and this saves his house from inspection. His house would have to be the size of an aviation hangar, since, according to the documents, 15 beds (full beds, judging by the price), 26 dinner tables, 40 night stands, 48 cushioned chairs, 40 quilts, bedspreads, and mattresses, 100 sets of bed sheets, 40 pillows, 150 towels, and many other items should be hidden there.

The director smiles with relief. He has been saved by the soldiers of the Smolensk OMON who guard the checkpoint at the entrance to Geldeken. After he explains something to them quietly, they embrace him in a brotherly manner and don't let any strangers into the village.

This is how things are done all over Chechnya. The officials' interest in the war is one of the biggest reasons for its continuation. The Khankala generals (the North Caucasian United Group of Armies) and the general staff in Moscow are equally interested in the war continuing. Middle-rank officers stationed at the edge of Chechen villages make friends with minor local officials; neither of them want anyone to meddle in their small but gainful domain. There is a perfect local method to do that: "special operations," or unauthorized purges, that you can launch whenever a village needs to be closed.

Nobody knows where the orphans' tables and beds are, and I'm afraid they never will. There is one other characteristic detail in the Kurchaloi foster home story. The reason the indefatigable Yakhyayev was appointed director is that he is a protégé of Kadyrov. They are either close friends or distant relatives. That is precisely how most appointments are done in Chechnya these days. And if you are given a post, you have to share whatever you happen to come across—dinner tables, bed sheets, blankets.

Even children's aid, a pitiful fifty-eight rubles and a few kopecks, is dispensed in the same manner in Chechnya, by the fifty-fifty method. As long as you give one half to an official by the budget trough, you can have the other half. If you don't want to share, off you go. The fifty-fifty business is flourishing to an amazing extent. Any official connected with the budget funds is supposed to share with other influential Chechens. So the cynical fifty-fifty rule quickly spreads to children's aid, invalids' prosthetics, and medicine for hospitals, where half goes to the hospital and half is sold in the market.

The overwhelming majority of the new Chechen officials, who arose in close contact with the military, strive to keep things in the "no war or peace" zone. Here, everything is allowed under threat of violence: illegal oil businesses, the fifty-fifty rule, humanitarian aid being sold in the markets, medicine that the republic got for free appearing in private drugstores belonging to Ministry of Health officials and their relatives.

This is simply sabotage—blatant, shameless stealing. The war conditions have made it very easy to silence anyone who is unwilling to participate, anyone too scrupulous. All you have to do is inform the FSS on them. Go to any village, and they will tell you who the local informer is and why. The soldiers and many civilians are depraved by the war to the utmost degree. They have formed a lethal combination: the military Chechnya ruled by the fist, zindan,* and submachine gun has fused with the ostensibly peaceful Chechnya where they prefer fraud, nepotism, and lack of control.

Westernizers and Easternizers

The army is gradually entering the third fall of the war and will soon greet its third winter in the trenches. Why is this such a long war? Who opposes the army in Chechnya? What is going on among the forces opposing the Federal soldiers? What do the so-called field commanders want? And if most of them have run to neighboring states to "prepare for the future struggle," cynically abandoning those of their people who cannot afford to flee, then who fights against the Feds? And what is their aim?

The Old Guard

The people known as Chechen field commanders can now be called this only conditionally. Many high-ranking, famous brigadier generals have turned into John Does surrounded by their own guard, whose goal is to protect their bosses, not to wage war.

"Detachments" of these field commanders are hardly capable of real fighting. However, one should not underestimate the danger of the situation either. It's true that some of the former large militant units barely exist today, but this does not mean they cannot expand again if the need arises. Brigadier generals have no troops today, but tomorrow they could turn into lieutenants with companies under their command.

---

*A zindan is traditionally a prison in Persia or nearby countries; the word now refers to a hole in the ground where prisoners are kept as part of Chechen antiterrorist operations. *Trans.*

We will discuss the mechanism of this growth later. Now, let's talk about some people, the field commanders of the first draft— Dudayev's—who fought for the independence of Ichkeria. First and foremost, they are Maskhadov, Gelayev, Arsanov,* Basayev, and Khattab.

In the fall of 1999, Chechen roads were flooded with torrents of refugees leaving the republic. Grozny was preparing for an attack. Detachments calling themselves resistance units were passing through the villages, after which the residents were shelled and bombed. At that time, Maskhadov could at least clearly formulate his thoughts about the situation. Now he always chooses silence, leaving his people wondering. Has Maskhadov forgotten about his suffering people? Has he betrayed them? Or does he simply have nothing to say?

There are serious reasons for this strange behavior. In the fourth year of the war, Maskhadov is no longer commander in chief, even though he is a legitimate president, as he knows very well. So what can he say? All the former field commanders are on different pages now; each has his own views.

Dissent among them was evident even in the beginning of this war. One might recall Maskhadov's infamous violent curses when he found out about Basayev's march to Dagestan and Basayev's insolent response. Now things are even worse. The gap between most of the commanders who are still alive is so wide that many of them are incapable of sitting at the same table. No matter how you pair them—Maskhadov and Basayev, Gelayev and Maskhadov, Arsanov and Basayev—they all viciously hate each other. Each of them always suspects the other of having FSS ties. The only "friendly" connection was between Khattab and Basayev, but the basis for their heartfelt mésalliance was money and "legitimacy." Basayev needed Khattab's money, which he can now get from whoever replaces him. Khattab needed Basayev's involvement in at least some sort of Chechen reality, since he lacked any other way to achieve this.

Thus, there is a schism within the "other side." Rumors regularly presented by some media about field commanders supposedly getting

---

*Vakha Arsanov: The vice premier of the Chechen Republic of Ichkeria during the time of Maskhadov (1997–1999).

together "to develop a unified strategy and tactic" are nothing but lies. The sources of this disinformation are, first, the FSS, who need to justify their own existence again and again, and, second, field commanders who are eager to raise their rating and image by any means.

Here is a secondary but important subject: the interests of the secret services are intricately interwoven with those of their opponents. The main question is along which lines the split lies and what it means for the country and the world.

Basayev versus Maskhadov

It would be wrong to think that field commanders disagree because of their bad attitudes or the difficult conditions of life in the mountains. The split among them is much more serious and principled—it concerns their views on the future of Chechnya. And on sources of financing, of course.

Some of the field commanders might be provisionally called "Westernizers," others "Easternizers" or "Arabs." The "Westernizers" mostly look hopefully toward Europe and the rest of the Western world. They strive to adapt European laws of social life, based on human rights in their traditional Western interpretation, to Chechnya. They appeal to the Council of Europe and international human rights organizations. Their strategic aim is to hold an international trial of war criminals and to collect material for a future court investigation, along the lines of the one steamrolling the former Yugoslavian leader Milosevic.

The main figure on this side is Maskhadov. His views are partially shared by Gelayev (which does not prevent them from hating each other) and Arsanov. However, the latter is a Westernizer out of spite, not because of a European orientation but because of his dislike of Wahhabism and Khattab's pro-Arabic stance. Arsanov supports future development of specifically Chechen ways of life, and the imported Islamic extremists, with their own agenda, cannot meet his approval.

The other side of the Chechen military and political elite, which the Feds are searching for and cannot find, is the "Easternizers." Their plans are first and foremost connected with the Arab Middle East. They are sure that further Islamization of Chechnya according to the Arab example and the inevitable repudiation of old Chechen traditions will be for the best: it will strengthen the people's morals and bring significant Middle Eastern and Arab-African funds into the ruined republic.

The most famous and ardent representatives of this clan are Basayev and Khattab. Khattab is simply a barbarian, and that's it. Basayev, though, is capable of anything for money; this has been no secret to anyone for a long time, both within his inner circle and outside of it.

Movladi Udugov provides the final touch to this picture of the Easternizer wing. He is the ideologue. Long ago, after winning the first Chechen information war, the cynical Udugov emigrated from Chechnya to become a legal resident of Qatar, where he manages the well-known Internet site kavkaz.org. If nothing else, the site gives you a few good laughs because of its Soviet propaganda style, now nearly forgotten. One interesting detail that sheds some light on the acuteness of the disagreement between the Westernizers and the Easternizers: Basayev's biography at this site has been cleansed of any mention of the role of Maskhadov in the past ten years of Chechen history, leaving Basayev as the one and indisputable leader of the Chechen people.

While the commanding elite is being torn by conflict, the third force is the one that really wages the war, planting mines, blowing things up, and ensuring an endless stream of funeral notices.

Blood Avengers

The third force of the Chechen military and political makeup is composed of numerous small detachments and groups that became militant in the course of the war to carry out their own and, usually, specific plans of revenge for their killed or missing relatives. There is only one principle guiding the birth of these fighters: the more people get humiliated and hurt, the more units are formed.

The essence of their activities is best described in modern Khankala terms: "point hits" and "address purges." These are designed to kill those who have destroyed their families. Members of these small units do not want to coordinate their actions to any serious degree; nor do they require a head command. They are independent. They wage a personal war against their enemies according to personal rules that are hard to understand, control, and predict, unlike, to a certain extent, Basayev and Khattab's or even Maskhadov, Arsanov, and Gelayev's.

The third force has its own commanders, of course. But their names don't mean anything to anyone. These units were born in the war, recruiting from Chechens who never thought of fighting before and were even hoping for the Russian troops to come and liberate them from the Wahhabis. It was the methods that the Feds chose for their antiterrorist operation that compelled them to take a different road. Also, most of these units will cease to exist as soon as their personal plans are fulfilled. Many already have. Of course, their places have been taken by others who have found out who killed their sons, brothers, and fathers.

How does the third force get its weapons and money? Clearly, unlike Khattab and Basayev's detachments, it doesn't get them from abroad.

Small units are supported mostly by the army inside Chechnya—they do the Feds favors and participate in their commercial projects. For example, they help the Feds escort the night routes of oil carriers and trucks with nonferrous metal. Sometimes, when their interests coincide, they take on completely confidential assignments. For example, one detachment was set up by members of one of the most influential families in Chechnya to execute a hit on Gelayev and his people in response to their insidious deceit and subsequent shooting of several members of this family in Kurchaloi. Now these militants are under the auspices of a Main Intelligence Department (MID) unit deployed in the Staropromyslovsky district of Grozny. They live in its barracks and are supplied with food and arms. The reason for this merger is one of the goals of the MID unit—eliminating Gelayev and his people. For that, you can't find better allies than these blood avengers.

Still, it is simply not true that these militants are in the service of the MID. You can say, though, that today in Chechnya, a club, united by a common interest, has been formed along the lines of the Afghan one: a heavily armed conglomerate of "avengers" and Feds. Each party needs and supports the other materially, despite the fact that they officially stand on opposing sides of the unseen front.

Of course, there is a more precise description of the situation: secret financing of the Chechen civil war in connection with antiterrorist needs. Any secret service in the world would verify that it is much better to destroy the enemy by someone else's hands than your own.

This idyllic coexistence is, of course, quite unique in Chechnya. It does not happen too often, since most of the third force units search for their enemies among the Feds. When they find them, they launch attacks on night transports, set up mines and explosions, and resort to kamikaze hits. Officially, these actions are attributed to Basayev's or Gelayev's people, but the fact that it is the third force's doing just can't be ignored anymore. The question is which side it will join.

Judging by my personal meetings with these people, I think that most of the present small detachments and groups are of the Westernizer rather than the Easternizer orientation. They do not accept Basayev or Khattab, but stick to Chechen traditions. A simple conclusion can be drawn from this: if Maskhadov finally wakes up and shows his determination to fight, he will have the support of most of the middle ground, which can result in much more serious military operations than the Gudermes attack.

Playing Russian Roulette

How do our secret services operating in Chechnya react to this split and the whole situation—all these numerous secret divisions, highly educated officers, the FSS, the MID, and others? It would be logical to suppose that, first, if we really want to do away with the international terrorists Basayev and Khattab (or his replacement), then we should make full use of the inner Chechen split for this aim. All the more so since all the necessary conditions are in place. Second, we should take the Westernizers' side. All the secret services in the world would probably do just that to ensure the safety of their citizens.

But our secret services in Chechnya are busy having a love affair with the Easternizers. Categorically refusing to negotiate with Maskhadov, they support the Basayev-Khattab group. They know very well that Basayev, for example, desperately needs this support, since his position among the Chechens is very weak. The Chechen Westernizers, having realized the need for some kind of consolidation so as to preserve the nation, are trying to set up a coalition, albeit ephemeral, against the Easternizers as a common enemy. They even managed to present a few of their firm demands to Basayev. The main requirement was that Basayev had to personally do away with Khattab (someone else did that), which was supposed to cut the financial umbilical cord connecting him to the Arab world (it did not do that) and provide Basayev with the only possible way to return to the Chechen traditions and military and political life as an almost equal partner (it did not do that either). The unavoidable alternative was for him to be killed by the Westernizers, along with Khattab, of course.

When the secret services found out about this ultimatum, they rushed to the rescue not of Maskhadov, who was trying to destroy Basayev, but of Basayev himself, who was trying to survive. For example, he was informed about when large sums of Federal money would be transported to Gudermes (this information provided the starting point for the September 16 attack on Gudermes). His people were also given safe passage to Gudermes and back, and even, according to some data, armaments. What does this all mean? Only one thing: those who are in control do not want peace in Chechnya.

The Kremlin's control of the smoldering conflict in the Northern Caucasus is its main governmental policy. You really cannot find a better partner in this business than Basayev, who, along with Khattab, is the main guarantor of new battles emerging in Chechnya. Need to make a stronger case by adding the Gudermes events to the American tragic bombing? Here he is to do that for you. Dozen of lives lost? Well, it is Russian roulette, after all!

In March 2002, a rumor war started in Chechnya that Khattab was removed from the game by the secret service, which had let him in in the first place. Soon the FSS announced that "Khattab is probably dead." Later, they made the same report about Basayev. And then what happened?

Nothing much. Peace in Chechnya was supposed to come as soon as they did away with those "cult figures," according to the long-standing promises of the military. But it has not come. The partisan avengers go on with their war while the Feds continue their purges. There are more and more corpses every day.

Chechnya as the Price for the UN Secretary-General's Post

May 2001 brought new evidence of how involved we have gotten in restoring the Brezhnev era during the time of Putin. The influential international organization Human Rights Watch (HRW) released its report of just one of the hundreds of mass graves of the

Chechen civilian population, timing the publication to coincide with UN Secretary-General Kofi Annan's visit to Moscow and demanding that the international community and, first and foremost, the UN start a full-fledged investigation. This immediately resulted in a wave of Kremlin denials, angry responses, and rebukes, with the high-ranking officials who usually shun TV cameras suddenly finding the time to share their belief that nothing of the sort is taking place.

Why would the government suddenly start fidgeting as if it were sitting on a pin? Could Annan's visit be considered such a pin? And finally, why did the highest UN official inappropriately keep silent when someone in his position was supposed to at least show some sympathy and say a few words, if only according to protocol, about the necessity of curbing the war crimes in Chechnya?

I have no doubt that we have witnessed a deal being made at the cost of many lives, a deal that was profitable for both high parties, the Kremlin and the UN secretary-general. And why all the anxiety? Why all the fuss, the comments by lying officials? It is quite understandable: the Russian side was none too sure about its distinguished guest, fearing that the deal might fall through at the last moment, after the HRW presented its report.

But let's start from the beginning. First, here are the main points in the human rights advocates' report, a detailed account of the mass grave found from January to February 2001 not far from Grozny, just across the road from Khankala, the main Russian military base in Chechnya. There are fifty-one corpses in the grave. How did they manage to find them? Information about the first corpse, that of Adam Chimayev, who disappeared on December 3, 2000, was obtained commercially by the Chimayev family: for three thousand dollars (in rubles) they bought the grave coordinates from the officer who had had something to do with guarding Adam on the territory of the military base. After paying, the family was allowed to take the corpse.

This set off a series of rumors in Chechnya, and soon Dachnoe was flooded by the relatives of other Chechens who had disappeared without a trace. This resulted in the identification of nineteen more corpses, leaving thirty-two unidentified. On March 10, 2001, these remains were buried by the soldiers without any notice. Biological samples were not preserved, as is required in such cases. In its report, the HRW cited a lot of testimony about the actions of the prosecutor's office, the Russian government, and the president's office, calling them inadequate.

The Russian government did not want any investigation about the mass grave and categorically denied that it was done by the military. The international community turned a deaf ear to the Dachnoe tragedy too. The United States, the European Union, the European Parliament, and the OSCE basically did their best to conceal the story. Alvaro Gil-Robles, the chief European human rights commissar, visited Chechnya for an inspection in the final days of February, right after the grave was found, but he did not even go to Dachnoe or meet the relatives of the identified victims. In addition, the HRW indicated which of the UN basic documents Russia has violated, and how the UN has diplomatically ignored being spat on.

The report concluded that the investigation of the Dachnoe mass grave must be renewed. To this end, it recommended that a special international committee be rapidly set up, whose first order of business should be to exhume the thirty-two hurriedly buried, unidentified corpses, with the participation of the International Red Cross, the OSCE aid group, European Council experts, and representatives of the UN Commission on Human Rights. In essence, the HRW called for the establishment of a sort of international protectorate for the investigation of the Dachnoe tragedy.

In order to understand the reaction of the Kremlin and the UN secretary-general to these suggestions, let's take a closer look at what was going on in the UN in the spring of 2001. Is this international protectorate under UN supervision in Chechnya possible in principle? And what could the secretary-general do?

It should be pointed out that long before the HRW report and the resulting public outrage, *Novaya gazeta* had tried to find the answer to these very questions in the UN Headquarters in New York, right in the heart of the diplomatic lobby, the recreation hall of the Security Council meetings, where international "humanitarian" politics is being cooked up. The *Novaya gazeta* correspondent was in fact illegally let into these places, concealed from strangers, and illegally introduced by a certain person. I am indebted to this person. He assisted me in this illegal intrusion into the Security Council lobby only because he realized how important my questions were: What can the UN do to resolve the acute Chechen crisis? How can the continual suffering of the Chechen people be stopped? What is the real, as opposed to official, reaction of the council? Is an international protectorate possible?

I did not come up with these questions by chance, but by analyzing a huge amount of information about the actual situation in Chechnya, not the reports carefully put together and submitted to Putin by his assistants, or the ones shown through the rose-colored lenses of the TV news. There is just one idea underlying these questions: how can we end the war and mass violation of human rights in Chechnya? And, can the rapid moral decay of the army be stopped?

My position is based on discussions of dozens of alternative peace settlements with hundreds of Chechen civilians—ordinary people and officials living in Grozny and the villages. Here it is: the international protectorate is absolutely necessary. And even though official Moscow is not willing to so much as consider such an outcome, it is crucial. A third party is needed like air—it must separate the opposing sides for some time (these are not, as the official Kremlin propaganda has it, the militants and the Feds, but the Feds and the civilians), appease passions as much as possible, and start working to soften both sides' positions.

But let's go back to New York. Most of the diplomats I talked to, who work in the Security Council and make decisions about introducing UN peacekeeping forces in all regions, expressed the opinion that it is practically impossible to "get the job done." To send in the peacekeeping forces mandated by the UN, an agreement of the two opposing sides is needed. According to the UN charter, in this case, civilians who suffer massive human rights violations every day cannot be considered one of the "opposing sides." And of course, it is useless even to speak of an agreement from the Russian side.

However, there is another way to get the UN mandate for a protectorate: a military operation to establish peace, as stipulated in article seven of the Charter of the United Nations. (It is according to this protocol that the well-known events occurred in Iraq and Yugoslavia that later resulted in big trouble for the United States, which lost its place on the UN Commission on Human Rights.) If article seven were to be applied to the Chechen crisis, the diplomats of the Security Council affirmed, there would be no need for an agreement of the "opposing sides."

But Iraq and Yugoslavia are not Russia. Iraq and Yugoslavia are merely members of the UN, whereas Russia is a permanent member of the Security Council with veto privileges. The decision on article seven is made by the Security Council. This means that anyone can submit such a proposal to the council, but no matter how long the discussion lasts, the Russian government will automatically veto the proposal. If Russia does not want this to happen, the council cannot do anything.

Most of the council diplomats came to the same conclusion: sending peacekeeping forces to Chechnya is impossible; to believe otherwise is an illusion. The only person who could change the situation and get around this dead end is the secretary-general.

But can we count on Kofi Annan? I posed this very question to the council diplomats. Back then, at the end of April, they predicted the scenario that is now in fact being staged in Moscow: Annan turns a deaf ear to the situation in Chechnya (and to the HRW report). These were not third-rate diplomats but those who work directly under Annan. They assured me that right now he does not care who suffers in what way on this tiny spot of our planet, since the spot is located on the territory of the Russian Federation. The most important thing for him is to be reelected for a second term, no matter what the price. In this case, the price is Chechnya. The secretary-general will continue to silently bless the North Caucasian war for as long as Russia helps him to stay in office.

There is no doubt, I think, that Russia is very happy with the office-loving Kofi Annan. Soviet policy (and now we are obviously experiencing its renaissance) was always based on the fact that communist leaders were convenient in some way to Western and international VIPs, which made the latter turn a blind eye to the nightmare of life in the USSR and feed the regime with grants and loans—anything to avoid social cataclysm.

Thus, everything in Moscow happened in accordance with established Soviet traditions. The deal on the summit was successfully closed—in essence, the same kind of deal they were closing in the communist years. Putin is happy with the compliant Kofi Annan as UN secretary-general, since while he is there Russia does not have to worry about any pressure in connection with Chechnya. Annan needs Putin's vote in the elections. Given that Russia's relations with the European Union, the European Parliament, the OSCE, and so on work the same way, there is simply no hope.

The international community and the Western world have stepped aside, allowing the Russian government to do whatever it wants in Chechnya, indulging in official lies and demagoguery. This leads to the further deterioration of the Chechen situation. You might recall that this has happened before. The silent agreement of the international community to have the "exemplary Chernokosovo" (a Chechen prison where interrogations took place, which slowly turned into a Potemkin village and left the high-ranking international visitors quite satisfied) provoked further plunder. Instead of being put in jail, dozens and then hundreds of people started to simply disappear, and their bodies were found only by chance.

So even if Moscow, under HRW pressure, agrees to continue investigating the Dachnoe mass grave, Dachnoe will inherit the Chernokosovo fate. It may sound sacrilegious now, but Dachnoe will soon be turned into an exemplary grave, toured by flocks of foreign journalists and parliament members.

This will be the result of the HRW report, designed to put pressure on the UN secretary-general.

And what is going on in Chechnya, which Kofi Annan has traded for his post? The same old things—lies and terror.

On May 14, 2001, an armored vehicle without license plates drove by the Bardukayevs' home in the district center Urus-Martan. During the January purge, six men had been taken from this house: three were soon released, but there was no news of the other three for half a year. An officer got out of the armored vehicle and, following the methods of Field Commander Arbi Barayev (remember the sliced-off heads of the Western engineers in the snow?) showed the photos of the Bardukayev brothers' corpses (the relatives identified the bodies). He demanded fifteen hundred dollars for revealing the burial site. Exactly the same story as the one in Dachnoe with the first body, that of Adam Chimayev.

Special Operation Zyazikov

The war that so many people profit by has grown up, has become a full-fledged living organism. The pro-Russian Chechen government wanted to drag its neighbor Ingushetia into the war, and therefore the Kremlin put someone in power there who could allow this to happen.

Ingushetia has lived near the war zone for ten years. Now its territory is turning little by little into a war zone. The process of civil peace turning into civil war is called presidential elections in a country with "controlled democracy," where the post of Ruslan Aushev, who in the winter of 2002 "voluntarily" retired as the president of the republic, is being contested. The second round was to take place on April 28. On April 7, two candidates were selected: Alikhan Amirkhanov, a State Duma deputy, and Murat Zyazikov, an FSS general and the first deputy of Putin's plenipotentiary representative in the Southern Federal District (SFD). Here is how Zyazikov was elected.

A Raped Court

Khasan Iragievich Yandiev, a judge in the Supreme Court of Ingushetia, has lived a respectable life, with ten years of court experience and two years as the republic's minister of justice. But it is terrible to look at him now. His eyes are empty, as if he has buried his own family. Indeed, there was a funeral—of principles and illusions about the place of judicial power in this country. There is no doubt that Yandiev will go down in modern Russian history as the judge who, in April 2002, experienced the pressure of the whole hierarchy of executive power that demanded that the court be turned into an organ of political manipulation.

"I didn't believe it when I heard about it," Henrich Padva, one of our most famous attorneys, will say later, in the halls of the Supreme Court of Ingushetia. He has a big frame of reference too, about half a century of practice going back, incidentally, to 1953.[*]

At the end of March, Yandiev was assigned a case involving the removal of one of the main presidential candidates, Khamzat Gutseriev, from the preelection race. All court sessions on this case were conducted under intense pressure from SFD officials, who were

---

[*] The year of Stalin's death. *Trans.*

shamelessly pushing the court to decide in favor of the other candidate, FSS general Zyazikov. Gentlemen with characteristically featureless faces darted through the corridors, walking the judge home and meeting him in the morning at the front door. But Yandiev took it all stoically. He has seen a lot in life.

On April 1, at the end of the day, the judge and two members of the jury went into the council room, a sacred place no one else can enter, to make a decision. On the morning of April 3, they were ready to make it public. Around eleven, Zyazikov's people, representatives of the SFD, entered the judge's council room, violating its confidentiality, along with the country's constitution and several laws (subject, by the way, to criminal prosecution). They handed the judge a telegram from the Russian Supreme Court signed by its deputy chair, Nina Sergeeva. The telegram instructed the judge to hand the case over to a courier who would take it to Moscow. The chair of the Supreme Court of Ingushetia, Dautkhasan Albakov, accompanied by his deputy Azamat-Hirei Chiniev, gathered the pages of the file from the desk and took them away. Soon the news agency ITAR-TASS announced that the Supreme Court of the Russian Federation had examined the case and annulled the registration of Khamzat Gutseriev as a presidential candidate.

Khamzat Gutseriev means nothing to me. He's just a functionary, the Ingush minister of the interior in the toughest times of the antiterrorist operation in the Northern Caucasus. His actions as a military minister in a country that borders on Chechnya have annoyed me personally several times in the course of over two years. However, what does it matter who dislikes whom? Laws are laws. On the other hand, Gutseriev, the brother of the oligarch Putin is fighting, definitely means a lot to the president. And in Russia today this is reason enough to have state officials rape the court and morally humiliate judges who do not want to accept the anticonstitutional rules of the game.

The Reign of Fear

"How serious is such an infringement of the election law?" I ask Musa Evloev, the attorney for the republic's election committee.

"These elections could be declared illegal," he says.

"Could be or must be?"

Musa silently hides his eyes. He want to live and work. The best way to ensure that in present-day Ingushetia is to keep silent and pretend that you are obedient to the SFD war machine that promotes Zyazikov, the candidate the Kremlin wants. Dozens of people have used these exact words to describe the situation in the republic.

It's April 19. These same esteemed colleagues of Putin and Zyazikov wander around the halls of the Supreme Court of Ingushetia, listening to who says and asks what, and how Musa Evloev answers my questions. When they're finished eavesdropping, they go down a few steps to report all this to someone on their cell phones. Just yesterday, in Moscow, this insolent FSS trick would have seemed almost a product of election-induced paranoia.

Under these circumstances, we wait for a new court session on annulling the registration of a number of candidates for bribing the electors. Judge Mohammed Mohammedovich Dourbekov is preparing to take the torch from Yandiev. He is nervous. He knows that Yandiev had to be taken to the resuscitation ward after what happened to him, and that he is still not fully recovered, even though he continues to go to work. He knows that Yandiev submitted a claim to the attorney general of Russia, demanding that the law be upheld. After circling over Moscow, this claim landed back in Ingushetia, right into the hands of those who should have been prosecuted for their crime. He knows that the only result of Yandiev's truth-seeking efforts was a request submitted to Putin to end the judge's life term in office.

Judge Dourbekov held his own that day, in spite of the often monstrous demands, pressure, and even insults from the Zyazikov party. The results of the first round of voting were not annulled. But who could guarantee a peaceful tomorrow?

"Why are they trying to twist our arms?" people asked. "We will never, ever accept this, no matter what."

And they would add right away: "Don't mention my name." Everyone said the same thing: "Please, don't mention it. I have kids. I could be fired."

There were no exceptions. They all asked about it—deputies of the Ingush parliament, members of the government, brave officers, lawyers, teachers, and journalists. The latter told me that these days in Ingushetia, their colleagues can be fired merely because of a chance appearance on TV near a presidential candidate other than Zyazikov. This is not an exaggeration.

"Who fires them?"

"Pyotr Zemtsov."

The public rape of the Ingush court system is beyond doubt the most cynical of the campaigns designed to appoint Zyazikov president of Ingushetia, to use the accurate description of one of my interlocutors. But it is not the only one. Another campaign was aimed against the freedom of speech that is also guaranteed by the constitution. Right before the election race started, Moscow had "replaced," as they put it here, the chairman of the Ingushetia TV and Radio Company, commissioning that very Zemtsov to ensure the correct election results.

And Zemtsov is doing a great job. They cannot even broadcast video material about any candidate besides Zyazikov, from Nazrani to everywhere else. In order for a report about any other candidate to appear in the Independent TV Channel news, the journalists have to go to Vladikavkaz, in Northern Osetia. And it's not all that simple to go there and come back at night, driving along the empty roads in a region that is raided day and night by a motorcade controlled by Musa Keligov, the so-called chief inspector of the Southern Federal District. The task of this motorcade (or gang, to be more precise) is to intercept those who have not yet been subjugated and put under control.

Now Keligov with his mob is not just another Khattab. He is Zyazikov's main promoter, an official who represents President Putin, whom he raves about everywhere, leaning against a Kalashnikov. He is Zyazikov's colleague in the SFD, a friend and deputy to Plenipotentiary Representative General Kazantsev. In addition, Keligov is a former vice president of the company Lukoil. At present, he combines state service with helping himself to the state-owned Ingush Oil Industry, whose headquarters are conveniently located in Malgobek, right next-door to the main oil wells of Ingushetia.

Deputy Landing Party

On April 20, a delegation of twenty Duma deputies representing various factions landed in Ingushetia to see how things were going. Divided into groups, the deputies went all over the republic, following four routes, to meet with people. In the district center Malgobek, which is quickly falling into Keligov's dominion, the deputies were not allowed to enter the district cultural center, where they were to meet with Malgobek residents. The reason was very simple: Keligov was not sure they would campaign for Zyazikov. By orders of Mukhazhir Evloev—the head of the district police and Keligov's son-in-law, the man who warned the voters that if Zyazikov does not win "we'll make things real bad for you"—the meeting with the deputies was cancelled.

However, the deputies did not lose their heads in Malgobek, which is now such a tough city. Vera Lekareva, Andrei Vulf, Vladimir Semyonov, Vladimir Koptev-Dvornikov, and Aleksandr Barannikov—members of the Union of Right-Wing Forces—talked with a few hundred people who had gathered for the outdoor meeting in pouring rain.

"Of course, we could have entered the cultural center by force," Vera Lekareva says, "but we felt that they were provoking us, that they wanted us to lose our cool. Some strange people with mean faces were wandering around. So we decided to just calm everyone down. Honestly, I'd never vote for a candidate who's being shoved down my throat this way."

Many people in Ingushetia feel that something is about to happen. They describe it as a provocation, a controlled outburst, bloodshed.

On April 19, a very bad sign confirmed all their fears. A secret official telegram came from the Ministry of the Interior in Moscow: "To Pogorov MI Nazrani: Commission to Russian MI Police Colonel Tamaskhanov Colonel Ilyasov Police Colonel Gireev Police Colonel Yaryzhev on business for ten days Arriving April 22, 2002 Gryzlov."

In normal language, this means that four deputies of Akhmed Pogorov, the minister of the interior of the republic, have been ordered by Boris Gryzlov, minister of the interior of Russia, to go to Moscow during the ten most difficult days for Ingushetia, the last week before the second round, when the votes are submitted and counted. Nothing like this has ever happened before. Usually it's just the opposite: to ensure order in any region, all higher police officers are usually asked to come back from vacations and hospitals for election time.

In this small republic, they know everything about everyone, including the aforementioned colonels and their potential orders to their subordinates about whose side to take. The special telegram was regarded as fateful. It meant that these several hundred FSS men who had come from everywhere and were now raiding the Ingush roads in strangely identical Tavria cars really were up to something. It would not be difficult to arrange either, with so many desperate refugees around. The only official left in the Ministry of the Interior was Pogorov, a Zyazikov man, so that when the riots were provoked, Pogorov would fail to control them.

Why? There can be no doubt: when the chances of an FSS general to win the election are close to nil, disorder is needed to officially proclaim that it is impossible to hold elections, and the head of state needs to be "appointed." This would be the end of the special operation to put Zyazikov on the Ingush throne. It's exactly what the SFD officials openly told people two months ago: "No matter what you do, Zyazikov will be your man. That's Moscow's decision. There's no other alternative. If you don't elect him, he'll be appointed."

Zyazikov and What He's All About

Who is this man who has already become a bogeyman for the Ingush children? As his main spokesperson Aleksei Lyubivoi put it, "I forbid him to talk with the press."

Nice policy. Let's take a look at the people who surround him, then. Zyazikov's supporters are divided into two groups.

First, there are the aforementioned FSS men who were summoned to Ingushetia for the election period from various Russian regions. When they talk to people, they do not conceal the fact that for them "Zyazikov's defeat in the elections would be a slap in the face of the entire counterintelligence system."

Second, there are the Ingush who were somehow wronged or failed to make it under ex-president Aushev. Most of them resettled in Moscow a long time ago because they could not work with Aushev. They now meet at Zyazikov's election headquarters on Oskanov Street in Nazrani. I ask the headquarters chairman Salman Naurbekov and his deputy Kharon Dzeitov:

"Why is Zyazikov a good candidate? Tell me about him."

"The main thing is, he's crystal-clear, unlike everyone else."

"Why do you think so?"

"Because he comes from a crystal-clear service."

Now isn't that a bit much?

In May, Zyazikov took the oath, and a week later, troops entered Ingushetia. In another month, they started to forcefully move refugees back to Chechnya. The Kremlin wants the war to go on. And so it does.

We Survived Again!: A Chronicle of Colonel Mironov's Luck

We were flying in a military helicopter from point A to point B. In the December night, Chechnya passed by slowly and inconspicuously below. It was gray, and there was no snow. All you could see was the wells and the flickering milky ways of the roads. Everything else was darkness. The middle-aged officer accompanying us peered habitually through the night vision device, his legs dangling in the open hatch. He was ready to fire his handheld machine gun.

You can't talk in a helicopter. It's too noisy, and your ears are clogged. But I managed to talk a little with my neighbor anyway, even though he was invisible, since they don't turn on the inside lamps at night. We took turns leaning to where the other's ear would be and shouting.

"Where are you from?"

"Moscow."

"Me too."

"Where do you live in Moscow?"

"Near the Garden Ring."

"I work there. I live in Maryino."

"That's a bit far away."

"It's OK, I have a big place."

"What do you do?"

"I'm an officer. And you? You're not wearing camouflage, are you?"

"I'm a journalist. What's taking so long? We should have reached Gudermes in twenty minutes."

The captain came out of the cockpit, stared into the dark helicopter belly where we've been held for the last two hours, and shouted something into the ear of the accompanying officer. The officer immediately closed the hatch, leaned back, and, judging by the sound, started dismantling his weapon.

We all needed to get to Gudermes, where everyone had arranged to have a place to stay for the night and a banya—a very important thing in these local conditions. But now something strange was going on. Why was he dismantling his machine gun? The helicopters always flew to Gudermes under guard. Also, the farther we flew, the more lights we could see below.

Twenty minutes later, it became clear that we weren't landing in Gudermes. What they call the military airport there is simply a field, but here, a real landing strip appeared below, and we saw a civil dispatcher tower, lit up as it can never be in a war.

"This isn't Chechnya," my neighbor said happily and even clicked his heels softly. He was a changed man: earlier he had talked as if he had the weight of the world on his shoulders, and now he was practically singing.

"Why are you so happy? Nobody's waiting for us here. There's nowhere to sleep, nothing to eat... Not to mention a banya."

But my neighbor didn't hear me; he had gone to the cockpit. In a minute, he ran out and gleefully yelled just one word:

"Vladikavkaz!"

The soldiers who took Berlin at the end of World War II yelled "Victory!" in this manner. Then he started tap-dancing gently right in the middle of the helicopter.

There was probably some kind of military trouble in Gudermes, shooting or something else. It was dangerous to land there, so the pilots changed plans, without asking their passengers, of course. It's always like this in the war: nobody cares about your plans, and you are often presented with a fait accompli that totally destroys them. My neighbor was laughing heartily over the engine's roar, dancing and rubbing his hands:

"Colonel Mironov, at your service!"

He stood in the aisle, calmly balancing himself by barely touching the helicopter plating with one hand. This was a miracle: why was he suddenly so strong? Just fifteen minutes ago, he was as subdued as everyone else; his body moved around in response to the helicopter's evasive maneuvers. But now, while the helicopter is landing, shaking feverishly, he's just standing right in the middle, like a handsome cadet on leave, "weight on your left leg, right leg slightly forward."

We went down the lowered ladder in a tired crawl, but the colonel flew down and ran around the air field in circles, laughing, jumping and turning his head with black curly hair above his wide forehead furrowed with deep, premature wrinkles. It was raining softly. In the landing lights, Mironov turned out to be a well-built, muscular man. He raised his hands and started to catch with his lips the water falling from a sky that was no longer scary.

Mironov's enthusiasm proved to be infectious. As they left the helicopter, the officers slowly lost the usual Chechen stupor, when you are equally afraid of what is on your right, your left, and ahead of you, and scared to death of what might be behind you. They were loudly discussing where to stay for the night. They started telling jokes, mocking each other, with a ringing, not at all "Chechen" laugh.

"Let's go to a restaurant!" Mironov shouted.

"What are we celebrating?"

"You still don't get it? You should come to Chechnya more often!" He shook me firmly by the hand, demanding my full attention. "We have just one thing to celebrate: We're alive! Still alive! We survived again! We're not in the war today, and I'm ali-ive! And you are ali-ive!"

His last words came from the distance. He was already running to arrange things, to find out where a good restaurant was and how to get there. The night dispatchers nervously looked down from the airport tower at the strange party that had unexpectedly descended from the Caucasian sky, wondering if it was time to call for the police and nip the drunken commotion in the bud.

Soon Mironov returned, easily picked up the bags and backpacks, and dragged us into the night, showing the way like a guiding star. "Ali-ive, ali-ive!" He roared with laughter, walking very fast. We had caught his mood and were able to keep up with him now. We became as weightless, young, and happy as he was. We felt his fire, intoxicated with the joy of our lives, which had been given to us anew. Our lives that had hung by a thread in the helicopter and that we would have had to defend during the night in Gudermes too. Here, we were surrounded by the Vladikavkaz sights: thick, sleepy acacias, quiet, clean little streets, soft light from the street lamps, people slowly strolling along, in spite of the late hour and our firm habit of hiding in corners after curfew. We became drunk on all this, although no one had had any wine or vodka yet.

By nine, the party reached its peak, although the bottles were still nearly untouched. We were on a natural high, happy to be in good health, sitting in this North Osetian café. We talked drunken nonsense. We became one family, even if we didn't know each other's names. We were going crazy together, understanding each other completely and not wanting tomorrow to come.

Mironov was still our leader. After wolfing down a bunch of local delicacies, he started dancing. He invited all the women there to dance, one by one, promising each his eternal love and friendship in a loud voice that everyone could hear. But he lived in the moment and didn't care who heard what. All the women seemed lovely, and he didn't want a single one to leave without him saying the most poetic things he could think of.

He ended every dance in a fiery flourish, lifting his partner in his arms and whirling fervently around the mirrorlike floor of the expensive restaurant, his lady leaning on his chest. He'd whirl even after the music stopped, and even if the lady was somewhat heavy.

"We're alive! Do you understand?" he whispered in my ear when it was my turn to dance. He said it the way others had once whispered "I love you."

It turned out that he had spent over a year in Chechnya without a break.

"How many times have you returned alive?"

"It's the sixth time tonight," he said putting me back on the floor. "Think I should try my luck a seventh time?"

He didn't wait for my answer, knowing that he shouldn't, and yelled loudly.

"Flowers for all the ladies!"

He ran up to the tiny stage and snatched the microphone out of the bewildered singer's hand with the sharp, quick motion officers use to grab their gun in a dangerous moment. The colonel wanted to sing. He sang for a whole hour, just for himself. He didn't care that everyone got tired of listening to him or that he seldom sang to the beat. He had his own music and his own rhythm in his head that night. His last song was, quite appropriately, a lullaby. After that he demanded cognac.

"Where are you going tomorrow?" he asked

"I've decided to go to Moscow."

"When are you coming back?"

"In two weeks or so."

"Don't hurry, things aren't too good here now."

"I know. And what about you?"

"I'm going to Chechnya in the morning. The pilots say the weather will be good."

"Good luck."

We've known each other for five hours, maybe six. And yet we talked as if we were very close to each other, happily married for thirty years. We talked in short phrases, and there was no need for explanation; we understood everything right away.

"You know, I can't get upset by things like not having any money anymore."

"Neither can I. Or that my husband left me."

"Your husband left you?"

"Yes."

"That's nothing."

"True."

This conversation took place very late at night, in the lobby of one of the Vladikavkaz hotels where we had gone from the restaurant. We could not get rooms in it for the money that we still had left.

"When did he leave you?"

"At the beginning of the war. He drank and partied a lot, and then he left. But this is all nonsense, in comparison."

"In comparison to what?" He wants to make sure.

"You know."

"Yes. To life and death."

"I'm thankful for this war. I got here by chance, and got stuck by chance as well. But now I know how to rise above all this nonsense. The war is horrible, but it has purified me of everything that was superfluous, unnecessary. How can I not be thankful?"

Mironov silently agreed. He told me nothing about himself, but I still understood, without any words. We shared the same blood that had been poured into our veins by the war. It rushed inside our bodies like hormones, all too often taking us nowhere, into a dark room without doors. When it let us go at the very last moment, we realized how lonely we were. Our fate was to look for people who were similar to us in this world, who knew something about life that most people would never experience. Perhaps we would like to share this secret with them, but they didn't want to know and didn't care.

Early next morning, Mironov came to see us off, we who were leaving for Moscow. He looked nothing like the fit, dark-haired man with rosy cheeks who had partied the day before in the Vladikavkaz restaurant. His hair had a noticeable streak of gray, and his face was gray too. He was depressed, apparently sunk in some sad thoughts, and answered haphazardly.

"Don't worry, I'll call your family and tell them you're OK." What else could I offer besides these clichéd "Chechen" phrases that people who are leaving always say to those who stay behind?

"Yes, call them... I'm OK..." he repeated mechanically. "My oldest son is a cadet at the Suvorov School, my youngest is three years old. My wife is young and beautiful. And what now?"

"Now, you have to believe in luck. We're nothing without it."

He kept silent. He didn't agree this time. He wished very much that he could go to Moscow. I wanted to give him something as a souvenir, but I didn't have anything, so I took off my scarf and gave it to him. But he didn't even smile.

The next time we met was at a hospital near Moscow. Mironov called me and said he was wounded.

"Is the wound serious?" That was a dumb question. Everyone knows that they only bring the severely wounded into hospitals near Moscow from Chechnya.

"No." A senseless lie.

I was scared. Did we not share the same blood anymore? Did we have to say unnecessary things now?

But the very first thing Mironov said when he saw me and waved from his squeaky hospital bed calmed me down:

"I've come to hate the word 'never' in this war. Because 'never' always happens right away."

Those were exactly my thoughts on my way upstairs to his room. So we were the same people as before. He understood me, and I understood him. Isn't that strange for people who barely know each other? Not a bit, even if we hadn't known each other, since we've been through what we have.

Then we just shot the breeze, enjoying each other's company. His young wife, who really was quite beautiful, was taking care of him. She watched the dripping of the IV, not understanding a thing. She didn't realize, for example, how lucky Mironov was to have been wounded but still alive.

"I came out alive again, see?" The colonel was obviously recovering. Forgetting his pain, he jumped up on his bed in the Vladikavkaz manner. He was ready to sing and dance.

"That's great!" I said, under his wife's unfriendly gaze. "That means you'll get a long vacation now. You have a lot of per diem money saved, and you'll get your insurance money. You'll live like a king. And while you're enjoying yourself, the war will probably end. I promise! I'll write extra articles so that the damn war will end and you'll never have to go there again."

This was all nonsense, of course. But why not, if that's what he wants to hear. So I went on:

"You'll be raising your sons. And you two will go to the theater." I smiled at his wife as sweetly as I could, knowing how much she wanted me to leave. "And you'll go visit your mother. There's a million things you can do while you're here."

"Now wait a minute," the colonel said. Those were his favorite words, always followed by something really important for him. "Do I understand correctly? In order for me to stay alive, you have to write and continue going to a place where you could be killed? And you want me to lie here waiting for this 'never' to happen?"

Thankfully, things turned out all right for us. We were both alive. Again. There was only one problem: while the colonel was recovering, I didn't write all that much. During that time, he managed to do everything: recover, get stronger, make use of all his military leaves, go to a resort, talk and play with his sons, go to the theater with his wife (more than ten times, in his words). But I let him down. The war did not end, as I'd promised. So he had to go back to the place where even adults have to learn the real meaning of the word "never." And we both waited in awe for it to happen to us. We were scared that the day would come when there would be no one to yell so loudly that the entire Vladikavkaz airport would hear: "We're alive, get it? We survived again!"

And that day did come. There is no one to yell it any more. In December 2001, Colonel Mironov died from wounds that were incompatible with life.

It's time to return to London, to our interview with Akhmed Zakayev, Aslan Maskhadov's special representative.

"There's been a lot of talk about so-called peace negotiations between you and General Viktor Kazantsev, President Putin's plenipotentiary representative in the Southern Federal District. Everyone, including the international community, wrote that the cause of peace in Chechnya had gotten a real jump-start. But the outcome was somewhat vague. What did these negotiations accomplish?"

"Nothing. The meeting was held on November 18, 2001, as a result of Putin's September 24 statement about surrendering arms. Both the statement and the meeting were for the most part propaganda aimed at Europe and Bush, since all this took place after September 11. We hadn't expected much from the meeting. Still, we considered it crucial as another attempt to start a dialogue. But this didn't happen. After all, Viktor Germanovich is not a politician who can make his own decisions. I don't even think he informed Putin later of our suggestions. And he had no suggestions at all. Except for 'give up, join us, and we'll live happily ever after.'"

"Did he offer amnesty to the militants then?"

"No. He didn't even mention that. All he said was, 'Enough is enough. Everyone's sick of the war. Let's unite.'"

"What was Kazantsev's goal in suggesting this on November 18?"

"One indivisible Russia. Nothing else. We talked for three hours, and he didn't make any of the suggestions that we'd expected. Not a single step to end this conflict. We, on the other hand, did have suggestions that could help stop the military activity and later normalize the situation in Chechnya."

"Is it possible to implement your suggestions now? Is there still time?"

"Of course."

"Tell me what they are."

"First, declare an immediate cease-fire from all sides. Second, set up a bilateral working group for negotiations, state or governmental committees—it's up to them. Third, immediately discontinue the purges, which only cause further mutual alienation. Fourth, renew negotiations with Maskhadov, of course."

"In what capacity?"

"As the chief Chechen negotiator, the indisputable head. I told Kazantsev then that we have a formula that would allow Russia to remain an indivisible state."

"Even without Chechnya? What is this formula?"

"It would be subject to negotiations. But we do have such a formula."

"Did you submit your suggestions to Kazantsev in writing? Or only orally?"

"In writing, of course. Since he didn't take any notes, it was clear that the meeting was being recorded too. He promised to report it all to Putin. I told him: 'Now you know what is acceptable for us. Do you think Putin will accept this?' And he said, 'I'm 99 percent sure he will, and there will be a follow-up to this meeting. But there's no guarantee, of course, since it's the president's decision."

"And?"

"And nothing. That was the end of it. We stayed in contact through our deputies and assistants, by phone. But I haven't talked to him since, even on the phone."

"Why not?"

"Because events took such a turn that it would be morally wrong for us to continue the dialogue. The purges, instead of being stopped, became more ferocious. We didn't make any attempt to meet and neither did they, although, practically speaking, it's not a problem to renew negotiations."

"Did you talk with Kazantsev one-on-one then?"

"Yes. We met in the international wing of Sheremetyevo Airport. Of course, I didn't fly to Moscow alone. I flew on a private jet with the leader of the Turkish Liberal Democrat Party, who was the guarantor of my security. The Turkish Embassy in Moscow was officially informed about our mission."

"What does the peace process look like today?"

"There is none. There simply isn't any peace dialogue. The war is still going on, and in my opinion, there is no one in the Russian government today who could take responsibility and stop it. Putin can't do it, and neither can the prime minister. No one can."

"Why not?"

"I'm convinced that they simply can't control the situation in Chechnya. It's the military that tells Russia what to do today. One essential difference between Yeltsin and Putin is that Yeltsin, for all his problems, had a very low approval rating but high authority, while Putin seems to have a high rating but no authority. A decision to stop the war is an act of political will, and for that you need authority."

"In April, presidential elections were held in Ingushetia. It's common knowledge that former president Ruslan Aushev, Maskhadov's advocate, resigned voluntarily because he was unable to fight Moscow's pressure any longer. This led to FSS general Murat Zyazikov, a henchman of the Putin administration, winning the elections. In your opinion, how could his victory influence the course of the Chechen war? How could it change the politics of the Maskhadov side?

"It will not affect our politics in any way. But what does it mean for Ingushetia to have an FSS officer appointed president by Putin? I think they are preparing to launch 'another Chechnya' in Ingushetia. The military needs to expand the war zone, since it's already cleaned out Chechnya. The Chechen war, if you compare the present situation with that from 1999 to 2000, is very unpopular among the military. The troops can't just go on hanging around in this territory anymore—the situation needs some kind of development. The military doesn't want to give up its leading position in the country, and the only way to keep it is to create new local wars and conflicts. A nation like Russia, which hasn't yet given up its imperial ambitions or adopted law as its foundation, needs an enemy. It doesn't have enough strength to deal with an external enemy but it can always 'appoint' an internal one. First it was the Chechens, next it will be the Ingush, who are supposedly loyal to the Chechens."

"When do you think the war in Ingushetia will begin?"

"Very soon. The terrorist act in Kaspiisk* was not an accident. I can assure you that neither the Chechens nor our allies had anything to do with that."

"And yet law enforcement officers started searching for field commander Rabbani Khalilov practically right after the terrorist act, as the media extensively reported. Why are you so sure that Khalilov had nothing to do with the bombing?"

"I don't know if he did or not. I only know for sure that he has nothing to do with the Chechens. We heard his name for the first time on TV just like everybody else, after the May 9 bombing."

"So you don't know this field commander?"

"No. No such man fought with us in the first or second Chechen war. He wasn't a member of any of our units, although there were many Dagestanis among us. All I know is that the Russian secret services have many such names at their disposal—unfamiliar and meaningless to me, but effective enough to create a public impression that an investigation and search really did take place."

"What about Maskhadov? Does he know Khalilov?"

"I'm 100 percent sure that he doesn't. I'm also certain that most of the Chechens don't know him either."

"What can you tell me about the deaths of Khattab and Basayev? Can you verify or disprove them?"

"Basayev is alive, and Khattab is dead. But the Russian secret services have nothing to do with his death, they just received a videotape showing his dead body. The secret services had nothing to gain by his death. It'll take them a lot of time now to invent a new Khattab for the Russian public. They'd received the video long before they showed it publicly. They didn't want to show it at all, but there was pressure from the American side. The Americans suspected Khattab of ties with al Qaeda and demanded some concrete results from the Russians in the joint fight against international terrorism. So they just couldn't keep silent anymore, and had to come up with this information about

---

*In Kaspiisk, Dagestan, forty-two people were killed in an explosion at the 2002 Victory Day (May 9) parade. *Trans.*

a 'supersecret operation.' Nothing of the sort ever happened. Khattab died a natural death."

"How?"

"He just didn't wake up one morning."

"But that's exactly what the secret service officers say. The 'super-secret operation' was about sending an agent who managed to poison Khattab. Do you know if a postmortem examination was conducted? Was a court medical expert present? Was an official death certificate issued? Where is he buried? If we don't know any of this, the Khat-tab story will end just like the Dudayev one: everything in a fog, no documents, no grave, and most Chechens believing that he's alive."

"There was no court medical expert and no official death certificate. He's buried in Chechnya in the mountain area of the Vedeno district. His brother's claim that Khattab's body was taken to Saudi Arabia is nonsense. It would have been impossible to secretly transport his body there."

"Which Chechen field commanders were at Khattab's funeral?"

"None of them. Just his inner circle."

"What do you think of the fact that when they discussed his death in the media, many called Khattab a 'cult figure,' following the lead of FSS representatives and the Putin administration?"

"Khattab has done a lot, but he was just one member of the Chechen resistance. I'll never agree that anyone—Dzhokhar Dudayev, Shamil Basayev, or Aslan Maskhadov—is a 'cult figure.' This approach of personifying our problem is nothing but propaganda. When Dudayev was alive, they said that once he died, the problem would go away. Then they made Raduev* into a cult figure and said that once he died, the problem would go away. I'm sure that even with Raduev, Maskhadov, Zakayev, Basayev, and Khattab all dead, nothing would change, since the Chechen problem is a political one. Until it is resolved, everything will continue."

"You said that Basayev is alive. Can you prove it? Does Maskhadov know that Basayev's alive?"

---

*Salman Raduev was a Chechen field commander from the Gudermes region who was famed for his exploits against Russian troops in the first Chechen war. He died in 2002 while serving a life sentence in prison. *Trans.*

"Yes, I talked to Maskhadov the day before yesterday, and that's what he believed. I'll repeat that even if all of us starting with Maskhadov died, Yastrzhembsky and Putin would have no fewer problems, in their sense of the word. The political problem between Chechnya and Russia cannot be personified. Those who try to do that are doing so only to drag out the madness that's going on in Chechnya."

"Does Berezovsky* play any role in the peace process, if there really is any secret process underway?"

"We know that Berezovsky is a real figure who acted in opposition to the Putin regime, but he simply can't play any role now. Only those who might influence Putin can. And those people want to continue the war. And they are the only ones in his circle."

"One of the biggest problems in Chechnya is that no one knows the exact numbers of who is dead and who is alive, or the total number of militants. Yastrzhembsky is officially unsure of his numbers."

"We've tried to do a count, but it's very difficult. We think that approximately three hundred thousand were killed in both wars, one hundred twenty thousand during the first war, and the rest during this one."

"And how many militants are operating now?"

"It's useless to give numbers here. This is a partisan war, and it'll continue for five, ten years until . . . "

"Until what? What would you consider the end of the war? Under what terms would you accept it?"

"A cease-fire. Our main condition is Maskhadov being allowed to come out from underground, with his security guaranteed. There will be no second Khasavyurt, of course, no pompous negotiations. But the Russian troops cannot stay in Chechnya. Of that I'm positive."

"I'm not, though."

"If we survive another year or two, you'll see, they'll be withdrawn."

"Why are you so sure?"

"It's simple logic. In the current Chechen situation, with the punitive role that the military has chosen for itself, it just has to withdraw. It can drag the war out for another year or two, but it can't

---

*A former Deputy Secretary of Russia's Security Council, Boris Berezovsky is in voluntary exile in London, where he critiques Putin's policies, including the Chechen war. *Trans.*

defeat the people. The Chechens have survived the most crucial time, when Putin's war was popular. Now it's very unpopular, and we'll continue to survive. Even those people who have emigrated recently will never forgive or forget. Even if the war ended today, but the political climate between Chechnya and Russia remained the same, it would start all over again in five years. New Dzhokhar Dudayevs, Basayevs, and Maskhadovs would appear and exhort the people to war, reminding them what had happened. Keep in mind that every new cycle brings forth even more deadly punitive action from Russia. For this reason, if we ended the resistance now without resolving the main question, we would be setting ourselves up for more horrible events. Now everyone is aware of that, even those who fought on Putin's side at the beginning of the war, like Ruslan Khasbulatov."*

"Who can conduct negotiations with the Kremlin from the Chechen side today?"

"Maskhadov is the only one who should do that."

"Are you sure that you and Maskhadov personally represent the Chechen people?"

"I was waiting for this question. True, I'm not there now. And I do feel uncomfortable because of that. But at the same time I'm relieved that Maskhadov is there. And I'm his ambassador. The Chechen people elected Maskhadov, so he represents them. And since I'm Maskhadov's special representative, I also stand for the Chechen people. The Chechens will never accept anyone appointed by Moscow. They've been trying to impose someone since 1991—now it's Kadyrov—and all in vain."

"What do you think of Kadyrov?"

"It's against both Russian and Chechen customs to speak ill of the dead. And I don't have anything good to say."

"What is his political future?"

"He has no future in Chechnya."

---

*A member of the Russian Academy of Sciences and a major Soviet economist. The only Chechen who held the post of chairman of the Supreme Council of the RSFSR (under Yeltsin). An organizer of the anti-Yeltsin putsch of October 1993. Later given amnesty. Influential in Chechnya as a pro-Russian figure. Moved closer to Maskhadov beginning in 2001; now promulgates the idea of Chechen independence as the only means of survival for its people.

"But he says neither you nor Maskhadov have a political future in Chechnya."

"I'm sure that those who allowed him to remain in power until the troops are withdrawn from Chechnya will kill him. By the way, I don't rule out the possibility of the troops leaving the country on their own. Kadyrov is a problem not for Chechnya, but for those who have promoted and appointed him. He is provoking people today, calling for civil war in Chechnya against his enemies. He's trying to do that because such a war, once it's started, would allow him to avoid being held accountable for all the horrible crimes that have happened in Chechnya."

"He isn't the only one who's trying to avoid responsibility."

"Maskhadov and I are ready to stand before the international tribunal and take responsibility and blame for our part in what happened in Chechnya, along with the war criminals. I'm sure that no matter how things play out, there will be such a tribunal. If the Chechens fail to arrange this, the war between Chechnya and Russia will never end. Up until now, the Russian generals have been advancing their military and political careers on Chechen blood, getting medals, promotions, and money. No one has ever been held accountable. If this doesn't happen, we're doomed to a vicious cycle. The Russian generals have grown used to feeding on Chechen blood, and they will never end this tradition of their own free will."

"But things are not perfect in your ranks, either. You aren't united, are you?"

"Did we ever have a chance, a single day of truce, for example, to verify that some units did not obey Maskhadov's orders? Did Maskhadov have a chance to order all the units to stop firing? And did anyone refuse to carry it out? Nothing like this ever happened. No such order was ever given. There was no truce, either, for any of his subordinates to break. So why do they say that Maskhadov doesn't control the resistance forces? Since 1991, the Chechens have been assured that they are their own enemy. But we have a different mentality from other Asian peoples. Blood brings us to our senses, not the other way around. We all know that someone will answer for this blood."

"And yet, at the end of April, eighteen soldiers of the Chechen OMON were killed in a bombing in Grozny. Their chief, Musa

Gazimagomadov, has to find and destroy the bombers. He's responsible to the families of those he recruited for the unit, only to get them killed. Isn't this the real Chechen civil war?"

"I have no doubt that the Russian secret services did that."

"Why do you think so? That's what everyone says, but is there any proof?"

"That's our mentality. You can't hide anything in the Chechen units. A man has to tell someone about what he did. And that person has to tell someone else that he knows who did it. But there's no such person in this case."

"These days we hear a lot of talk on all levels, including among the Chechens, about finding a sort of compromise figure to be the head of Chechnya, someone most of the Chechens and the Kremlin would accept. What do you think of that?"

"There can't be any compromise figures. We have a president who was elected by the people."

"But what if he resigns? Many Chechens are discussing this."

"He won't."

"What makes you so sure?"

"He is not Shamil Basayev. There's a huge difference between a president who has been elected and one who has been appointed. Dudayev was elected, and he didn't resign. He was killed. Maskhadov is not going to run away, resign, or abdicate. And whether he lives or dies is in the hands of the Almighty."

"But let's be honest, there's a scenario outlined by the Chechens themselves, that on the first day after the end of the war, Maskhadov would come out from underground and resign. And he would hand his authority over to the compromise figure that they are now searching for. What do you think of this scenario?"

"Aslan will not leave in this manner. It's not his decision, but the will of the people. He can't hand it over. No one will allow this."

"But there are people—for example, deputy Aslanbek Aslakhanov and Ruslan Khasbulatov—who have received such suggestions from the Kremlin and are ready to become these compromise figures."

"It's not the Kremlin's decision. The Chechens will decide this."

"How will they decide?"

"Through elections. If the people choose Aslakhanov in the course of future elections, then he will be president."

"What do you think Maskhadov's worst mistake was?"

"His worst mistake was also our worst mistake, the mistake of all his friends who fought with him in the first war. We fell for the propaganda trick that the Kremlin pulled after Khasavyurt, saying that we'd won the war. That was our tragic mistake, and we're still paying for it, along with all of the Chechen people. The truth is, it was no victory. One hundred twenty thousand dead, the infrastructure ruined, villages and cities wiped off the map ... And we were celebrating victory, giving out medals and promotions. If we had claimed, from that day on, that we are victims of a genocidal war, perhaps the second war wouldn't have happened."

"Do you still insist on Chechen sovereignty?"

"If there is any other way that security could be guaranteed for the Chechen people, we're ready to accept it. But Putin isn't a leader we can talk with about that."

"Then you won't talk for a long time—Putin is counting on being reelected."

"That's Russia's problem."

"Russia's problems are Chechnya's problems too."

"Of course. But the thing is, not much depends on the Chechens now. All we can do is go on with the resistance. Please understand me. I'm not comfortable talking about resistance here, in a hotel lobby very far from Chechnya. That's not my style. I've always been in the middle of things. Now it's turned out that I'm here. Many Chechens have come to realize that their only choice is to continue the resistance, and this has nothing to do with me, Maskhadov, or Basayev. The main thing is, the younger generation has come to realize this."

"Suppose Putin invites Maskhadov to the Kremlin for negotiations. What would he do, refuse?"

"Yes, he'd refuse. Not out of fear; it's just that Maskhadov cannot make another mistake."

"All right then, suppose Kazantsev calls you and says: 'Let's have another meeting.'"

"I'd tell him no, too. I'm not going to play his political games on account of Bush coming for a visit or something else. The answer is no."

"Aren't you personally tired of the war?"

"Do I have a choice?"

"How do you see yourself coming back to Chechnya?"

"That's a personal question. I can't answer it. But it would have to be as a victor."

"Where will Maskhadov live after the war?"

"In Chechnya, no doubt about it. I'm not in Chechnya now only because I've been assigned to represent Maskhadov in Europe and to international organizations. I didn't leave Chechnya. I was brought out wounded. And I'll come back—that's my life's goal."

"Who do you think memorials should be erected to in Chechnya after the second war?"

"No one. There are no heroes or winners in this war. The nation has been thoroughly humiliated and insulted. Heroes don't let this happen to their people."

Here I am, back in London. We seem to be doomed to return to this city.

January 8, 2003. An interrogation about *Nord-Ost* * has been scheduled for the fifteenth in Moscow. An FSS investigator will be coming. He'll ask questions about what happened in what way, and aggravate the wound once again. Right now, though, I'm leaving the Heathrow passport and customs area, looking for the person I agreed to meet. But nobody is there. Very strange. Did something go wrong? Suddenly Yasha jumps out from behind. After a short exchange of greetings, he quickly walks ahead. "He's here, waiting in the car." That's all Yasha says to me.

"He" is Akhmed Zakayev. I brought him here from Copenhagen last December 7, after he was released from jail. But Russia has demanded that Zakayev be extradited from London too. He is under British surveillance, and is not allowed to leave London. His passport has been taken away, and he can't go to any public places.

I am almost running to keep up with Yasha. Finally, he leads me to a car. There, in the back seat in the dark, is Zakayev.

"We couldn't wait to see you. How is it there, at home? Tell us."

"At home" means in Chechnya.

He is a Chechen who has wandered the globe, for the last three years unable to walk down the Urus-Martan street where he was born. But it is I, a Muscovite, a Ukrainian of Russian citizenship, who tell him how a tunnel under Minutka Square has been restored, how victims of the terrorist act of December 27 are in the Ninth Municipal

---

*The Russian musical playing at a Moscow theater that was taken over by Chechen rebels on October 23, 2002. Taking the staff, actors, and audience hostage, the Chechens demanded an end to war in their country. Many of the rebels and the hostages were killed when Russian troops stormed the theater wielding guns and poison gas on October 26. *Trans.*

Hospital, how Gantamirov is building a new market in Grozny, and how Gantamirov's people are tearing down the Krasny Molot factory to get bricks for the construction. This factory, before all these wars, was Europe's biggest producer of oil drilling equipment.

Zakayev cannot leave the car. It is highly unadvisable for him to be in a London café, as the British authorities are afraid that the Russian FSS will steal him. It's just like in Soviet spy films. That's how bad things have become again. What have we turned into? What has happened to the country that Putin pushed into war, that was then so jolted by the *Nord-Ost* October tragedy and left with so little chance for normal life?

I believe less than ever in the usual way of measuring time. More and more, it seems to me that each of us has his or her own personal calendar, and that we all live by these calendars—and not from January to February to March—depending on the circumstances that we find ourselves in. Or perhaps we choose them ourselves.

I have a calendar like this, for the 2002 *Nord-Ost* year, which has passed so quickly, and for the beginning of 2003. This calendar has no chronology and no external logic. It has nothing but images tied together by the logic of feelings surrounding this tragedy.

"Feelings?" someone might say, dragging the word out disappointedly. "What about analysis? Practical conclusions? A sober prognosis?"

I'm not very good at prognosticating. Besides, we live in the time of Putin, when it is once again permissible to sacrifice thousands of lives "in the name of a bright nonterrorist future." There are people who can analyze this, but few who can sympathize. And since feelings are so rare now, they are the most important thing in my calendar.

EARLY DECEMBER. It's been forty days* since the *Nord-Ost* hostage crisis has passed. And it seems like it's time for everything to go back to normal. But this doesn't happen at all. Maybe it's because of the weather? Moscow in December is bitter and freezing, with no snow. The relentless cold really gets you down. It makes you feel so sad ... Sometimes hostages who survived the nightmare musical visit

---

*The Russian word in the original refers to the wake that is held forty days after a death in Russian Orthodox tradition. *Trans.*

me at the newspaper. There is Ira Fadeeva, for instance, in a black beret, coat, and sweater. She has something yellow in her hands. It's a big bouquet of long yellow roses in memory of her son, who was killed. Ira is thirty-seven. She went to *Nord-Ost* on October 23 almost by chance. They lived nearby, and were getting ready to go to another theater when they realized that the tickets had expired. But they already had their coats on, so she persuaded her fifteen-year-old son Yaroslav, a tenth-grader, to go with her to *Nord-Ost* instead.

Ira survived, and Yaroslav was killed. She fled the hospital, identified his body in the morgue, found the bullet's entrance and exit wounds, and received a death certificate with a dash under "Cause of Death." You can understand that any way you want; he's dead, but there's no reason. Why? Because the official version is that "only four were shot, and all of them by Chechen terrorists," and Yaroslav was the fifth.

That's why there's a dash. And what about his mother? His grandparents? The government suggests that they stop whining, and not disturb the investigation with questions that are tactless, from the point of view of official ideology. All the hostages were supposedly killed by gas that was used to save others, and there was no other solution. For the umpteenth time in our history, ideology wins out, and the people who don't fit in with it are on their own.

Ira left the morgue and jumped off a bridge. Former hostages committing suicide are a terrible reality that we are faced with this December. But Ira was rescued from the Moscow River. Now she suffers so much that there are no words to comfort her. At least I don't know any . . . And naturally, there is no help from the government that sentenced her son to death. If you're not a victim of terrorism, there are no rehabilitation centers, psychotherapists, or psychiatrists for you. Ira is a victim of her government's ideology.

NOVEMBER 23. It is a month after *Nord-Ost*, probably about six in the morning. I'd love to doze off after a sleepless night. But the telephone rings. "Anna Stepanovna, come get me from the police station . . . I'm in trouble again." I rush to my car. God, it's cold, I'm shivering terribly. Smug cops at the Novo-Alekseevsky Street station are saying nasty things. Ilya is in the depths of their spit-covered, stinking cell, hounded, dirty and unshaven.

Ilya is an old friend of my children. I've known him since he was a boy. Back then he was a sturdy little red-cheeked kid who went to the music school on Merzlyakovsky Street with his cello tilted over his shoulder and made a lot of mischief with my son, pestering the teachers. Later, when he was sixteen, he started to go out with my daughter, who played the violin. Their romance did not last long, but we all stayed good friends. A year ago, the twenty-four-year-old Ilya joined the *Nord-Ost* orchestra. And of course, he was playing that cursed evening.

How well we understand misfortune when it strikes our dear ones! "Mom, Ilya is there!" my son shouted to me over the phone on October 23. "What should we do? Can you help him? Talk with the Chechens! Please, mom!" But I couldn't help him at all. Because you couldn't use personal connections there; you couldn't plead for just one of them and probably end up sacrificing the rest. You could only plead for everyone. Ilya was held there for three days; he had seen the gas come in, and passed out. But he was lucky. One of the very first Luzhkov ambulances took him to the toxicological ward of Sklifasovsky hospital, the best one in Moscow, and he was saved. But now, a month after the gas attack, something is wrong with him. His nerves are on edge. He is reexamining his whole life, but he can't come to terms with it, and sees a reason to fight everywhere. "Anna Stepanovna, I feel like a teenager again . . . What's wrong with me?" "You just need to be treated." "I can't stand seeing injustice. How can the hospital help with that?"

Right now, early in the morning, Ilya needs some very practical help. He is at the police station because he threw a toaster at someone. And the evening before, he had tried to lecture an Azerbaijani vegetable salesman on the street because the salesman had peed on a church fence on Sukharevka Street right in front of him. After that, he stopped at a night club frequented by a very cultivated crowd, where poets recite new works, and got into a fight with someone who said something he didn't like. "What's wrong with me, Anna Stepanovna? Take me away from here. They've been holding me in this cage like a monkey, forcing me to stand."

One policeman at the station, who seems reasonably bright, goes into details about the terrible shock to the *Nord-Ost* musician's fragile psyche, and asks me, "Can you get him to shape up? If you promise to do that, I'll let him go." How can I promise him anything? I'm not a psychiatrist. But I promise anyway. And the policeman continues, "Keep him at your place for now, for a while at least. Let him cool off a bit, otherwise he'll wind up here again, and things will be more serious." In the meantime, it's already nine.

I take Ilya to my car, and he immediately falls asleep; the whole night he's been fighting with windmills. At 9:30, I have to give a talk at an annual conference called "The KGB: Yesterday, Today, and Tomorrow." I've been invited to speak about how the secret services acted from October 23 to 25 as they tried to fight the terrorists. I go there with Ilya and seat him in the far corner of the beautiful Moscow Helicon Opera Theater on Bolshaya Nikitskaya Street, which the KGB conference has rented. Ilya quickly falls asleep again, and I give my talk, assigning Sasha Petrov, a very nice activist from Human Rights Watch, to look after him. Sasha understands everything without a word, but I don't let Ilya out of my sight anyway, worrying that he might wake up and decide that everyone around him is an enemy. "What's wrong with me, Anna Stepanovna?"

OCTOBER 25. Today is the day before the twenty-sixth, with its early morning gassing. It's raining hard, typical for a Moscow fall: protracted and inescapable. I'm standing on the first floor of the captured building, as a negotiator. The terrorists bring out male hostages, pointing automatic weapons at them. They go downstairs single file from the second floor to get the water and juice that has been brought to the theater building as agreed. The hostages haven't eaten or drunk in three whole days. They're also coming down because I asked them to. I insisted on seeing the hostages before talking with the terrorists. So now the men and boys are coming down gloomily to meet me, one after the other. One of them, with a sharp nose and wearing a gray sweater, suddenly begins to shout: "You there! Bring us disinfectant! I asked for it this morning!" But the terrorists cut him off rudely: "What do you mean, you asked for that?" A young man nearby in a black tuxedo and white shirt, an orchestra member, whispers: "They said that they would start killing at ten ... Please ... pass it along."

Later, after everything was over and the government announced "victory" despite the many human casualties, I couldn't find this young man in the black tuxedo anywhere. However, the man in gray who was shouting about disinfectant gave an ideologically correct interview that was broadcast on all the TV channels, and of course, was invited to the Kremlin. There he thanked Putin on behalf of all the hostages for his care and attention.

OCTOBER 25. Once again, the day before the attack. Abubakar, terrorist number 2 in the siege of *Nord-Ost,* his submachine gun tilted forward, is a muscular OMON soldier in military camouflage, like all the troops in Chechnya on both sides. He wants to speak his mind before dying. He is sure that he will die here, that he won't come out alive. Abubakar is a young man who already looks old. He explains what brought him here. "You live very well here!" he says to me. "And we live in the forests! But we also want to live like people. We want to, you hear? We'll force you to listen to us!" This last part echoes on all sides from somewhere above, where the terrorists have established posts throughout the building.

The hostages are taken back upstairs. Then they are brought downstairs again, in single file. "I passed along what you said." "I see," the orchestra musician in black and white says, barely moving his pale lips. A fellow I never met anywhere again. "Starting at ten... Pass it along... Plead with them..."

A CHEERFUL AMERICAN OCTOBER 23. Lightly dressed, I run into my hotel in Santa Monica. This ocean suburb of Los Angeles is incredibly bright and beautiful, with many colors and palm trees. I just gave a lecture at the local university to journalism students and their instructors. The lecture was about our life, and of course, the endless civil war going on in my country without any truce: the second Chechen war, which has been generating nonstop terrorism for internal use for four years now.

The students are astonished. They ask "How can this be?" And I tell them about the sharp radicalization of the Chechen resistance units, about how these units are being joined by those who want to avenge their tortured, kidnapped, and murdered relatives. I tell them that Maskhadov's moderation no longer satisfies the young militants, that Basayev has gotten the best of him. After the lecture, I run to the hotel and the desk clerk tells me that I got a call from the Moscow paper I work for, that something has happened there. When I call, they tell me: "Hostages have been taken at *Nord-Ost.* Nobody knows what to do." "Nobody knows?" "Nobody." "What about Putin?" "He's not saying anything." It is night. Lena Milashina, our correspondent, calls the hotel: "The terrorists want to see you. They just made this demand. You have to tell them if you're coming or not live on the REN-TV channel; you'll be called from there." They call. I say "yes." My son manages to get through to me in the midst of all the people calling me: "Please don't do this! We can't take it anymore! You don't understand what's going on here!" It's a difficult conversation. My son feels desperate; he is very upset. He's tired of worrying about me. He can't even express in words how tired everyone around me has gotten from these experiences that take up their whole lives as I cover this infernal, endless second Chechen war. My son gets furious when he doesn't get a definite promise that I won't do it. But later, he will help me more than anyone else with the negotiations, talking with the terrorists on the phone until my arrival from Los Angeles. After the attack, the FSS will put him under surveillance, listening to his phone conversations.

But that's down the road, later. In between my trips to *Nord-Ost*, I will be sitting at headquarters. What headquarters? What is their task? I couldn't tell you that. More likely the seizure of the building than rescuing people, as it turns out later. So I'll sit there on the twenty-fifth until late at night with an officer called Zhenya. I'll be shaking feverishly from cold and fear. The rain is pouring down, as luck would have it. My coat is soaked and there's nowhere to dry off. And right then my son calls again and says that he has thought it over, and that it would probably be best for the situation if he's the one who takes water and juice to the building with me, since he is just my son, and not from the secret services. "The terrorists won't mind, right?" He looks like me, and it's clear from his passport that he's my son, which will "calm down the terrorists." I pass our conversation along to the officer, Zhenya—maybe that's what would really be best for everyone? After all, at this moment everyone is thinking of only one thing: what can be done to help, for heaven's sake? What can be done?! Zhenya looks very closely at me and asks, "*That's* what you want to do?" And only then do I come to my senses and answer "Over my dead body." Next morning, when they start taking the corpses to the morgues, and relatives plant themselves against the locked doors of the hospitals, we're all tortured by our inability to help them. I go to the newspaper and tell my colleagues about my son and his suggestion late last night. Dima, the editor in chief of our oppositional paper, which is being persecuted by the government, starts to cry. "What terrific kids we have!" And I suddenly realize that I almost roped my son into this, and that I don't even have any tears left. Not after living in Chechnya through 2002 with its endless purges, not with the constant series of corpses I've witnessed and had to deal with, as if I were part of a military burial team . . .

DECEMBER 2. Again, early in the morning. A call from the Moscow Echo radio station: "Last night Malika Umazheva, the head of the Alkhan-Kala village administration, was killed in Chechnya. Could you comment on this, please?"

"What, she was killed?"

The troops drove around the village in armored vehicles all evening yesterday. At the midnight curfew, unknown masked men in camouflage entered Malika's home and took her into the barn. Her teenage nephews, whom she had raised after the death of her brother, grabbed hold of the camouflaged men and begged them not to kill her, but in vain. Malika was shot. Those beasts, who had become adept during the war at killing off people like this woman in her fifties with high blood pressure, heart problems, and constantly swollen legs, went away. Another of my heroines was dead.

Malika was the administrative head of one of the toughest Chechen villages, Alkhan-Kala (Barayev's village with endless purges, shootings, and disfigured corpses), after the previous head was killed. And reason should have told her to stay put, be careful. But she did the very opposite. She became the boldest, bravest village head in this zone of military lawlessness, where it's so difficult to survive.

And acting that way was a real feat. Alone and unarmed, she stood up to the tanks that rolled into the village. She was the only village head to shout "You beasts!" right to the faces of the treacherous prosecutors who had been intimidated by the generals and simply kept records of the torture and killing. And she cried "Bastards" at the generals who had tricked her and secretly killed residents of her village. She fought desperately for a better life for Alkhan-Kala. No one else dared to do so in present-day Chechnya, not even the men.

The chief of our general staff, General Kvashnin, with his big stars and red-striped pants, fiercely and personally hated this modest village official, who had been elected by the villagers. What's more, he hated her so much that he spread all kinds of slander about her, using his access to TV cameras for this purpose. And what did she do? She stuck to her guns and sued him in response to his lies, knowing very well that almost everyone was afraid to defy Kvashnin. This includes even people from the Kremlin, not just residents of Alkhan-Kala. They know that Kvashnin doesn't forgive those who don't fear him.

Kadyrov drove her away from his "high" government doorstep in Grozny, because he was deathly afraid of talking with this woman, who was never at a loss for words with any authorities. He knew that she would say only bad things about him: that he sold out his own people and that he looked good only compared to his Kremlin sponsor but not to the people he was supposed to take care of. He also knew very well that Malika would do everything she could to stop him from becoming the Chechen president "chosen by the people." And twenty thousand votes depended on her. The Alkhan-Kala villagers worshipped her. And Kadyrov didn't forgive those whom the people worshipped, because the people hated him.

I remember Malika's words: "Anya, what a dirty war this is! Who do I fear most of all? The Feds, of course. Our militants are bandits, it's true, and nothing is sacred to them either. But the Feds act badly in the name of the constitution." That day, it rained cats and dogs in Alkhan-Kala. Malika sat in her office in the administration building, constantly putting her stamp on papers that were brought in and taken away by villagers. They all winced slightly, either from the dampness or from the knowledge that right here, behind this very desk, unknown people shot the previous administrative heads of Alkhan-Kala and that Malika herself was constantly being threatened. So at any moment, people said, someone with a submachine gun could crash through the window.

That evening, after we had discussed the frightening events, Malika and I went to the graduation at High School No. 2. She made a farewell speech to the twelve graduating students—three boys and nine girls. All of them, together with Malika and the rest of the villagers, had dug in the ruins where the Feds had blown up the bodies of their fellow villagers. They had picked out hands, feet, and pieces of clothing, and the boys had taken part in the funerals. Malika said the usual words about choosing a worthy path, but in the Alkhan-Kala context, they were full of meaning that had been lost in our everyday lives. About how their lives depended on the choices they made—they had to sink or swim. And that there was no room for error, or even compromise. I remembered these words on October 25: Movsar Barayev, the leader of the terrorists who seized the *Nord-Ost* theater, was from Alkhan-Kala.

DECEMBER 5. Copenhagen. Akhmed Zakayev has been in a Danish prison for a month, at the demand of the Russian authorities, supposedly for helping plan the *Nord-Ost* terrorist act. We found out that on December 5 he'd be released. I'm standing by the walls of the Copenhagen prison, waiting for him. These walls are very gloomy and medieval, with lighted torches. An old woman with a shopping bag comes up and asks me to follow her. I never follow anyone I don't know, but here for some reason I obey. We walk for a long time through twilit Copenhagen. Finally, we get to a door, an entranceway, another door, some people speaking a language I don't understand, a long hallway, and an entrance to a room. There, Zakayev gets up from a couch.

We both would have cried, if we were still capable of it.

His Danish lawyer brought him here, to a private apartment, straight from jail. Akhmed doesn't understand a single word of any language other than Chechen and Russian. It's been very uncomfortable for him too. But right now we feel that we're together in uncomfortable Copenhagen.

We get up, thank everyone, say good-bye, and leave. But where are we going?

Zakayev is an eternal wanderer in Europe. The year 2002 was coming to an end. The holidays approached unnoticed, as always. I wanted to live, but I wanted to wail even more. I returned to Moscow. The weather in Moscow was cold and biting, with no snow. Irina's yellow roses still hadn't withered; they stood on the floor by my desk, as if they were frozen. As if it were a desert winter: wind, earth hard as rock, without any white fluff. Will we all survive 2003?

I have no affirmative answer. And therein lies the whole tragedy.

CPSIA information can be obtained
at www.ICGtesting.com
Printed in the USA
LVHW030753170719
624369LV00015B/239/P